AF842544

BRIDGES TO NEW BUSINESS

This monograph is a publication of the research programme
'Indonesia across orders; The reorganization of Indonesian society'

Netherlands Institute for War Documentation

NEDERLANDS INSTITUUT VOOR OORLOGSDOCUMENTATIE

The programme was realized by the Netherlands Institute for War Documentation (NIOD) and was supported by the Dutch Ministry of Health, Welfare and Sport

Published in this series by Boom, Amsterdam:

- Hans Meijer, with the assistance of Margaret Leidelmeijer, *Indische rekening; Indië, Nederland en de backpay-kwestie 1945-2005* (2005)
- Peter Keppy, *Sporen van vernieling; Oorlogsschade, roof en rechtsherstel in Indonesië 1940-1957* (2006)
- Els Bogaerts and Remco Raben (eds), *Van Indië tot Indonesië* (2007)
- Marije Plomp, *De gentleman-bandiet; Verhalen uit het leven en de literatuur, Nederlands-Indië/Indonesië 1930-1960* (2008)
- (forthcoming) Remco Raben, *De lange dekolonisatie van Indonesië*

Workshop proceedings, published in Indonesia:

- Freek Colombijn, Martine Barwegen, Purnawan Basundoro and Johny Alfian Khusyairi (eds), *Kota lama, kota baru; Sejarah kota-kota di Indonesia / Old city, new city; The history of the Indonesian city before and after independence.*Yogyakarta: Ombak (2005)
- 'Indonesianisasi dan nasionalisasi ekonomi', Special issue of *Lembaran Sejarah; Jurnal Sejarah dan Ilmu-Ilmu Sosial Humaniora* 8-2 (2005)

In the same series will be published by KITLV Press, Leiden:

- Freek Colombijn, with the assistance of Martine Barwegen, *Under construction; Urban space and housing during the decolonization of Indonesia 1930-1960*
- Robert Bridson Cribb, *The origins of massacre in modern Indonesia; Legal orders, states of mind and reservoirs of violence 1900-1965*
- Els Bogaerts and Remco Raben (eds), *Beyond empire and nation; The decolonization of African and Asian societies 1930s-1960s*

Other titles are in preparation

Indonesia across Orders

J. THOMAS LINDBLAD

BRIDGES TO NEW BUSINESS

The economic decolonization of Indonesia

KITLV Press
Leiden
2008

Published by:
KITLV Press
Koninklijk Instituut voor Taal-, Land- en Volkenkunde
(Royal Netherlands Institute of Southeast Asian and Caribbean Studies)
P.O. Box 9515
2300 RA Leiden
The Netherlands
website: www.kitlv.nl
e-mail: kitlvpress@kitlv.nl

This book is volume 245 in the Verhandelingen Series of the Koninklijk Instituut voor Taal-, Land- en Volkenkunde

KITLV is an institute of the Royal Netherlands Academy of Arts and Sciences (KNAW)

Cover: Creja ontwerpen, Leiderdorp

ISBN 978 90 6718 290 4

© 2008 Koninklijk Instituut voor Taal-, Land- en Volkenkunde

No part of this publication may be reproduced or transmitted in any form or by any means, electronic or mechanical, including photocopy, recording, or any information storage and retrieval system, without permission from the copyright owner.

Printed in the Netherlands

Contents

Preface

Indonesia is very much alive in the Dutch psyche. Not only do many Dutch people have roots in the former colony, but there is also a seemingly boundless interest in the colonial past, particularly in the events leading to Indonesia becoming a sovereign nation. In 2002 the Dutch government decided to support a large-scale historical research programme aimed at enhancing the understanding of this transition. This programme, entitled 'Indonesia Across Orders' (*Van Indië tot Indonesië*), was officially launched in December 2002 in Amsterdam and officially concluded with a public presentation in January 2007 in The Hague. This monograph is one of a number of results of the programme.

Generous financial support was provided by the Ministerie voor Welzijn, Volksgezondheid en Sport (Department of Welfare, Health and Sports). The entire research project was designed and administered by the Nederlands Instituut voor Oorlogsdocumentatie (NIOD, Netherlands Institute for War Documentation) in Amsterdam. The project's aim was to provide a multifaceted view of the process of emancipation from colonial rule, including aspects such as law and order, urban life and its symbols, labour relations, and economic decolonization. In addition, two issues specifically relating to the Japanese occupation and the Indonesian Revolution were focused on, namely war damage and reconstruction, and the issue of backpay to former colonial civil servants. The project on economic decolonization, entitled '*Indonesianisasi* and Nationalization', was executed under the auspices of the International Institute of Asian Studies (IIAS) in Leiden. This book is the culmination of six years of work on that project.

An important aspect of the research programme 'Indonesia Across Orders' was the close cooperation with Indonesian historians, who participated in part through the Lembaga Ilmu Pengetahuan Indonesia (LIPI, Indonesian Academy of Sciences). This resulted in a number of regional case studies undertaken by junior Indonesian historians, some of which had immediate relevance to the research project '*Indonesianisasi* and Nationalization', as well as a series of workshops and academic meetings, mostly in Indonesia.

Indonesian interest in the main topics of 'Indonesia Across Orders' has been overwhelming, and there are plans to translate the monographs, this one included, into Indonesian.

For three full years, from late 2002 until late 2005, the main research for the '*Indonesianisasi* and Nationalization' project was carried out by myself and by my chief assistant Jasper van de Kerkhof in archives and libraries both in Indonesia and the Netherlands. Two international workshops were devoted to the topic of '*Indonesianisasi* and Nationalization', the first in Yogyakarta on 18-19 August 2004, the second in Leiden on 18-19 November 2005, with proceedings appearing in separate publications. There were many opportunities to present research findings while work was in progress. Presentations were given to a Dutch audience at NIOD in Amsterdam, at IIAS in Leiden, at the public presentation of the research programme in The Hague (11 January 2007), and at the Bronbeek Museum in Arnhem (22 April 2007). Presentations were given to an Indonesian audience during workshops in Jakarta, Surabaya (26-27 August 2004), and Padang (3-4 August 2005).

Research findings were discussed during international conferences organized by NIOD in Amsterdam (11-13 December 2003), the International Association of Historians of Asia (IAHA) in Taipei (6-10 December 2004), the International Convention of Asian Scholars (ICAS) in Shanghai (20-25 August 2005) and Kuala Lumpur (2-5 August 2007), the University of Auckland (1-3 February 2006), and the International Economic History Association (IEHA) in Helsinki (21-25 August 2006). Seminars on this topic were also offered at Leiden University, Gadjah Mada University in Yogyakarta, the Australian National University, and the University of Adelaide. I benefited immensely from the feedback received on these occasions.

Most of the manuscript for the final book was compiled in 2006 during a six-month stay as a research fellow at the Research School of Pacific and Asian Studies at the Australian National University in Canberra. Revisions were finalized in mid-2007.

Several institutions facilitated the preparation and completion of this book. With a minimum of bureaucracy and hierarchy, NIOD provided the ideal institutional setting for this research. With its unsurpassed combination of efficiency and informality, IIAS was a perfect host for the activities undertaken by Jasper van de Kerkhof and myself. LIPI in Jakarta rendered invaluable support in helping me gain access to archival materials at Bank Indonesia and the Arsip Nasional Republik Indonesia (ANRI, Indonesian National Archives). The Research School of Pacific and Asian Studies at the Australian National University offered the most pleasant environment imaginable for focusing exclusively on writing. The Departments of History and Southeast Asian Studies of Leiden University, with which I am affiliated, demonstrated admirable flexibility in facilitating this research effort.

I am indebted to several people. As coordinator of the research programme 'Indonesia Across Orders', Els Bogaerts went far beyond regular duties in offering continuous and substantive support. It was a pleasure to deal with such a devoted and able coordinator. Other NIOD staff, notably Marije Plomp, Remco Raben and Peter Post, also contributed in organizational matters, on occasion even sharpening the focus of my research. Wim Stokhof, then director of IIAS, offered encouragement without fail. As the representative of Indonesian historians on the steering committee of the entire research programme, Taufik Abdullah, former chairman of LIPI, gave valued comments on the manuscript. Bambang Purwanto at Gadjah Mada University once again displayed his great organizational talents when hosting the first ever workshop focusing specifically on the economic decolonization of Indonesia.

The research project '*Indonesianisasi* and Nationalization' was carried out in the wider context of teamwork. It was a privilege to work alongside highly qualified, amiable scholars such as Freek Colombijn, Robert Cribb, Ratna Saptari, Peter Keppy, and Hans Meijer. Freek Colombijn offered insightful comments on parts of the text and Robert Cribb made a lasting contribution to historiography by weeding out mistakes and misunderstandings in my chapter on the Japanese occupation and the Indonesian Revolution I was also able to rely on his skills in drawing the maps included in this book. I was fortunate in being able to work closely with Jasper van de Kerkhof, a devoted and cooperative young economic historian who took primary responsibility for organizing the second workshop on the economic decolonization of Indonesia. I am particularly grateful to Martijn van der Loos, MA, and Jeroen Bouterse, BA, who loyally and with unfailing diligence assisted me during the final phase of writing. Others made valuable contributions too, notably Undri from Padang, who with great zeal located materials in Indonesian archives, Cyril Flohr, who consulted newspapers in the KITLV library in Leiden, and Marc Buijnsters, MA, who translated Japanese-language materials.

I am especially indebted to two great scholars who read the entire manuscript and supplied extensive comments and suggestions for improvement. As a leading economic historian of Indonesia and somebody who personally lived through Indonesia's transition across orders, Thee Kian Wie offered insights that no one else could have provided. With his exceptional knowledge of the topic and superb feeling for style, Howard Dick offered the kind of constructive criticism that can only lead to a marked improvement of the end result. My use of the English language, finally, was corrected with great skill and devotion by Rosemary Robson and Rita DeCoursey; their suggestions on style and grammar significantly enhanced the quality of the entire text. The index was diligently prepared by Alexander Tetteroo. Needless to say, remaining errors remain my responsibility.

Abbreviations

ANIEM	Algemeene Nederlandsch-Indische Electriciteits-Maatschappij
ANRI	Arsip Nasional Republik Indonesia
AVB	Algemeene Volkscredietbank
AVROS	Algemeene Vereeniging van Rubberplanters ter Oostkust van Sumatra
BAPPHAR	Badan Pusat Penguasa Perusahaan2 Pharmasi Belanda
BAPPIT	Badan Penjelenggara Perusahaan-Perusahaan Industri dan Tambang
BDN	Bank Dagang Negara
BDP	Biro Devisen Perdagangan
BE	Bukti Ekspor
BI	Bank Indonesia
BII	Bank Internasional Indonesia
BIN	Bank Industri Negara
BKTN	Bank Koperasi, Tani dan Nelajan
BNI	Bank Negara Indonesia
BPM	Bataafsche Petroleum Maatschappij
BRI	Bank Rakjat Indonesia
BUD	Badan Urusan Dagang
BUN	Bank Umum Nasional
BUNEG	Bank Umum Negara
BVM	Bataafsche Vervoers Maatschappij
CTC	Central Trading Corporation
DEIP	Dewan Ekonomi Indonesia Pusat
DIY	Daerah Istimewa Yogyakarta
DPR	Dewan Perwakilan Rakjat
DPRD	Dewan Perwakilan Rakjat Daerah
DPV	Deli Planters Vereeniging
Finec	Financieele en Economische Overeenkomst
Gaperti	Gabungan Pertenunan Indonesia
GAPPERSU	Gabungan Pengusaha Perkebunan Sumatera Utara

GDP	Gross Domestic Product
GIA	Garuda Indonesian Airways
GKBI	Gabungan Koperasi Batik Indonesia
GMB	Gemeenschappelijke Mijnbouwmaatschappijen Billiton
GNP	Gross National Product
HSBC	Hongkong-Shanghai Banking Corporation
HVA	Handels Vereeniging 'Amsterdam'
Ikini	Ikatan Importir Nasional Indonesia
Indestins	Indonesian Estates and Industrial Supply Corporation
Indevitra	Indonesian Development Industrial and Trading Corporation
Internatio	Internationale Crediet- en Handelsvereeniging 'Rotterdam'
Intraport	Indonesian Trading and Transport Company
ISC	Indonesian Service Company
ISTA	Indonesian Shipping and Transport Agency
KENSI	Kongres Ekonomi Nasional Seluruh Indonesia
KINSI	Kongres Importir Nasional Seluruh Indonesia
KLM	Koninklijke Luchtvaart Maatschappij
KNIL	Koninklijk Nederlandsch-Indisch Leger
KPM	Koninklijke Paketvaart Maatschappij
KPUI	Kantor Pusat Urusan Impor
LAAPLN	Lembaga Alat-Alat Pembajaran Luar Negri
LMOD	Landbouw-Maatschappij Oud-Djember
NEFIS	Netherlands Forces Intelligence Service
NEP	New Economic Policy (Malaysia)
NHM	Nederlandsche Handel-Maatschappij
NIAM	Nederlandsch-Indische Aardolie-Maatschappij
NICA	Netherlands Indies Civil Administration
NIVAS	Nederlandsch-Indische Vereeniging voor de Afzet van Suiker
NU	Nahdlatul Ulama
OGEM	Overzeese Gas- en Electriciteits-Maatschappij
ORI	Oeang Republik Indonesia
ORIDAB	Oeang Republik Indonesia Daerah Banten
ORIDAST	Oeang Republik Indonesia Daerah Sumatera Timoer
ORIPS	Oeang Republik Indonesia Propinsi Sumatera
ORIPSU	Oeang Republik Indonesia Sumatera Utara
ORITA	Oeang Republik Indonesia Tapanoeli
P3B	Panitia Pengawasan Perusahaan2 Belanda
P4P	Panitia Penjelesaian Perselisihan Perburuhan – Pusat
PAM	Pendidikan Ahli Minjak
PELNI	Pelajaran Nasional Indonesia

Perbana	Perhimpunan Bank-Bank Nasional
Permindo	Perusahaan Minjak Indonesia
PIR	Persatuan Indonesia Raya
PKI	Partai Komunis Indonesia
PN	*Perusahaan Negara*
PNI	Partai Nasional Indonesia
PP	*Peraturan Pemerintah*
PPN	Pusat Perkebunan Negara [Poesat Perkeboenan Negara]
PRRI	Pemerintah Revolusioner Republik Indonesia
PSI	Partai Sosialis Indonesia
PSII	Partai Sarikat Islam Indonesia
PT	*Perseroan Terbatas*
RI	Republik Indonesia
RTC	Round Table Conference
Sarbupri	Sarikat Buruh Perkebunan Indonesia
SBBI	Sarekat Buruh Bank Indonesia
SBBSI	Serikat Buruh Bank Seluruh Indonesia
SBLGI	Serikat Buruh Listrik dan Gas Indonesia
SKK	Saibai Kigyô Kôdan
SKKK	Saibai Kigyô Kanri Kôdan
SOBSI	Sentral Organisasi Buruh Seluruh Indonesia
SPA	Sumatra Planters' Association
Stanvac	Standard Vacuum Petroleum Company
STEM	Samarinda-Tenggarongsche Electriciteits-Maatschappij
TNI	Tentara Nasional Indonesia
Usindo	Usaha Industri Indonesia
YPTE	Jajasan [Yayasan] Pembangunan Teritorium Empat

CHAPTER I

Introduction

Historians can learn from fiction. Suparto Brata's novel *Saksi mata* ('Eyewitness') is set in Surabaya in 1944, or the year 2604 by the Japanese calendar. The twelve year old protagonist of the story, Kuntara, happens to witness Raden Bulik Rum, a young woman staying with his family, making love with her Javanese husband Mas Wiradad, who is secretly conspiring against the Japanese military authorities. Kuntara becomes a bit confused when later Bulik Rum shows great affection for him too. He later discovers her dead body and becomes entangled in highly complex machinations helping the Japanese military commander, Tuan Ichiro, solve the murder while at the same time trying to absolve his family of conspiracy charges as well as protecting Mas Wiradad, who has gone into hiding in the neighbouring kampong. In the process, young Kuntara witnesses how the Japanese in Surabaya, including his enigmatic teacher Pak Okada, adjust to conditions in Indonesia while imposing their will on the Javanese. He becomes a witness to the great historical change in Indonesia: *sejak sekarang bendera Merah Putih bisa dikibarkan di samping Hinomaru, dan lagu Indonesia Raya dikumandangkan* ('from now on the Indonesian flag can fly alongside the Japanese one and the Indonesian national anthem is heard') (Suparto Brata 2002:4).

Japanese hegemony over Indonesia was short-lived, from March 1942 to August 1945, but the emancipation from Dutch colonialism it initiated endured. Although much has been written about the political aspects of decolonization, only a few works deal with the economic losses of the Dutch, whether real or perceived. This book chooses a different angle. It tells the story of what Indonesia gained from economic decolonization, for better or for worse, with respect to future development. It is not a novel like Suparto Brata's *Saksi mata,* but it does give testimony to a wide range of changes, on macro and micro levels of observation, some irreversible, others ill-fated.

This introduction focuses on the key concepts of analysis, the international dimension of the topic, and its historiographic context. It concludes with an outline of the structure of the book and a note on sources consulted.

Key concepts

'The economic side of the Indonesian Revolution has yet to begin.' This saying is attributed to Haji Agus Salim, a leading figure in the nationalist movement, spoken with the intention of damping down Indonesian euphoria after achieving political independence (Higgins 1957:102). It is a simple but important statement, because it acknowledges that political and economic decolonization, although obviously interrelated, are two separate processes, each with a rhythm and time-span of its own. The two may coincide in time, but they may also unfold with a considerable time lag. Delayed economic decolonization is not necessarily the same as neo-colonialism, a favoured topic in the international literature on Third World economics. The former refers explicitly to the one-time colonial power, whereas the latter refers to a dependence on foreign, that is, mostly Western, economic interests in general. This book is about economic emancipation from the Dutch, not about alleged or actual interests of foreign capital in Indonesia under the New Order.

As with the political train of events, nationalism lies at the core of economic decolonization. One definition of economic nationalism goes as follows: 'the national aspiration to have nationals own and control the productive assets owned by foreigners, or residents considered to be aliens, and perform the important economic functions hitherto performed by foreigners or resident aliens' (Johnson 1972:26). This definition is especially useful for Indonesia, as it encompasses more than just those whose origin lies in the colonial mother country. The designation 'residents considered to be aliens' fits two important population groups in colonial and newly independent Indonesia: Indo-Europeans and ethnic Chinese. The other label, 'resident aliens', refers to Dutch people born and raised in Indonesia and also to foreign immigrants of non-Dutch origin. Economic nationalism flourishes whenever actual command over economic assets is at odds with political aspirations. As such, this situation was a creation of colonialism.

Further operationalization of economic nationalism brings us to the concept of *Indonesianisasi*, as it has become known in the literature, though there are several variants of the term and of its spelling. The classical definition is given by John Sutter, a political scientist who prepared his PhD thesis while on secondment with the American Embassy in Jakarta in the 1950s. Sutter's *Indonesianisasi* is 'a conscious effort to increase the participation and elevate the role of the Indonesian – and more particularly the "indigenous" Indonesian – in the more complex sectors of the economy' (Sutter 1959:2).

Sutter was a highly systematic scholar. He identified no fewer than nine forms of *Indonesianisasi* (Sutter 1959:2), which have been rearranged here, so as to list them in order of appearance in this book. The following six forms of *Indonesianisasi* are discussed later in detail:

1. establishment of new enterprises in sectors previously closed to Indonesians (Chapter IV);
2. transfer of formerly colonial public enterprises to the Indonesian government (Chapter 5);
3. establishment of state-owned enterprises (Chapter V);
4. increased government control over foreign-owned businesses (Chapter VI);
5. increased participation by Indonesians in the management of foreign-owned companies (Chapter VII);
6. transfer of private foreign-owned enterprises to the Indonesian government (Chapter VIII).

Three of Sutter's forms of *Indonesianisasi* are of less immediate relevance to the situation in Indonesia and do not warrant further analysis here. They are:

7. transfer of private foreign-owned enterprises to Indonesians and Indonesian organizations;
8. increased Indonesian equity ownership in corporations established by foreigners;
9. return of landholdings to the Indonesian community by foreign enterprises.

Sutter was writing prior to the seizure of Dutch firms in December 1957. At that time, there appeared to be no compelling reason to give priority to the expropriation and change of ownership of foreign-held property (number 6 above). Nationalization can be viewed as the most extreme form of *Indonesianisasi.* But such a line of reasoning easily blurs the distinction between the voluntary nature (at least nominally) of most forms of *Indonesianisasi* as identified by Sutter and hostile take-over and nationalization. Thus a conceptual separation between *Indonesianisasi* and nationalization is useful. Such a distinction invites several interesting historical questions which are addressed in this book: Did nationalization become inevitable because too little progress was made in implementing *Indonesianisasi*? Did successful *Indonesianisasi* pave the way for nationalization? What were the costs of opting for nationalization before *Indonesianisasi* had run its course?

In its narrow sense, *Indonesianisasi* refers to the promotion of Indonesians to supervisory and managerial positions in private enterprises controlled by foreign nationals. It is in this sense that it was applied in the 1930s by the Dutch colonial administration under the awkward term *indianisatie*. It gained general acceptance during the 1950s in the public debate on foreign investment in Indonesia. This book follows Sutter in his original broad definition, but considers nationalization a separate conceptual category.

Goeboeng railway station in Surabaya where, Kuntara, the hero in Suparto Brata's novel *Saksi mata,* lingered around during the Japanese occupation (KITLV 30272)

The distinction in Sutter's definition between Indonesians in general and indigenous Indonesians is essential. In the 1950s the latter were usually labelled *asli,* suggesting an ethnic Indonesian origin. Only several years later, in the mid-1970s, was the term *asli* replaced by *pribumi,* with its current, unambiguous reference to an ethnic origin ranging from Acehnese to Papuan (*Kompas* 24 March 1976).

Although *Indonesianisasi* applied primarily to indigenous Indonesians, it did not by definition exclude non-indigenous Indonesians. The same cautious approach is adopted here. I intend to devote most of my attention to the changing position of indigenous Indonesians in the newly independent nation's economy. However, changes affecting non-*pribumi* businesses, especially those of ethnic Chinese, will be considered too, albeit in less detail. It goes without saying that a history of economic decolonization cannot possibly do full justice to the contributions made by ethnic Chinese and other non-indigenous minority groups towards the economic development of Indonesia.

The pivot of decolonization remains the achievement of political independence. Yet profound change in the economic structure constitutes a vital auxiliary. The economic structure inherited by Indonesia in 1945 was singularly ill-suited to the provision of sustained economic growth for large segments of the rapidly growing population. It was unilaterally geared towards the export production of raw materials and had already begun to crumble during the worldwide economic depression of the 1930s, the true turning point in the economic development of modern Indonesia (Dick et al. 2002:153). The need to reduce extreme dependence on world markets for primary products was acknowledged by the colonial government's launch of a belated industrialization policy towards the very end of undisputed Dutch rule. Successive cabinets during the 1950s assigned a high priority to change within the economic structure and attempted to accelerate industrialization.

In 1949 a booklet appeared, with in its title the phrase *dari ekonomi kolonial ke ekonomi nasional* ('from colonial to national economy'). The author, Soejono Hadinoto, had been active in the nationalist youth movement during the late 1930s and would become Minister of Trade and Industry in 1951 in the Sukiman cabinet. Soejono Hadinoto's message was clear: Indonesia had to change from one type of economy to another. In the conflict with the former colonial power, a solution had to be found that was in the interests of both parties and, as far as possible, in accordance with the needs of Indonesia's own economy (Soejono Hadinoto 1949). Although the expression *dari ekonomi kolonial ke ekonomi nasional* became a catchphrase in the public discourse of the 1950s, its precise meaning remained ambiguous, with some stressing *Indonesianisasi* in its narrow sense of introducing Indonesian supervisory and management personnel, and others urging nationalization and a substantially wider role of the state in economic life. In this study the transition from a colonial to a national economy is conceived as a three-pronged process embracing *Indonesianisasi*, nationalization, and structural change. The three prongs formed a bridge to new business in Indonesia, both literally and figuratively.

International dimension

However reluctantly at first, Sukarno and Hatta did seize the opportunity arising from the Japanese capitulation to declare Indonesia independent on 17 August 1945. But they were, however, not acting in a vacuum. Ho Chi Minh followed suit on 2 September 1945 with the installation of his cabinet in Hanoi, in which the Communists held a majority. The royal rulers of Vietnam, Laos, and Cambodia had already been encouraged by the Japanese to formally renounce French suzerainty in March 1945 (Lockhart 2003:53-60). The Philippines gained full independence on 4 July 1946, according to plans made prior to the Pacific War, under the leadership of Manuel Roxas, appointed President of the Philippine Commonwealth in 1935. Burma (now Myanmar) became a sovereign state on 4 January 1948 in the wake of British withdrawal from the Indian subcontinent, but chose not to join the Commonwealth. On 1 February 1948 the new Federation of Malaya was born on the peninsula, but independence was delayed for almost another decade due to Communist insurgence during the period called the Emergency (Hack 2003:116-22).

In 1945 Thailand was the sole sovereign nation-state in Southeast Asia. Fourteen years later, after the establishment of Malaysia and Singapore in 1957 and 1959 respectively, virtually the entire region was independent. Exceptions to the rule included the three British protectorates in western and northern Borneo (Sarawak, Sabah, and Brunei), the western part of New Guinea, and Portuguese-held East Timor. It is against this background of momentous change among its neighbours that economic decolonization unfolded in Indonesia.

Paths of decolonization differed, not least with respect to economics. Active American support of decolonization in the Philippines was accompanied by the Laurel-Langley Agreement, offering protection to American investment in the former colony while retaining free trade between the two countries for 28 years, from 1946 until 1974. British cooperative policies in their dealings with Malaysia and Singapore served to safeguard vested interests of British capital and the continuity of revenue flows to the Commonwealth from Southeast Asia (Lindblad 2003:41-8). This situation was diametrically opposed to the one prevailing in Vietnam, where direct military confrontation continued until the French defeat at Dien Bien Phu in May 1954. The subsequent peace settlement at Geneva did not include any agreement on future economic relations.

Burma is a particularly interesting case. Although British capital dominated in the vital oil, timber and rubber industries, Sao Shwe Thaik's government, which took office in January 1948, instantly adopted a hostile attitude towards foreign capital. An exodus of British capital followed during the 1950s, as official rhetoric grew ever more anti-Western and pro-socialist. In March 1962 the self-styled 'Buddhist socialist' Ne Win seized power and any remaining British enterprises were nationalized (Lindblad 1998:99-101). The shift of newly independent Burma to a socialist dictatorship illustrates the importance of ideology and the influence of the Cold War in the process of decolonization.

The Communist uprising in Madiun, Central Java, in September 1948 is often considered a turning point in the history of the Indonesian Revolution. Apart from its domestic impact, the forcible suppression of the rebels had the effect of considerably enhancing Sukarno's credentials with the American government. It turned vague American sympathy into active support precisely at a time when the international political situation was growing more tense because of events such as the Soviet blockade of Berlin and Communist advances in China. Only a couple of months later, in January 1949, the United States government led the way in increasing international pressure on the Netherlands to cease hostilities against Indonesia and start negotiating terms of independence (Ricklefs 1981:217-8; MacMahon 2003:216-8).

American policies towards Indonesia under Sukarno were strongly influenced by the priorities of the Cold War and plans for the reconstruction of the world economy. American fears that Indonesia would, in the footsteps of Vietnam and Myanmar, end up in the Communist camp were widespread. Initiatives taken by the Indonesian government to foster capitalist enterprise were invariably greeted with enthusiasm and could count on funding through American aid. John Foster Dulles, Secretary of State in the Eisenhower administration, entertained a hierarchical view of a global capitalist economy in which supplies of raw materials and market outlets in Southeast Asia played an important part (Pruessen 2003:231-5). In such a conception, active state participation in economic life met with suspicion. American apprehension heightened when Dutch firms were seized and nationalized in the late 1950s. The threat of nationalization of private enterprises stemmed from the Russian Revolution in 1917 and resurfaced after the Chinese Revolution in 1949. Political allegiance during the Cold War could have far-reaching ramifications for the economic structure taking shape under the banner of decolonization.

Sukarno himself skilfully maintained a balance between the two power blocs in his effort to postpone choosing sides for as long as possible. His finest hour was in April 1955, when he hosted the Asia-Africa Conference in Bandung and appeared to emerge as the leader of the non-aligned bloc of Third World nations. Afterwards, he moved more towards the left in the ideological spectrum. Socialism became an increasingly important source of inspiration for both his rhetoric and his policies, illustrated by the amalgamation of nationalism, religion, and communism in Nasakom (*nasionalisme, agama* [religion], *komunisme*), a doctrine officially launched in 1960 (Ricklefs 1981:256, 263). The deepening rivalry between the Partai Komunis Indonesia (PKI, Indonesian Communist Party) and the armed forces in the late 1950s and early 1960s should also be understood in the light of the Cold War confrontation between Western capitalism and socialist ideology.

Historiography

Did it pay off to become independent? In searching for a systematic relationship between political and economic change, two Italian scholars writing on Africa confirm that economic growth performance usually improved after independence had been achieved, although former colonies continued to pay for the consequences of their colonial past.[1] Taufik Abdullah, a leading historian of the Indonesian Revolution, poses the question as to how much economic loss Indonesia had to suffer as a consequence of the 'radical' version of *Indonesianisasi* which was implemented in the late 1950s. He argues that had this policy been pursued to its conclusion with the original ideological zeal of achieving a fair (*adil*) society, it would have resulted in economic bankruptcy (Taufik Abdullah 2005:12). Such a critical note does not sit comfortably with the conventional wisdom in Indonesian historiography that economic decolonization had a value of its own, irrespective of repercussions on future economic performance. The Dutch strand of the historiography, by contrast, tends to stress the harm inflicted by Indonesians upon the Dutch and themselves. This book aims to give a fuller assessment than the existing historiography has thus far offered.

National historiography is not impartial, especially not when the struggle for independence is still a vivid memory. In addition to meeting the international requirements of history as a science, a national historiography serves to explain and legitimize past acts. Sartono Kartodirdjo, the grand old man among historians of independent Indonesia, readily admits that such legitimi-

1 Bertocchi and Canova 2002. I am grateful to Daan Marks, then PhD candidate at the University of Utrecht, for drawing my attention to this publication.

zation was a major purpose of the first round of an official Indonesian national history, *Sejarah nasional Indonesia,* presented at a seminar of Indonesian historians in 1970 in Jakarta (Sartono Kartodirdjo 2001:15). In this light, it is of singular importance that a younger generation of Indonesian historians is now working towards a new paradigm in Indonesian history-writing, based on a post-Indonesian-centric point of view capable of liberating national history from 'sacralization and mythologization' (Bambang Purwanto 2004:23-4, 2006:48-9). I hope this book will contribute to a rejuvenation of Indonesian historiography along these lines.

There has been a certain rehabilitation of the period of constitutional democracy during the recent years of democratization in Indonesia. Nevertheless, historiography immediately after the fall of the Soeharto regime in May 1998 did not experience a major upheaval, a radical revision of the past, as historians both at home and abroad had expected (Van Klinken 2001:325-6). The problem with the 1950s in Indonesian history is that they were followed by the 1960s. Praise for achievements during the early Sukarno years inevitably reminds us of the cataclysmic conclusion of the era in 1965-1966. Considerable courage is needed to tackle this dramatic and horrific event (Bambang Purwanto 2006:270-4).

Another revision of the historical canon concerns the involvement of the Indonesian military in the country's economy. The conventional view is that it all began during the 1950s, the main example being the business dealings between Soeharto and Liem Sioe Liong when the former was serving as a commander in Central Java (Robison 1986:259). But there is evidence that the business interests of the Indonesian armed forces were of an earlier date, having developed very soon after 1945 under General Sudirman, although these activities were probably not commercially viable. The economic arm of the military served primarily to collect revenue for the struggle against the Dutch (Bambang Purwanto 2005; Salim Said 1991:101-8).

Outline

This book is arranged in a loosely chronological fashion which permits a focus on a series of themes. The account begins with a stage-setting overview of major changes in the economic and political structure between the late-colonial period and early independent Indonesia (Chapter II). The emphasis is on the colonial economy and society as they had developed by the 1930s, while tracing the origins of *Indonesianisasi.* The chapter moves on to the shifting political constellations and main macroeconomic trends during the 1950s without, however, pretending to offer an exhaustive history of this period.

Rapid and often violent change in the period 1942-1949 becomes the topic of the next chapter, covering both the Japanese occupation and the Indonesian Revolution (Chapter III). It demonstrates that more progress was made towards economic decolonization during these tumultuous years than has often been appreciated.

Several chapters are then devoted to various aspects of *Indonesianisasi* as described above. The development of new entrepreneurship in Indonesia is surveyed against the background of economic restructuring and efforts to achieve industrialization (Chapter IV). A key question here is whether indigenous entrepreneurship flourished despite or because of the economic policies pursued.

Nationalization of foreign-owned firms served as a major vehicle for the Indonesian government in its endeavours to secure control over vital sectors of the economy. Early nationalization was largely voluntary and differed markedly from the forced government take-over which hit Dutch firms in the late 1950s (Chapter V). Sometimes, as in shipping, the path of competition was chosen in preference to cooperation or take-over. As a logical corollary to voluntary nationalization, the grip of the Indonesian state on the economy was strengthened.

Economic nationalism in Indonesia in the 1950s gained its most notorious expression in the policy of positive discrimination known as Benteng (literally 'fortress'), aimed at accelerating participation by indigenous Indonesians in economic life (Chapter VI). The Benteng policy basically failed, but why was this and what were the consequences? The chapter focuses on the 1950s and touches on the anti-Chinese sentiments re-emerging in the wake of economic nationalism.

Reactions of foreign – especially Dutch – business are portrayed in a separate chapter focusing on *Indonesianisasi* in its narrow sense of replacing foreign personnel with Indonesians (Chapter VII). Examples are drawn from major trading firms, agricultural estates, oil, and mining. Perceptions of progress in *Indonesianisasi* varied widely between Indonesian and Dutch observers. It is instructive to briefly compare similar developments in non-Dutch foreign firms.

The final phase of economic decolonization consisted of the take-over and nationalization of the remaining Dutch-owned enterprises. Chapter VIII gives a full description of this dramatic event, including its prelude and aftermath, while briefly outlining the take-over of British and American companies in the conflict with Malaysia during the early 1960s. By way of conclusion, I return to the issues addressed in this book and review the entire process of economic decolonization (Chapter IX).

Sources

This study is based on original research using a variety of primary and secondary sources. The primary sources may be divided into the following five categories:

1. archives of government departments kept at the Arsip Nasional Republik Indonesia (ANRI, National Archives of the Republic of Indonesia) in Jakarta;[2]
2. business archives of private Dutch firms with operations in Indonesia, including Internatio (Internationale Crediet- en Handelsvereeniging 'Rotterdam', International Credit and Trading Association 'Rotterdam'), Handels Vereeniging 'Amsterdam' (HVA, Trading Association 'Amsterdam'), Billiton, and Landbouw-Maatschappij Oud-Djember (LMOD, Estate Company Oud-Djember, all in the Netherlands;[3]
3. archives of two leading Dutch banks operating in Indonesia, the Javasche Bank (Java Bank) and the Nederlandsche Handel-Maatschappij (NHM, Netherlands Trading Association), at respectively Bank Indonesia and Bank Mandiri in Jakarta;[4]
4. archives of Semen Padang, at the company premises in Padang, West Sumatra, and Gabungan Pengusaha Perkebunan Sumatera Utara (GAPPERSU, North Sumatra Planters' Association, SPA), kept at Bank Agro in Medan;[5]
5. unpublished daily news reports, *Antara*, consulted in the National Library (Perpustakaan Nasional) in Jakarta.

Secondary sources include daily newspapers such as *Harian Rakjat*, *Merdeka*, *Soeara Asia* and *Suluh Indonesia*, along with a wide range of magazines and journals published at the time.[6] Limited use was made of Japanese language

2 Research in the ANRI was sponsored by Lembaga Ilmu Pengetahuan Indonesia (LIPI, Indonesian Institute of Sciences) in Jakarta and in part carried out by Martijn van der Loos, MA, then a staff member of the Department of Southeast Asian Studies at Leiden University.

3 Research in business archives in the Netherlands was carried out by Jasper van de Kerkhof, MA, then a Fellow at the International Institute of Asian Studies at Leiden University, resulting in several separate publications (Van de Kerkhof 2005a, 2005b, 2005c).

4 Research at Bank Mandiri was sponsored by LIPI and in part carried out by Martijn van der Loos, MA.

5 Research in Padang and Medan was carried out by Undri, BA, then a student of history at Andalas University, Padang, West Sumatra.

6 Cyril Flohr, MA, then a student in the Department of Southeast Asian Studies at Leiden University, assisted in consulting Indonesian language newspapers available in the Netherlands.

materials in libraries in Japan.[7] Interviews were conducted with Indonesians, mainly in North and West Sumatra, who had in one way or another been participants or eyewitnesses of relevant events.[8]

Our research group was fortunate in being able to draw on findings presented at two international workshops, held in Yogyakarta (18-19 August 2004) and Leiden (18-19 November 2005).[9] Our study also incorporates results from two related research projects on indigenous entrepreneurship in Yogyakarta (Hersumpana 2004, 2005) and on the nationalization of Dutch estates in Jember, East Java (Tri Chandra Apriyanto 2004, 2005).

A final note on spelling. Expressions in Indonesian are rendered in modern spelling, but Indonesian personal names remain unaltered. Geographical designations follow modern Indonesian usage except where the name has changed altogether, as in the case of Batavia/Jakarta. Chinese personal names are given in their original order, that is, with surname preceding given name.

7 All Japanese language materials were translated by Marc Buijnsters, MA, lecturer in the Department of Japanese and Korean Studies at Leiden University.

8 Interviews in Padang were conducted by Undri, BA.

9 Proceedings from the Yogyakarta conference were published as a special issue of the historical journal *Lembaran Sejarah* 8-2 (2005) :1-143. Publication of the Leiden conference proceedings is forthcoming.

CHAPTER II

From colonial to national economy

E. du Perron's novel *Het land van herkomst* ('Country of origin') was acclaimed as a masterpiece of Dutch literature on its publication in 1935. The author offers a classical description of Sukabumi, the place where his alter ego, Arthur Ducroo, grew up in the 1910s. It was 'one of the loveliest (*liefste*) places' in the Priangan, West Java, 'full of delightful houses, an abundance of greenery, with a characteristically large main square (*alun-alun*), a tidy (*zindelijke*) Chinese quarter with new shops, as well as suburban neighbourhoods (*buitenbuurten*) with indigenous (*inlandse*) houses, idyllic and testifying to prosperity' (Du Perron 1996:147). This is how many Dutch people wished to remember colonial society: idyllic and stable, with firm lines of demarcation between the various ethnic groups. It was this type of society which disappeared as a consequence of Indonesia's decolonization.

As perhaps no one else has ever done, Du Perron gave expression to the fundamental ambivalence of colonizers who feel completely at home in the tropical colony, more so than in the distant and cold European mother country, while fully realizing that they are trespassers. Arthur Ducroo starts working as a journalist at the fictitious *Nieuwsbode* ('The Messenger') in Batavia (now Jakarta). He adopts the conventional political attitude shared by the journal, his father, and 'every ordinary Dutchman in Indonesia', which saw in a rebellious Javanese their natural enemy (*een opstandige Javaan was vanzelfsprekend onze vijand*), a standpoint easily reconcilable with the idea that 'we still had no business in Java' (*dat wij nog altijd niets op Java te maken hadden*). Later, in Europe, Ducroo (or indeed Du Perron) regrets his youthful arrogance and grows more sympathetic to the political aspirations of Javanese nationalists (Du Perron 1996:270-1). Such contradictory feelings were not the sole preserve of one young intellectual. They were characteristic of the colonial economy as a whole.

This chapter sets the stage for my account of economic decolonization in Indonesia. It begins with an overview of the colonial economic structure prevailing up until 1942, which was subsequently inherited by independent Indonesia. Particular attention is paid to profound changes set in motion by the Depression of the 1930s. Subsequently, the colonial roots of *Indonesianisasi*

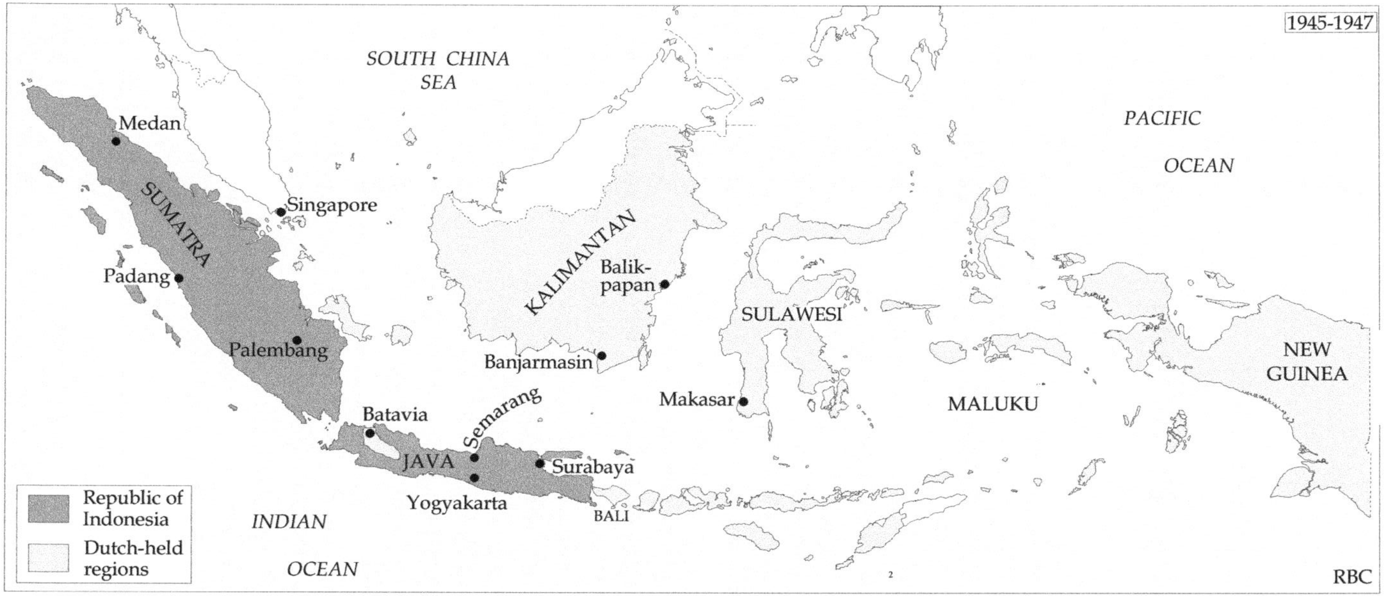

Map 1. The Indonesian archipelago in 1945-1947.
Source: Cribb 2000:157

in both its narrow and its broad sense are traced. The chapter concludes with a bird's-eye view of post-colonial trends in macroeconomic performance and politics.[1]

The plural economy

In 1930 colonial Indonesia had a population of 61 million, roughly two-thirds of which lived in Java (including Madura) and one-third in the rest of the country, conventionally known as the Outer Islands. Indigenous peoples claiming an ethnic origin in the archipelago made up more than 97 per cent of the total, while ethnic Chinese, by far the largest non-indigenous ethnic minority, numbered almost 1.3 million, alongside only 235,000 Europeans, including Indo-Europeans of mixed descent (Boomgaard and Gooszen 1991:121, 133-7, 224-30; see also Claver 2006:422-4). Ethnic divisions between the huge indigenous majority and the tiny non-indigenous minorities had been legally sanctioned and institutionalized in the mid-nineteenth century in a government regulation (*Regeeringsreglement 1854*) that served as the colony's constitution. Right up until independence stratification along ethnic lines remained a defining characteristic of colonial society (Fasseur 1994:36, 54; Coppel 1997:566-8).

Amongst others, social differentiation by ethnic origin had an economic function. A well-informed visitor from the British colonial administration, J.S. Furnivall, coined the term 'plural society', defining this as the coexistence of two or more 'social orders living side by side, yet without mingling'. In this type of society, production enjoyed a higher priority than consumption, while fostering a 'sectional division of labour' or a 'distribution of production among racial castes' (Furnivall 1939:446, 450-1). The outcome was a pyramidal hierarchy of economic activity with a top layer dominated by Western private enterprise and the huge sector of subsistence agriculture remaining a virtually exclusive indigenous domain. The Chinese and Arab minorities acted as intermediaries between the two. Although such a division of labour was based on complementary functions of ethnic groups, it presupposed colonial rule and it failed to guarantee an equitable distribution of gains from growth.

Economic segmentation by ethnic group was reflected in the very composition of the labour force. In 1930 the total registered labour force numbered 20.8 million, of whom 20.3 million (97.5 per cent) were indigenous Indonesians

1 It is not within the scope of this book to provide an in-depth coverage of economic and political trends in the immediate post-colonial era. The modern economic history of Indonesia is dealt with in recent comprehensive surveys (Booth 1998; Dick et al. 2002), while the story of constitutional democracy in Indonesia has been told in classic historical works (Feith 1962; Ricklefs 1981).

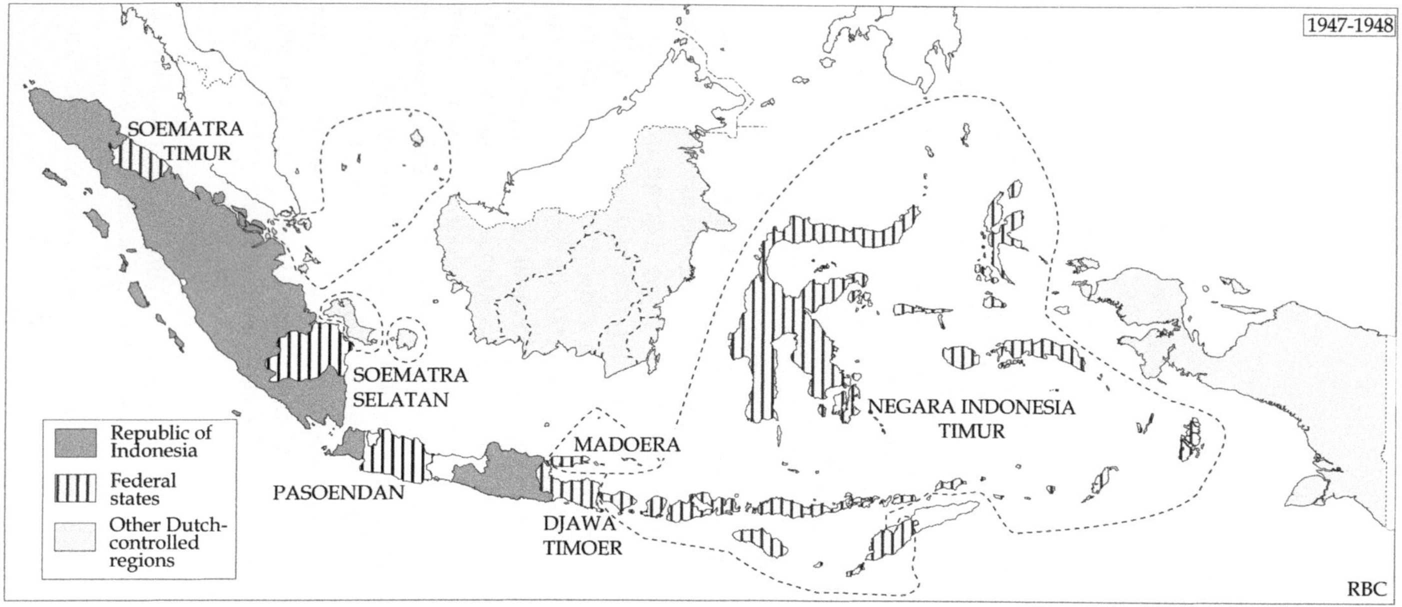

Map 2. The Indonesian archipelago in 1947-1948.
Source: Cribb 2000:160.

and fewer than 100,000 were Europeans. The majority of indigenous workers, more than 60 per cent, were engaged in agriculture, whereas the single most important sectors of employment were commerce among ethnic Chinese (36 per cent) and public service among Europeans (25 per cent). The contrast was particularly great between indigenous and European employees in non-agricultural pursuits. Trade, transport, and professional services each attracted about one-eighth of European employees; corresponding proportions in the indigenous work force were 5 per cent for trade and scarcely more than 1 per cent for transport and professional services (*Indisch Verslag* 1935, II:133-5).

For many years the discourse on the colonial economy was strongly influenced by the idea of economic dualism, first expounded by the Dutch scholar J.H. Boeke in his Leiden University dissertation of 1910 and subsequently reiterated in publications into the 1950s. This concept, with its Kiplingesque undertones, presupposes that the Western and Asian sectors of the economy were separated by an unbridgeable gap. The former was depicted as modern and dynamic, in contrast with the latter, which was viewed as traditional and stagnant. The modern sector existed by virtue of colonial rule. The indigenous Indonesian was considered by Dutch observers to be 'not an active participant but a passive object' (*geen actief deelnemer maar passief object*) in the process of modernization (Boeke 1953:203; see also *Verslag Commissie staatsrechterlijke hervormingen* 1941:68). Even at the time, however, a perceptive observer such as Furnivall wondered whether Boeke was not exaggerating the difference between Western and Asian modes of production (Furnivall 1939:460).

Subsequent research has shown Boeke's dichotomy to be essentially wrong. Indigenous smallholder producers of rubber in Sumatra and Kalimantan, and of copra in Sulawesi proved highly responsive to signals from the world market and were quick to reap benefits from the export boom in agricultural commodities in the early twentieth century (Touwen 2001:163-223). By 1940, to cite just one isolated statistic, the area under cultivation by indigenous smallholder rubber producers outside Java was twice as large as that in use by Western estates (Creutzberg 1975:94). Economic pluralism under colonial aegis thus also applied to entrepreneurship.

The structure of the colonial economy was highly traditional, geared towards primary production rather than manufacturing. Nevertheless, the economy was not stagnant. A spectacular economic expansion, driven by exports, took place between 1905 and the onset of the Depression in 1930. The increase in export volumes was impressive. Deliveries of Java sugar rose from one million tons in 1905 to 2.8 million tons in 1930, a nearly threefold increase. Exports of crude and refined oil products increased tenfold during the same period, from less than 500,000 to 4.5 million cubic metres. Rubber was added to the range of exports in 1912 and export volumes trebled during the 1920s alone. In the late 1920s, exports of tobacco, coffee, and copra were double what they had been in 1905 (Lindblad 1988b:284-8; Korthals Altes 1991:72-5; Dick et al. 2002:124-5). The story of the export industry's success was reflected in a juxtaposition of a favourable external market and flexible internal production capabilities. Or, in the words of the economist Kindleberger (1962:211), 'demand was right abroad and supply was right at home'.

The 1920s saw the zenith of export expansion from the colonial economy, a time years later still affectionately remembered by indigenous rubber producers in South Kalimantan as the 'golden rain' (*hujan emas*) (Lindblad 1988a:68-71). The expansion in the volume of exports was sustained in response to a fall in world prices for primary products after 1925. The drop in unit prices was more than compensated by the volume increase. This response to market signals applied equally to Western producers and to indigenous smallholders; it reflected rational entrepreneurial behaviour: working harder to retain the same level of income.

The export boom obviously had a positive effect on national income. According to estimates by the economic historian Pierre van der Eng, total national income increased by 37 per cent between 1920 and 1930 (Van der Eng 2002:171-2). Considering the simultaneous population growth of about 13 per cent, there must have been considerable scope for improvement in average per capita income. But the distribution of gains from growth was marked above all by the highly skewed distribution of income and wealth across ethnic groups.

So far no systematic attempt has been made to break down total national income by ethnic origin of producers. Van der Eng's method of reconstructing Indonesia's historical national accounts does not lend itself readily to such an exercise, since it estimates gross value added from undifferentiated total quantities of goods and services produced, flavoured with inferences and bold assumptions (Van der Eng 1992, 2002:168-70). An experimental study targeting one single region, Southeast Kalimantan (today's Kalimantan Selatan, Kalimantan Timur and part of Kalimantan Tengah), reveals how a fundamental dualism on ethnic grounds pervaded the economic structure, distorting gains from growth in such a way that far less was generated in terms of aggregate demand than what was potentially possible considering total regional income (Lindblad 1988a:202-15).

In 1943 the Dutch economist J.J. Polak published the first comprehensive attempt to estimate total national income in the Netherlands Indies, an exercise drawing on production statistics for the indigenous population and income tax returns for non-indigenous population groups. According to Polak's calculations, in the interwar period (1921-1939) indigenous Indonesians received 70 per cent of total national income compared to 20 per cent for Europeans and 10 per cent for residents of Chinese or Arab origin. Taking into account the difference in size of the population groups, this estimate translates into average per capita incomes in which one European earned as much as eight Chinese or 45 indigenous Indonesians (Creutzberg 1979:71; Dick et al. 2002:141-2).

Several important characteristics of the export industry came together to form a unique combination. First, although the range of exports continued to be heavily dominated by primary products, colonial Indonesia was less dependent on a few leading commodities than most tropical countries. In the early twentieth century, export goods such as sugar, coffee, tobacco, and tin were supplemented by oil, copra, and rubber, almost exclusively produced outside Java. In 1900, the share of the five top-ranking export goods was already less than 70 per cent; it remained at that level until the end of colonial rule (Booth 1998:207-8). Some export commodities were delivered exclusively by Western firms, notably sugar from Java, oil from Sumatra and Kalimantan, and tin from Bangka and Belitung. Other exports, such as rubber, coffee, and tobacco, were based on Western and indigenous production lines developing alongside one another and usually catering to different segments of the market. Finally, copra exports were virtually monopolized by indigenous producers in Sulawesi.

A second characteristic is a logical corollary of the first. The extended export range shifted its emphasis in production from Java to the Outer Islands. From the early 1920s the Outer Islands earned more than half of all export revenues (Dick et al. 2002:130), a feature of the Indonesian economy which has been consistently reinforced since independence. Eventually, in the very early twenty-first century, it formed the economic background of far-reaching reform in favour of decentralization of revenues and expenditures.

A third characteristic of the industry concerns the destination of exports. There was a successive shift away from the colonial mother country as the chief outlet (and also as a supplier of imports). The Dutch share in exports from colonial Indonesia fell from an average of 35 per cent in 1900-1904 to 19 per cent by 1939. Other foreign markets gained prominence, in particular Singapore, British India, the United States, and non-Dutch destinations in Western Europe (Korthals Altes 1991:100-3; Lindblad 1996b:112). This may be seen as a commercial emancipation of the colony from the mother country. From the perspective of the entrepreneur, the restructuring of export flows reflected an increasingly international outlook among Dutch enterprises in the colony as well as strong commercial links with mainland Southeast Asia, maintained by indigenous producers.

Restructuring also applied to imports. By 1933, when the colonial government introduced protectionist measures to stem rising volumes of imports from Japan, the Dutch share in total imports had fallen to 15 per cent (Dick et al. 2002:128). This was not the first wave of globalization to affect the Indonesian economy, nor was it the last, but it did give the Dutch version of

Indonesian employees in the colonial civil service, Algemeen Departement of Binnenlands Bestuur, in Batavia in 1937 (KITLV 29010)

colonial capitalism its distinct flavour of openness and confrontation with international competition.

A fourth and final characteristic of the export industry involves the balance of trade. Except for one single year (1921), the entire late-colonial period shows a consistent and often very substantial surplus in the balance of trade. Calculated over the period 1905-1930 the proportion of export revenues not spent on imports averaged about 38 per cent, reflecting a substantially higher share (53 per cent) in the Outer Islands than in Java (24 per cent) (Lindblad 1990:219-20). This is very high by any comparison. In the discourse on the economic effects of colonialism, the surplus in the balance of trade has come to serve as a proxy for 'colonial drain', the flowing away of resources from the colony to the mother country, enriching the latter but thwarting development in the former. Following Angus Maddison, Anne Booth extends the concept to include not only profit remittances by Western investors but also transfers benefiting Chinese intermediaries and overseas recipients. This 'double drain' perhaps explains why there was so much expansion yet so little sustained economic growth in late-colonial Indonesia. However, the assessment is challenged by Van der Eng, who considers most of the remittances to Western firms as a conventional or 'normal' return on employment of foreign capital, labour, and technology in colonial Indonesia. Moreover, the Chinese 'drain' remains almost impossible to substantiate or quantify (Booth 1990:291-3; Maddison 1990:326; Van der Eng 1998).

Non-indigenous players were of paramount importance in the colonial economy. The door to private foreign direct investment was wide open after the colonial government switched to liberal economic policies around 1870, symbolized by the gradual dismantling of the Cultivation System in Java and the introduction of individualized contractual relations between Western entrepreneurs and indigenous landowners-cum-labourers. Nevertheless, a protracted gestation period was required before private foreign investment reached a substantial volume. The quarter of a century between 1870 and the mid-1890s was also a gestation period in a different sense. It marked the transition from a reluctant or gradual kind of Dutch imperialism in the Indonesian archipelago to a forceful and rapid subjugation of territories not yet under effective colonial rule (Lindblad 1989a:23; Locher-Scholten 1994:110-1). The simultaneous breakthrough of foreign direct investment and the advent of aggressive imperialism was no coincidence.

Foreign direct investment in the colony remained unimpressive until the early twentieth century, when it began to rise rapidly, eventually reaching a level of 1.7 billion guilders in 1914. Further expansion brought the accumulated total to four billion guilders in 1930, which was subsequently reduced to about three billion guilders during the 1930s (Lindblad 1996b:113-4). An important proportion of the investment effort was financed by retained earnings from operations at existing production facilities. Dutch investors accounted for at least 70 per cent of the total. Three-quarters of all foreign direct investment went into estate agriculture (56 per cent) and mining, in particular oil (19 per cent). With data now available, it is possible to reconstruct annual new foreign investment going back as far as 1910, and to establish a statistically significant relationship between new foreign investment and yearly export revenues, which underscores the strong export orientation of foreign-owned enterprises in colonial Indonesia (Creutzberg 1977:17-8; Korthals Altes 1987:41; Lindblad 1996b:115, 1998:13-55).

Foreign investment assumed a peculiar shape in the colonial setting. Foreign investors were not always equally foreign. It is useful to identify five categories of alienness. First we may differentiate between indigenous Indonesians and those Indonesians who were considered aliens, in particular ethnic Chinese. A second type of differentiation separates Dutch-owned enterprises firmly rooted in the colonial economy from companies managed from the Netherlands – the former can be identified by the fact that their headquarters are located in the colony and may for convenience be labelled 'Netherlands Indies' undertakings. The fifth and final category covers foreign investors from third countries, notably Great Britain, the United States, and Japan, who were likely to be less familiar with legal institutions and informal connections than their Dutch competitors (Lindblad 1998:72-3). Annual firm-level data permit us to analyse the corporate network in the colony along these lines, with the caveat that indigenous entrepreneurs are hugely underrepresented since they were generally not inclined to choose Westernized forms of incorporation.

The total number of incorporated companies increased from 2,800 in 1914 to 3,700 around 1920, then declined successively to 3,300 in 1925, 2,800 in 1930, and fewer than 2,200 in 1940. Unrestrained optimism in the 1910s and 1930s apparently gave rise to a great many endeavours which in the long run did not prove viable, especially after the Depression had taken its toll during the 1930s. The single largest category of companies was the one labelled 'Netherlands Indies', accounting for 43 to 44 per cent of the total number in 1930 and in 1940. But many of these companies were small, as were the firms run by ethnic Chinese. Genuinely Dutch corporations with headquarters in the Netherlands claimed more than 70 per cent of total registered equity in 1930 compared to 14 per cent for 'Netherlands Indies' firms, and only 4 per cent for enterprises owned by ethnic Chinese, whereas British-owned companies alone commanded almost 10 per cent of the total.[2] In the corporate network

2 Lindblad 1998:72-9. The share of companies owned by ethnic Chinese in total equity is grossly underestimated in these calculations. Evidence suggests that earnings were not ploughed

of the colony a small number of large firms managed from abroad operated alongside a large number of small firms with a strong local entrenchment.

The prospect of making big profits lured foreign investors to the colony. There were indeed examples of spectacular returns. The small tea estates Santosa and Kertasarie in Priangan (West Java), for instance, paid out 200 per cent in dividends around 1930, the large tin-mining business Billiton offered its shareholders 70 per cent during the second half of the 1920s, while estate concern HVA guaranteed dividends at an average rate of 30 per cent throughout the 1920s.[3] Nevertheless, payments were usually far more modest. The ratio between paid-out dividends and registered equity amounted to 11 per cent around 1930. Rates were significantly higher among Dutch firms with headquarters in the Netherlands and lower for all other categories of incorporated companies. Different industries also showed considerable variation. The range was markedly better for sugar factories, with 9 to 20 per cent, than in manufacturing and rubber estates, with 5 to 10 per cent, whereas trading and tobacco offered less scope for a quick road to riches (4 to 7 per cent).[4] Profitability in colonial investment was high, but usually fell short of being extraordinary.

Ethnic Chinese played a unique role as intermediaries between foreign investors and the indigenous population. The most obvious manifestation was in trading, in which a conspicuously large proportion of ethnic Chinese found employment. Long-range international commerce was largely controlled by Dutch shipping and trading houses, whereas interregional trade and much local trade was handled by ethnic Chinese. Their intermediary role had been systematically reinforced by the Dutch in the nineteenth century, when ethnic Chinese were accorded a legally sanctioned position above indigenous residents but below Europeans. Ethnic Chinese were recruited by the colonial government as tax collectors. Managing tax firms for the Dutch often offered fertile ground for further economic expansion. Into the twentieth century this European-Chinese partnership in business continued and grew stronger (Claver 2006:167-8, 393). The most stunning example of success among ethnic Chinese was Oei Tiong Ham, owner of the largest sugar mill in Java, Redjoagoeng, as well as a shipping company, a bank and much real estate, mainly in his home town, Semarang. On his death in 1924, he left a business

back into such firms in the form of additional equity. Efforts were made to account for the most conspicuous cases of multiple nationalities in equity ownership such as the Anglo-Dutch concerns Bataafsche Petroleum Maatschappij (BPM, Batavian Petroleum Company) and Unilever.

3 ANRI, Jakarta: Algemeene Secretarie 808; Lindblad 1998:58, 82.

4 Bank Indonesia, Jakarta: De Javasche Bank (DJB) 126; Lindblad 1998:78, 80. Average rates could only be calculated for firms reporting non-zero dividend payments. A zero dividend may reflect either a decision by management to retain earnings or a reluctance to disclose this kind of information to outsiders.

empire worth 40 million guilders, which easily rivalled the leading Dutch trading houses in size and influence (Liem 1979; Dick 1993b).

Dutch colonial capitalism was defined by the juxtaposition of a high degree of integration in the world economy with an extreme degree of segmentation of functions in the domestic economy. Economic decolonization entailed sustaining the capacity to reap the benefits of the former without suffering from the disadvantages of the latter.

Seeds of transition

A young but perceptive observer, Suparto Brata's hero Kuntara does not fail to notice that the times are changing. On his walks through the Ngagel neighbourhood in southeast Surabaya, he is reminded of how his geography teacher used to refer to that area as the *Rührgebied van Soerabaia*, thus comparing it to the heart of industrial production in Germany (Suparto Brata 2002:250). Half a century later, in the early 1990s, the Surabaya metropolitan region had indeed asserted itself as a spearhead of industrialization in Indonesia. The momentous transition from a primarily agrarian to an industrial economy is arguably the single most important structural change in the Indonesian economy during the second half of the twentieth century. It is in more than one way linked to the process of economic decolonization.

In a provocative article the economic historian Howard Dick argues that at the end of the nineteenth century Indonesia had a real chance to launch itself into sustained economic growth through industrialization. Surabaya had the potential to pursue the same path as, for instance, Osaka or Bombay did at the time. But it did not happen. The domestic market was too small and unprotected from outside competition to permit a leading sector to reach maturity (Dick 1993a:137-8, 2003:253-80). Economic expansion in the colony remained strongly geared towards the export of primary products, although industrial activities, such as sugar-milling and oil refining, were becoming important too. Serious efforts to build up a manufacturing sector were by and large delayed until the 1930s. There are two sides to such a delay, which, by Dick's yardstick, would not have had to be protracted. One refers to colonial economic policy, the other to a macroeconomic trend rupture. Both are touched upon in this section.

The opening up of the Dutch colony to private foreign investment as of 1870 was accompanied by exceptionally liberal trade policies which remained in place for more than six decades, up until 1933. Free trade provided the maximum scope for export-led expansion, but it also exposed embryonic efforts at domestic manufacturing to fierce international competition. Under such conditions import substitution was not an option. Imports grew, albeit less rapidly than exports, and eventually encompassed not only rice, in which colonial Indonesia was not self-sufficient, but also a wide range of consumer and capital goods (Dick et al. 2002:127-8). Imports from third countries rose faster than those from the Netherlands, with Great Britain and Japan emerging as leading suppliers of, for instance, textiles. Occasionally, liberalism in the colonial trade policy was defended on the grounds that it safeguarded convenient market outlets for Dutch manufacturing, particularly the textile industry in the region of Twente in the eastern part of the Netherlands. Yet the true beneficiaries were third-country exporters, in particular those in Japan. The main party to be disadvantaged continued to be potential manufacturers in the colony, whether indigenous Indonesians, ethnic Chinese, or even Dutch-owned firms with a strong local basis.

During the second half of the 1920s goods procured from Japan constituted less than 10 per cent of total imports, but this changed rapidly after 1930. The high degree of integration into the world economy implied that Indonesian producers and consumers were almost instantly affected by the Depression. Purchasing-power for foreign consumer goods was seriously eroded. The squeeze on incomes for all population groups in combination with low Japanese prices and the steep depreciation of the yen caused a massive shift in import trade in favour of Japanese consumer goods. Japan's share in total imports climbed from 15 per cent in 1931 to 30 per cent in 1933 (Post 1991:184-9, 315).

In 1933 the colonial authorities switched to protectionism by issuing the Crisisinvoerordonnantie (Crisis Import Ordinance). Quotas were introduced as the regulatory instrument to curb imports. This departure from liberalism in colonial trade policy was predictably defended in the States-General of the Netherlands with a rhetorical reference to jobs at stake in Twente. Although ostensibly directed against foreign imports in general, scrutiny of the quota regulations reveals that Japanese imports were in fact specifically targeted. The intended effect soon materialized. By 1936 the Japanese proportion of imports had already dropped to one-quarter and it would fall still further during the remainder of the decade (Post 1991:315).

Protection against Japanese imports favoured not only more expensive imports from the Netherlands but, unintentionally, also domestic production set up to encourage import substitution. The more restrictive trade policy coincided with unprecedented initiatives by the colonial government to promote and accelerate industrialization. In 1934 a Bedrijfsreglementeringsordonnantie (Industrial Regulations Ordinance) was issued and in 1936 the first small industrial centres with shared facilities for local producers were established. They preceded the small production centres called *induk* which served to promote industrialization after independence.

The most conspicuous mechanization occurred in the textile industry. The number of weaving mills increased from fewer than twenty in 1930 to almost 2,000 in 1938, and factory employment rose from scarcely more than 6,000 in 1934 to 80,000 by 1941 (Baudet and Fasseur 1977:338). The number of modern handlooms in the production centres in Bandung and Majalaya, West Java, to cite just one more statistic, rose a hundredfold during the 1930s (Sitsen 1943:33). In Kudus, Central Java, indigenous and Chinese producers competed fiercely with one another in the booming *kretek* cigarette industry. Foreign firms also participated. Philips built a light bulb factory in Surabaya, General Motors opened an assembly line for motor cars in Batavia, Goodyear established Indonesia's first tyre factory, Bata started producing shoes for the local market, and Unilever brought locally produced margarine into Indonesian households. By the end of the 1930s colonial Indonesia was virtually self-sufficient in the supply of consumer products such as copra oil, beer, cigarettes, footwear, soap, and frying pans, but still highly dependent on textile imports (Segers 1987:34; Dick et al. 2002:160-1).

At long last, a colonial industrialization policy of some sort began to take shape, albeit far from consistent. Leading Dutch trading houses participated from the start. Internatio invested in local production, and plans were made to relocate part of Twente's textile manufacturing to Indonesia through the Java Textiel Maatschappij (Java Textile Company), which ran a pilot plant in Tegal, Central Java. After 1936 the emphasis shifted from light industry and consumer goods to heavy industry and the production of industrial goods. Self-sufficiency in terms of response to the threat of a Japanese invasion, became a priority, pushing the substitution of imports into the background. The urgency of this strategy was even more pressing following the outbreak of the Second World War in Europe in September 1939 and the German occupation of the Netherlands in May 1940. Ambitious plans included an aluminium plant in Asahan, North Sumatra, and a second cement factory, in addition to the one already operating at Padang, West Sumatra. Most of these plans did not reach implementation in the short period before the Japanese occupation in March 1942. However, some were realized decades later, notably the cement factory in Gresik near Surabaya in the mid-1950s and the aluminium smelter at Asahan in the early 1980s (Taselaar 1998:472-83; Dick et al. 2002:162; Dick 2003:291).

A second inconsistency concerned the ethnic origin of the entrepreneurs expected to take on the new industrial ventures. The colonial authorities were indecisive about whether to give preference to indigenous Indonesians or to ethnic Chinese or, alternatively, to large Dutch firms or multinationals from third countries. Discussions were invariably intertwined with a discourse about future modes of economic cooperation between the Netherlands and its colony. A powerful industrial lobby in the Netherlands urged that priority be given to the investment of Dutch capital, use of Dutch technology and Dutch management, all in order to revitalize direct economic links between the two countries. Industrialists in the Netherlands proposed schemes for joint ventures with British and even German capital (Van Oorschot 1956:39-59; Taselaar 1998:473-4).

The Netherlands also increased pressure for more direct state participation. Prime Minister Hendrikus Colijn, a former colonial administrator and one-time executive of the oil firm Bataafsche Petroleum Maatschappij (BPM, Batavian Petroleum Company), the colony's largest industrial enterprise, formulated a plan to increase the government's share in the tin exploitation on Belitung from 62.5 to 90 per cent. A leading nationalist figure, Muh. Husni Thamrin, headed the opposition when the matter was raised in the Volksraad (People's Council) in February 1937, after which the whole idea was abandoned (De Graaff 1997:536-7).

During the 1930s a rupture occurred in Indonesia's macroeconomic performance. The high degree of openness to the world market carried with it an extreme vulnerability to external price shocks. The main export commodities from colonial Indonesia had already fallen since 1925, but this downward movement was accelerated as soon as the Depression made itself felt in 1930. The decline in unit prices was so steep that the time-honoured strategy of compensating by increasing volumes in order to retain value levels no longer worked. Total exports, expressed in current prices, fell by 19 per cent in 1930, by another 36 per cent in 1931, and yet another 29 per cent in 1932. By 1932 rubber fetched only one-seventh of its 1929 price, whereas sugar, coffee, and copra were all down to one-quarter of pre-Depression price levels. The steep decline in exports was mirrored in reverse flows of trade, since purchasing power had dramatically eroded for all population groups. Annual rates of decline in imports amounted to 20 per cent in 1930, 33 per cent in 1931, and 35 per cent in 1932 (Korthals Altes 1991:56, 75; Dick et al. 2002:155).

Recovery was delayed for several years by the stubborn insistence of the Netherlands on maintaining the gold standard up until September 1936. Since the colony's currency, the Netherlands Indies guilder, was by law tied to the Dutch currency, the colony could not export itself out of its predicament in the same way as, for instance, neighbouring British colonies were able to, benefiting from the depreciated pound sterling from as early as 1931. The colonial economy was, in the words of one contemporary observer, suffering under 'the leaden burden of the golden guilder' (*de loden last van de gouden gulden*) (Meyer Ranneft 1937, I:296). Recovery came only in 1937, after the joint depreciation of the Dutch and Netherlands Indies guilder. The value of total exports climbed by almost 70 per cent, again approaching the one billion guilder mark already reached in 1930.

Income developments during the Depression were adverse for all. The greatest hardship was experienced by the indigenous population, for whom nominal incomes fell to a mere 40 per cent of the 1921 level. The decline in per capita Gross Domestic Product (GDP) in real terms has been estimated at 16 per cent for the first half of the 1930s, which, incidentally, is just a little more than the drop in incomes during the Asian crisis year of 1998 alone, when Indonesia's GDP dropped by 14 per cent. Per capita GDP did not regain its pre-Depression level until 1940 (Creutzberg 1979:70; Booth 2002:74; Dick et al. 2002:156). Supplementary qualitative evidence on consumption confirms that during the years 1933-1935 those worst hit in Java were the indigenous population (Boomgaard 2000:46).

The sugar export industry in Java virtually collapsed and would never fully recover. The key position of this export commodity was superseded by rubber, in which indigenous smallholders proved more successful than estates in adjusting to deteriorating market conditions. The share of smallholders in total output climbed from 30 per cent in 1932 to 50 per cent in 1939, despite government efforts to control indigenous production increases by imposing an unpopular special export duty on rubber produced by smallholders (Creutzberg 1975:94; Booth 1990:291). The oil sector was another major export industry staging a recovery, with refining capacity substantially increasing during the 1930s. Even so, by 1940 revenues from total oil exports had still not achieved the levels reached in 1929 or 1930 (Lindblad 1989b:76-7).

Throughout the entire 1930s total income in colonial Indonesia increased by 23 per cent when corrected for price fluctuations. Assuming an average population growth of 1.6 per cent annually or 16 per cent for the whole decade, we may infer that the scope for improvement of income levels was very limited during the decade of the Depression and its aftermath (Van der Eng 2002:171-2). The slowdown in economic expansion compared to the preceding quarter of a century was prolonged by the Japanese occupation and the Indonesian Revolution. These factors help us to better understand the enormous challenges of economic policy facing the Republican government immediately after independence, but the significance of the macroeconomic rupture in the 1930s reaches farther. In the long run its repercussions affected the structure and the very foundations of the Indonesian economy.

The tendency for terms of trade to turn against primary producers is a well-documented long-term trend in economic development. It applies in extreme form to colonial Indonesia during the Depression of the 1930s, and it also constrained the scope of possible economic growth later on. The export-oriented economy with its high degree of openness and dependence on demand for primary products under the aegis of colonialism could not offer a viable path for future economic development. Structural change and the creation of a more solid foundation for economic growth could be postponed for a while if prospects for oil and rubber on the world market were favourable, as was indeed the case in the 1950s. Sooner or later, however, Indonesia would have to face the necessity of a profound change in its economic structure. This was the most important lesson learned from the hardships of the 1930s.

Industrialization was the sole option for transcending the constraints of an inherited colonial economic structure. It was therefore unfortunate that initiatives in this direction materialized too late to have a significant impact. As a result, industrialization became an integral part of economic decolonization. It can be argued that the decisive turnabout in Indonesian economic development, as opposed to the nation's political development, took place in the 1930s rather than in the 1940s.

Early Indonesianisasi

On the threshold of Malaysian independence a Malay ruler, the Yang di-Pertuan of Negri Sembilan, dismissed indigenous entrepreneurship in an astonishingly blunt way. 'To teach a Malay to keep a shop', he said, 'you might as well teach a chicken to swim' (Harper 1999:248). Such attitudes fitted perfectly into the mental framework defined by Boeke's economic dualism, and were often voiced by officials in colonial Indonesia, at any rate informally. The economist J. van Gelderen has argued that 'the inhabitant of the tropics is further removed from the classical *homo economicus* than the Westerner' (Van Gelderen 1961:144). Others, such as G.H. van der Kolff, an agricultural extension officer, attributed the apparent lack of business rationality among indigenous entrepreneurs to poverty and the inherent constraints of an economic structure favouring Western sugar estates at the expense of Javanese rice farmers. There was considerable confusion in the colonial discourse about indigenous participation in the economy's modern sector, reasons for the lack of it, and how this might be redressed (Van der Kolff 1961:246-50; Booth 1998:290-3).

This section concerns two forms of *Indonesianisasi*, anticipating the emergence of indigenous business and the active promotion of indigenous management following independence. Prior to independence more was happening than caught the eye of contemporary European observers.

One obvious manifestation of successful indigenous entrepreneurship was the production of rubber for export by smallholders in Sumatra and Kalimantan. Although their alertness to signals from the world market did not differ from that of Western estates or ethnic Chinese traders, they generally did not opt for formal incorporation when setting up and running their business enterprises. This type of indigenous entrepreneurship was scarcely in need of promotion. The colonial government even showed reluctance to support smallholders for fear that this would cause rice cultivation to be neglected, necessitating costly imports. Along with colonial Indonesia's participation in the international rubber restriction scheme, from 1934, the colonial authorities also imposed a surtax on rubber exports to be paid only by indigenous smallholders (Touwen 2001:294-6). Indigenous business strategies were similarly successful among copra producers in Sulawesi, although conditions and regulations here were markedly different.

Indigenous business in the colonial period was not confined to export agriculture and smallholders. There were also successful ventures in manufacturing and services, where indigenous pioneers more often than not faced stiff competition from ethnic Chinese (Twang Peck Yang 1998:33). For illustrious examples of indigenous business success we need to return to the early decades of the twentieth century. A good example is provided by the Javanese Nitisemito.

In 1910 Nitisemito founded the *kretek* cigarette factory Nodjorono in Kudus, Central Java. The choice of location was no accident. Founded on an old and far smaller plant, run by H. Djamhari, Kudus quickly developed into a primarily industrial town, a unique feature in the Indonesian countryside at the time. Nitisemito was joined by other *kretek* producers, both Javanese and ethnic Chinese. By 1933 the Kudus cigarette industry boasted 15 large factories, 8 of which with indigenous proprietors, 48 medium-sized plants (60 per cent Chinese), and 800 small production units (two-thirds indigenous). The rising share of factory workers had already reached more than one-third of the industry's total labour force by the early 1930s. The Nodjorono factory alone was reported to employ 10,000 workers. However, competition from capital-rich ethnic Chinese intensified and the initial indigenous headstart vanished during the late 1930s and 1940s. Kudus increasingly resembled the other major production centre for *kretek* cigarettes in Java, located in the Brantas Valley of East Java, with factories in Blitar, Kediri, and Tulungagung. In 1934 41 out of 43 large and medium-sized *kretek* factories in the Brantas Valley were owned by ethnic Chinese (Van der Reijden 1936:115-6; Sutter 1959:4, 48-9; Robison 1986:26, 35, 58).

In 1912 three Javanese gentlemen named Raden Ng Dwidjosewojo, M.K.H. Soebroto and M. Adimidjojo met in what was then Batavia to establish the Boemiputera 1912 life insurance company. This was a precocious example of indigenous entrepreneurship choosing the legal format of a Western-style business firm yet catering exclusively to indigenous customers. The company survived mid-century turmoil and was eventually, in 1962, incorporated as PT (*Perseroan Terbatas*, Limited Liability) Bumiputera 1912, with activities extending into office management, leasing, and engineering contracting (Data Consult 1991:175). Bumiputera 1912 is the oldest indigenous conglomerate among the top business groups in present-day Indonesia.

Access to credit was obviously crucial to the success of enterprising new businessmen of whatever ethnic background. Here, however, indigenous entrepreneurs were at a disadvantage compared to ethnic Chinese, not to mention their European rivals. The financial sector in the colonial economy was poorly developed, with a small number of lending institutions and a high degree of reliance on overseas mobilization of capital, in particular in the Netherlands. Credit policies at the four Dutch-owned banks – NHM, the Java Bank, Nederlandsch-Indische Handelsbank, and Nederlandsch-Indische Escompto-Maatschappij (Netherlands Indies Escompto Company) – were requiring substantial collateral, thus effectively barring indigenous businessmen from borrowing significant amounts of money. Ethnic Chinese, by contrast, were able to draw extensively on credit provided by the four Dutch banks, as well as by a small number of other foreign banks (Claver 2006:286-91).

From 1912 the colonial government sought to stimulate the development of credit institutions for indigenous businesses by establishing and continually expanding the Volkscredietbank (People's Credit Bank). An elaborate network evolved including various small-scale credit institutions in villages or specifically for rice cultivation. Foreign visitors, including Furnivall arriving from British Burma, were impressed. On balance, however, the results were rather disappointing. Interest rates were high and investment in new production facilities was slow, since village banks in particular focused on financing short-term trade conducted by local women. The chief effect was to reinforce existing disparities between Western or Chinese channels of credit on the one hand, and indigenous ones on the other (Soemitro Djojohadikoesoemo 1943; Alexander and Alexander 1991:386-7; Booth 1998:303-7). Banks owned by ethnic Chinese enjoyed a strong lead over indigenous Indonesian banking. Besides the Oei Tiong Ham concern in Semarang, there were smaller ethnic Chinese banks, for instance The Fak Tong, set up in 1920 in Pontianak, West Kalimantan, in order to finance export trade (Ranken 1989:203).

Eventually private indigenous banks did emerge. The first of these was Bank Nasional Indonesia, founded in Surabaya on 20 October 1928 with an initial capital of 5,000 guilders. Its very location reflected Surabaya's long standing as one of Java's two financial centres (Dick 2003:417). A second bank soon followed. On 27 December 1930 Bank Nasional Boekittinggi was established in Fort de Kock (now Bukittinggi), West Sumatra. The founding fathers comprised a collective of ten local businessmen; the bank had been preceded by an association of traders, Himpoenan Saudagar Indonesia (Indonesian Merchants' Association), operating out of Padang. The bank's main activity was to deposit savings and give credit. With only 1,000 guilders, initial capital was even less than that of the bank in Surabaya. The primary aim of the new institution was to 'counter pressure from large-scale Chinese traders supported by the Dutch' (*untuk menghadapi tekanan dari pedagang besar Cina yang didukung oleh Belanda*) (Erniwati 2004:10).

At Bank Nasional, as it was known after 1931, when 'Boekittinggi' was dropped from its name, total outstanding credit rose to 115,000 guilders in 1945 and over 600,000 guilders in 1951, the increase in part being attributable to high inflation during the Indonesian Revolution. In 1946 the bank was incorporated as a limited liability company with eight shareholders, including two of the founding fathers, Anwar gelar Soetan Saidi and H. Muh. Jatim. Anwar served as a director together with Sofjan gelar Soetan Berahim, who was also a trader from Bukittinggi (Narny 1996:41). These two remarkable initiatives in banking, in East Java and West Sumatra, preceded the larger institutions set up by the Indonesian government after independence to provide sufficient financial backing for emerging indigenous entrepreneurship.

The textile industry, arising out of traditional home weaving and batik painting, began to flourish during the 1930s. It was promoted by the colonial government through the newly established Textiel Inrichting Bandoeng (Bandung Textile Institute), which in 1922 had introduced a mechanical weaving loom with a productive capacity five times larger than that of a traditional machine. In the late 1920s this type of loom gained acceptance among Sundanese landowners and merchants, who became the pioneers of the weaving industry in West Java, in particular in and around Majalaya near Bandung. Dramatic expansion followed after 1933, when imports of cheap Japanese textiles were being curbed by the newly introduced protectionism in the Netherlands Indies. By the late 1930s 81 per cent of all weaving mills and handlooms in Java were found in the area around Majalaya. This town alone had 275 weaving mills and almost 3,300 handlooms (Booth 1998:284; Keppy 2001:24-67). Yet rapid expansion was accompanied by fierce competition, and many indigenous textile producers were allegedly pushed out by ethnic Chinese entrepreneurs. On the eve of the Japanese occupation Sundanese pioneers owned three-quarters of the handlooms in the region, but controlled less than one-quarter of the larger production units and increasingly served as subcontractors to firms owned by ethnic Chinese. The latter owned one-third of all handlooms in Bandung (Antlöv and Svensson 1991:117).

As in the case of textiles, the colonial government actively supported indigenous prahu shipping during the 1930s (Dick 1987b:120), a decade which witnessed the establishment of a great variety of manufacturing and trading firms by indigenous businessmen who were to play a prominent part in Indonesian economic life following independence. A few typical examples are Tjandra Djojonegoro, who founded a rice wine distillery named PT Perindustrial Bapak Djenggot, the nucleus of the later ABC conglomerate; Sekar Djaja, forerunner of the Sekar conglomerate, who in 1933 began with agro-industrial production in Surabaya; and Raden Mas Koesmoeljono, who received his education in the Netherlands and worked briefly as a lawyer in Kalimantan before becoming the director of a coconut oil plant in Tegal, West Java – in 1945 he became the founder of Bank Perniagaan in Yogyakarta (Data

Consult 1991:52, 631).

Sumatran traders were equally important. H. Rachman Tamin began trading in Bukittinggi (then Fort de Kock) in 1914, moved to Padang in 1923, and to Batavia in 1932, where he collaborated closely with Chinese merchants (Robison 1986:54). Around 1935 Agoes Moesin Dasaad from Lampung joined forces with Djohan and Djohor and H. Abdul Ghany Aziz in a successful attempt to break the Chinese monopoly in textile imports from Japan. Although he quickly made plenty of money, his true breakthrough as a top indigenous businessman came later, during the Japanese occupation. Several of the successful Sumatran traders functioned in the 1930s as intermediaries for Japanese export firms penetrating the local Indonesian market (Post 1997:97-9).

On a local and more modest scale, a whole host of manufacturing activities was set up by indigenous business firms, especially in and around Yogyakarta. They often chose modes of incorporation that were not fully compatible with European business law. Only in 1939 a legal format was introduced tailored specifically to indigenous business. This legal entity, called 'Inheemsche Maatschappij op Aandeelen' (*Maskapai Andil Bumiputera,* indigenous shareholding company), could be established without the involvement of a notary, with indigenous participants each owning up to 75 hectares of land. The timespan of operations was shorter than for firms incorporated under European law, 30 years instead of 75 (Sutter 1959:104).

Kretek factories, weaving mills, and embryonic beginnings of later conglomerates in manufacturing and trading all underscore the new spirit of indigenous entrepreneurship emerging towards the very end of colonial rule. A keen observer such as D.H. Burger, preparing to enter colonial civil service, felt confident to assert in 1939 that an indigenous business class was finally emerging in the colony (Burger 1939:239).

The other form of *Indonesianisasi* prior to independence was the promotion of indigenous Indonesians to higher positions in private Western companies and in the colonial civil service.

The record for Western private business is straightforward. Rarely, if ever, do we encounter an indigenous Indonesian employee in a supervisory or management position above the level of overseer of production (*mandur*). One example may be cited from the Java Bank, formally a private corporation but with a public function as the colony's central bank. Throughout the 1920s and 1930s one or at most two out of about 100 supervisory employees listed in the annual reports were indigenous Indonesians, whereas, strikingly, almost all of the cashiers were ethnic Chinese (Lindblad 2004b:33). Social segregation based on ethnicity was even stricter in private business than in government institutions.

A major stumbling block was language. Proficiency in Dutch was the chief criterion for gaining access to higher positions. This 'artificial' language barrier perpetuated the strict segregation along ethnic lines in colonial society and effectively blocked upward social mobility for indigenous Indonesians (Sartono Kartodirdjo 1986:199). Paradoxically, therefore, *Indonesianisasi* in the colonial setting presupposed a command of the Dutch language and was thus closely linked to educational policies pursued by the Dutch colonial authorities.

The Ethical Policy, launched in 1901, placed a high priority on education. In its wake, government expenditure on schools increased, although still not amounting to more than 2 per cent of the total colonial budget in 1913 (Booth 1998:142; Dick et al. 2002:117-21). Many schools were founded and opportunities for indigenous Indonesians increased. Yet the structure of the educational system continued to be highly segregated. The primary level consisted of four types of schools: the European primary school, reserved for Dutch children and a handful of offspring of the non-European elite; the Dutch-Native (*Hollandsch-Inlandsche*) school with teaching largely in Dutch and pupils from the indigenous middle class; the Dutch-Chinese (*Hollandsch-Chineesche*) school; and, finally, the exclusively indigenous primary school with all instruction in Indonesian or a regional language.[5] A full-fledged secondary education was only available to those who had completed the European primary school. At a higher level still, there were facilities for vocational training in Java, for instance technical schools in Surabaya, Yogyakarta and Bandung, as well as the school for the training of indigenous doctors, STOVIA (*School Tot Opleiding Van Inlandsche Artsen*), renowned for the part played by its students in the emergence of the Indonesian nationalist movement in 1908. University students went to the Netherlands.

Intentions were sincere but results could not fail to disappoint observers. By 1920 European primary schools had only 2,630 pupils, of whom 50 per cent were Europeans, 43 per cent indigenous, and 7 per cent ethnic Chinese. The Dutch-Indonesian schools had 38,000 pupils, whereas the purely indigenous primary schools had 780,000 pupils (Sartono Kartodirdjo 1986:210; Booth 1998:270). In relation to the total population at the time, nearly 54 million, these numbers translate into a crude enrolment ratio of only 1.5 per cent. Numbers were smaller still at higher levels of education. The school year 1938-1939 saw 800 pupils in secondary and 267 students in tertiary education, respectively one-quarter and one-half of whom were indigenous Indonesians. The ever-observant Furnivall noted that enrolment rates were lower than in British Malaya, Thailand, and the Philippines (*Verslag Commissie staatsrechter-*

5 The term 'native' with its unmistakable condescending undertone is the most appropriate translation of the Dutch term *inlander* (or *inlands*), which was widely used in colonial society and traditional historiography. Its use today is discouraged among serious scholars.

lijke hervormingen 1941:62-3; Furnivall 1943:111; Booth 1998:271-5). Very few indigenous Indonesians could nurture the ambition of obtaining a higher position in colonial society.

The deliberate and successful policy of segregation by language served a political function. Especially after the first large-scale outburst of militant Indonesian nationalism, in 1926-1927, the colonial government considered it essential to prevent the creation of an intellectual proletariat of well-educated Indonesians who shared Western values and expectations but for whom Western incomes remained out of reach (Kahin 1952:55). In the event, however, almost all pioneers of the nationalist movement had received their training in the Dutch language section of the educational system and were highly proficient in Dutch. Whatever the political undertones and implications of the colonial educational policy may have been, it did determine the scope for effective *Indonesianisasi* prior to independence.

Almost half of all indigenous Indonesians with a Dutch language education between 1900 and 1928 ended up working in the colonial civil service (Sartono Kartodirdjo 1984:123). Private foreign-owned business simply did not offer much of a career path for talented Indonesians. Therefore the only appreciable progress in *Indonesianisasi* occurred within the ranks of the civil service.

In 1928 the colonial civil service consisted of about 108,800 people distributed across three different but partly overlapping salary classes. Those with the lowest pay were in Class A, with annual salaries ranging from 150 to 2,500 guilders, while at the other extreme, in Class C, most salaries were between 2,500 and 16,000 guilders per year. Civil servants in Class B earned more than 500 but less than 9,500 guilders (*Indisch Verslag* 1932, II:377).

The ethnic composition of the salary classes is revealing. Class A with 84,300 members (77 per cent) consisted almost exclusively (99.6 per cent) of indigenous Indonesians. Their share dropped to 30 per cent in Class B, totalling 16,200 employees (15 per cent). The share of European civil servants, on the other hand, rose from being negligible in Class A to 69 per cent in Class B and 97 per cent in Class C. Scarcely more than 200 of the 8,100-odd members in the highest-paid class were of non-European origin, with most of these being ethnic Chinese (*Indisch Verslag* 1932, II:377). Indonesians did find employment in the colonial civil service but only in the lower ranks.

Around 1930 a cautious awareness had dawned that it might be a good idea to redress the extreme imbalance in the ethnic composition of the colonial bureaucracy. Instead of *Indonesianisasi* the late-colonial discourse would, on occasion, include the awkward term 'Indianization' (*indianisatie*). The fact that the term had at least three different definitions caused further confusion. *Indianisatie* could be used to refer to 'extreme' nationalist standpoints, it could also imply that everything Indonesian was of an inferior 'indigenous level' (*inlandsch peil*), and yet another meaning was 'the elevation of the Indies to the heights of a civilized nation' (*het opheffen van Indië tot de hoogte van cultuurstaat*) (*BBL* 1931:17).

Some progress was made in the early 1930s, just when the colonial authorities began cutting expenditure in response to the Depression. Between 1928 and 1932 the total number of civil servants was reduced, albeit by only 5 per cent. Some European employees in Class B were replaced by indigenous Indonesian employees and by 1932 the proportion of Europeans in Class B had fallen to 58 per cent, with the proportion of indigenous Indonesians now exceeding 40 per cent (*Nota* 1935:15; *Indisch Verslag* 1936, II:395). Initial progress in implementing *Indonesianisasi* in the colonial civil service was aided by the possibility of offering indigenous Indonesians a lower salary than their European predecessors, as is demonstrated by the wide range covered by Class B. One of the very few examples of an indigenous Indonesian occupying a position at the apex of the bureaucracy was Muh. Husni Thamrin, who in 1927 was elected as the first indigenous alderman in Batavia (Abeyasekere 1989:126).

Indonesianisasi of the colonial bureaucracy continued throughout the 1930s, particularly in administrative positions, and to a lesser extent in financial and technical positions. A different type of classification, based on educational background rather than salary level, reveals that the highly skewed distribution was still largely intact in 1938. Proportions of indigenous Indonesians and Europeans were inversely related to the level of education. Among colonial civil servants educated to only primary school level, 99 per cent were indigenous Indonesians, but that proportion fell to 64 per cent for those with lower secondary school education and to 40 per cent if secondary school had been completed. Civil servants with tertiary education were 92 per cent Europeans, and 7 per cent indigenous Indonesians, which left a mere 1 per cent for ethnic Chinese (*Verslag Commissie staatsrechterlijke hervormingen* 1941, I:55-6; *Japanese military administration* 1963:51-2; Baudet and Fasseur 1977:330). It was a hierarchical arrangement mirroring colonial society at large.

Post-colonial trends

The slogan 'from a colonial economy to a national economy' (*dari ekonomi kolonial ke ekonomi nasional*), coined by Soejono Hadinoto in 1949, primarily meant wresting economic power from the Dutch. In a broader sense, this transition also entailed getting rid of other features of the economy closely associated with colonial rule, in the same way as the establishment of constitutional democracy required a decisive break with authoritarian colonial rule. The transition from a colonial to a national economy during the 1950s was accompanied by new developments in macroeconomic performance and political constellations which need to be kept in mind in order to fully understand the process of economic decolonization. This section sketches some trends in population, labour force, national income, foreign trade, foreign investment, money supply and foreign exchange, public finance, and the political arena.

It is useful to start with the demographic dimensions. Around 1940 the total population can be estimated at 66 million, close to 45 million in Java and 21 million in the Outer Islands (Lindblad 1993:246; Gooszen 1999:43). By 1950 the total population had increased to 77 million, reaching 85 million in 1955 (Ricklefs 1981:225). Slow growth, at an average annual rate of 1.2 per cent during the 1940s, reflected the extreme hardships of the Japanese occupation and the Indonesian Revolution. The population of Java and Madura is reported to have fallen by 2.5 million during the Japanese occupation, not taking into account hundreds of thousands never to return from forced labour.[6] There was an acceleration in population growth which peaked as conditions improved in the 1950s.

In 1961, when the first nationwide census in the post-colonial era was held, Indonesia had 96.4 million inhabitants, an increase of 25 per cent since 1950. The labour force numbered 35 million, a low degree of participation due to the young average age of the population. According to the 1961 census 72 per cent of the labour force was engaged in agriculture, 7.5 per cent in manufacturing, 9 per cent in trading and transport, and the rest, 11.5 per cent, in other services, including government. Such an occupational distribution is typical of a traditional economic structure in which subsistence farming and exports of primary products prevail. However, the pattern had changed since the early 1950s, but not in the expected direction. The share of the labour force population working in agriculture had even risen whereas the share of those working in manufacturing and services had fallen.[7] Inaccuracies in measurement may explain part of the difference, but not enough to reverse the observed trend.

The trend away from, not towards, modernization of the economic structure has been labelled 'structural retrogression' by Anne Booth, an authoritative historian of the Indonesian economy (Booth 1998:70). Structural retrogression suggests a high or rising share of peasant agriculture in the national income and a share of manufacturing which at any rate did not exceed levels

6 De Jong 2002:280; ANRI, Jakarta: Algemeene Secretarie: 806, 15-4-1946. This estimate was based on extrapolation from a mortality surplus in the Batavia region of 22 per 1000, caused by a decline in the birth rate to 18 per 1000 and a simultaneous increase in the death rate to 40 per 1000.

7 Suhadi Mangkusuwondo 1976:30. The 1961 census shows some notable idiosyncrasies in occupational distribution. Agriculture includes mining (0.3 per cent of the labour force), whereas manufacturing also encompasses construction and public utilities (together 1.9 per cent). The dividing line between public service and a range of various private services is not clear-cut.

at the end of colonial rule (Robison 1986:64).

The case for structural retrogression becomes less clear-cut when we consider the composition of net domestic product at factor cost. The share of agriculture was very high, at 57 per cent in 1952-1954, but then fell, to 53 per cent in 1957. The share of manufacturing rose from an average of 8.5 per cent in 1952-1954 to 12 per cent in 1957. In 1958 agriculture accounted for about 50 per cent, manufacturing for 13.5 per cent, and services for 32 per cent of national income.[8] The tendency towards structural retrogression had been halted.

The lopsided structure of the economy is borne out by a differentiation of exports by type of production. There were really only three lines of export production. Oil claimed a share in total exports increasing from less than one-fifth in 1950 to one-quarter by 1956. Two parallel lines of export production in agriculture, smallholders and estates, combined to supply almost 90 per cent of non-oil exports. Smallholders traditionally produced more than estates, but the proportion changed from 65:35 in 1950 to 55:45 in 1956 (Appendix 2, Table 3).

The oil industry was monopolized by three foreign-owned companies; most estates were also foreign-owned until the late 1950s. Assuming for the sake of argument that the estate sector was fully owned and managed by foreign capital, we may surmise that the foreign-controlled share of total export earnings increased from 53 per cent in 1950 to 70 per cent in 1956. The tendency towards a larger share of foreign capital in the export industries, the economy's engine of growth, ran counter to all the objectives of *Indonesianisasi*.

Regrettably, the rough approximation of the ratio between foreign-controlled and domestically owned lines of export production cannot be extrapolated to the entire economy. No calculations of national income in Indonesia during the 1950s provide a breakdown by ethnic origin. According to one single global estimate, the 'modern' sector occupied one-quarter of the economy and was strongly dominated by Dutch and other foreign investment (Higgins 1992:51).

The Sukarno period has acquired a singularly bad reputation for macroeconomic performance which is not entirely deserved. The cataclysmic ending of the regime, amidst negative growth, skyrocketing inflation, and widespread misery, makes it easy to overlook that performance at an earlier stage was not at all bad. National income, expressed as GDP, rose in real terms (after correction for inflation) by on average 6 per cent between 1951 and 1957; the pre-war level of 1941 was fully restored by 1953 (Van der Eng 1992:369). The result was an annual increase in real per capita GDP of about 2 per cent despite

8 Suhadi Mangkusuwondo 1975:13; Bank Indonesia 1966:3. The remainder, 4.5 per cent, was in mining and construction, listed separately in the statistics for 1958.

rapid population growth (Dick et al. 2002:178, 192). Growth performance was impressive compared to other Third World countries, let alone the dismal record of Indonesia itself during the 1940s and mid-1960s. External conditions were favourable, with the Korean War boom bolstering demand in world markets for oil and rubber.

Indonesia's foreign trade performance was especially impressive in the very early 1950s, but tapered off in 1952 and then remained at a rather constant level for several years (Appendix 2, Table 2). Total exports rose by more than 60 per cent in 1951, but 1952 saw a sharp drop, from $ 1.3 billion in the previous year to $ 930 million, or from Rp. 14.7 billion to Rp. 10.6 billion when denominated in Indonesian currency at the official exchange rate after the steep devaluation on 4 February 1952.[9] The years 1954 and 1955 saw constant export revenues but severely reduced expenditures on imports. As a consequence, the surplus in the balance of trade resurfaced.

Rubber and oil continued to play the role of prime earners of foreign exchange. Their combined share in the total never fell below 57 per cent during the years 1950-1957 and rubber alone accounted for 40 per cent on average, higher in 1951, 1952, and 1955 but lower in other years (Thomas and Panglaykim 1973:86). Production capacity in the rubber sector was almost twice as high in 1952 as it had been in the late 1930s. Nearly 700 estates produced one-third of total output while smallholders supplied the rest, albeit at a lower price per ton.[10] Such information testifies to both the rapid reconstruction of foreign-owned estates and the versatility of smallholder producers outside Java.

There are various important aspects of Indonesia's comeback as a major supplier of raw materials on the world market. One relates to the base for export production, which had become narrower than ever before. Large segments of the export-oriented economy outside rubber and oil were in fact performing badly. Recovery was especially slow on the sugar estates. The number of mills in operation in Java rose from 31 in 1950 to 54 in 1955, a far cry from the 84 which had been working in 1939. By the mid-1950s output still amounted to only half of pre-war levels. The slow recovery of the once so vital sugar industry was ascribed to changing prospects in foreign markets and adverse internal production conditions, aggravated by widespread theft

9 The exchange rate changed from parity between the rupiah and the guilder (Rp. 1 = one guilder) or Rp. 3.80 per dollar, to Rp. 3 per guilder or Rp. 11.40 per dollar. The official new exchange rate announced in February 1952 was roughly equivalent to the rate already prevailing on the black market in late 1950. Bank Mandiri, Jakarta: Jaarverslag NHM Factorij 1950-51, I:58.

10 Bank Indonesia, Jakarta: DJB 184, 19-9-1952; Bank Mandiri, Jakarta: Jaarverslag NHM Factorij 1953, II:45-6; Bank Indonesia 1954:134.

and cane burning.[11] Similar difficulties were reported from tobacco and palm oil estates in the plantation belt of North Sumatra.

The traditional structure of the Indonesian economy was also reflected in imports (Appendix 2, Table 4). The share of raw materials was disturbingly large, never below one-third, and on occasion climbing to one-half of total imports. This category included rice, which implies that productivity in food agriculture was still distressingly low (Booth 1988:1). Textiles may serve as a proxy for consumer goods in general. The high share of textiles, exceeding that of raw materials in all years except 1954 and 1955, conveys the message that the capacity of domestic textile manufacturing was insufficient for import substitution on an appreciable scale. The low share of capital goods, less than one-fifth, reflects a limited demand for advanced machinery and equipment in processing industries. A decisive step in the direction of raising productivity and levels of technological sophistication would have pushed the imports of capital goods upwards, both absolutely and relatively, whereas imports of basic foodstuffs and simple manufactured goods would have become less important.

Consequently, Indonesia remained excessively dependent on a small number of export products, basically rubber and oil, while importers faced high international prices for goods which to some extent could have been produced domestically. Indonesia's competitive edge in the world market, expressed in commodity terms of trade (export price level divided by import price level), was potentially subject to deterioration as a result of adverse price movements in the world market. This is indeed what happened after 1951. Terms of trade in 1952 and 1953 were down to less than 80 per cent of the 1950 level. Although some recovery followed in 1955 and 1956, for the remainder of the decade terms of trade remained significantly below the level of 1950 and 1951 (Bank Indonesia 1954:116, 1959:182). Within a short span of time Indonesia became an almost perfect illustration of the Singer-Prebisch hypothesis in economic theory, which predicts a long-term development in terms of trade in favour of the developed world, where industrialization has already taken place.

Almost all of Indonesia's foreign trade was with other countries in Asia, Europe, and the Americas, in that order. A reduced dependence on Western markets, or at any rate West European markets, for export sales and purchases of imports would have resulted in an increase in the Asian share in total Indonesian trade, possibly also in the proportion of the Americas. In the event, trading patterns did change in the short run but not in the long run (Appendix 2, Table 5). American export destinations gained at the expense

11 Bank Indonesia, Jakarta: DJB 1583; Bank Indonesia 1954:144; Sutter 1959:704-6.

of those in Asia in 1952 and 1955, whereas European destinations gained at the expense of American ones in 1956. By 1957 the share of Asian buyers was slightly above the 1951 level but not enough to speak of a sustained reorientation. The import side showed more stability. Major changes included a shift away from American sellers as of 1954. At first Asian rivals gained the most, but in 1955 European suppliers experienced a short-lived boom. Compared to 1951, the situation in 1957 was more favourable to Europe and less favourable to the Americas.

Although statistics are scarce, the evidence suggests that flows of fresh foreign investment remained very modest during the 1950s and would virtually dry up during the final phase of Sukarno's rule. The sole exception was the oil industry, in which three foreign firms, Royal Dutch/Shell, Caltex, and the Standard Vacuum Petroleum Company (Stanvac), continued to expand under 'Let Alone' agreements exempting them from many of the regulations affecting operations of other foreign-owned companies at the time (Lindblad 1998:104-5).

In 1950 one of the first tasks of the Indonesian government was to impose a uniform currency throughout the nation. In a spectacular manoeuvre in March 1950 the circulating paper money was literally cut in half: the left half could be exchanged for newly printed rupiah bills, the right half for government bonds. This operation was popularly known as *gunting Sjafruddin* ('the Sjafruddin cut'), after Minister of Finance Sjafruddin Prawiranegara. In one stroke the operation achieved both a purge of unwanted currencies and a reduction of the money in circulation, to stem inflationary pressures (Sjafruddin Prawiranegara 1987:102).

The most extraordinary part of monetary and exchange policies in Indonesia was the system of multiple exchange rates in use during the 1950s and early 1960s. The rate depended on the type of transaction, at first in exports only, later also in imports. Eventually the system grew even more complex. Differentiation of foreign exchange rates arose from either the exchange rate itself or from a whole host of taxes, tariffs, and surcharges imposed on, notably, imports of luxury goods and transfers of profits (Corden and Mackie 1962; Mackie 1971:63-7; Dick et al. 2002:191-3; Dick 2004:178-80). In 1954 the official rate of exchange was Rp. 3 per guilder. Yet due to all kinds of surcharges, the actual rate of transfers to foreign countries became Rp. 9.50 per guilder.[12] Indonesia was not the only country to make use of multiple exchange rates. At the time this regulatory instrument was not uncommon among Third World nations. However, it is unlikely that the complexity of the system in Indonesia was matched elsewhere in the world.

12 Bank Mandiri, Jakarta: Jaarverslag NHM Factorij 1954, I:2.

Under the international monetary system agreed upon at Bretton Woods, nations were expected to refrain from adjusting their exchange rates. Therefore it is not surprising that the official international exchange rate of the Indonesian rupiah remained constant at Rp. 11.40 to the dollar throughout most of the 1950s. What did change, however, was the actual market value of the Indonesian rupiah, as it was reduced by inflation and by a rapid enlargement of the domestic money supply. The system of multiple exchange rates and vigorous trading in foreign exchange certificates only widened the gap between the official exchange rate and the rate prevailing on the black market (Appendix 3).

In 1957 the dollar was worth four times the official rate. In August 1959 a dramatic attempt was made to redress this increasingly anomalous situation. The value of the rupiah dropped to one-tenth of the nominal denomination and the new official exchange rate was Rp. 45 instead of Rp. 11.40 per dollar. This was still far above the black market rate (Perbanas 1974:54; Dick et al. 2002:192). Widespread circumvention of complex regulations and the widening gap between official and black markets reinforced each other in undermining the trading system and fostering rent-seeking and corruption (Dick 2004:187-9).

A final word needs to be said about political constellations – political parties, the succession of cabinets, the armed forces, trade unionism, and regional responses to central government policy.

The provisional constitution coming into effect in Indonesia on 17 August 1950 made the cabinet directly accountable to parliament and limited presidential power. In 1950 the 232 seats in the Dewan Perwakilan Rakjat (DPR, Council of People's Representatives) were distributed across a large number of political parties and individuals in anticipation of general elections. Between them the two largest parties had only 85 seats in the DPR, scarcely more than one-third of the total. No single political party was strong enough to form a cabinet outright. All cabinets had to be based on coalitions of continuously varying composition.

With 49 seats the Islamic Masjumi was the largest party in the DPR. Founded during the Japanese occupation, it appealed to nationalists and moderate Muslims alike. Its leaders, Moh. Natsir and Sukiman Wirjosandjojo, were modernist politicians who did not wish to associate themselves with the ideals of an Islamic state as propagated by the rebellious Darul Islam movement. The same pragmatism was espoused by Sjafruddin Prawiranegara, who later became the first Indonesian president of the nation's central bank. In 1952 a split occurred in the ranks of Masjumi when the party's orthodox faction merged into the previously apolitical Islamic organization, the Nahdlatul Ulama (NU, Rise of Religious Scholars).

With 36 seats in the DPR the Partai Nasional Indonesia (PNI, Indonesian

National Party) was second largest. This was the party most closely affiliated to President Sukarno and Hatta, considering itself the rightful successor to the party founded by Sukarno in 1927 under the name Perserikatan Nasional Indonesia (Indonesian National Association). It was endorsed by the government bureaucracy and by direct supporters of the President, including non-Muslims outside Java. In the general elections of 1955 PNI even won more votes than Masjumi, 8.4 million to 7.9 million, resulting in an equal number of seats in the DPR, 57. NU ranked third, after PNI and Masjumi (Appendix 1).

Alongside nationalism and Islam, socialist concepts provided a powerful source of ideological inspiration for politicians in Indonesia immediately after independence. A moderate social democratic variant was offered by the Partai Sosialis Indonesia (PSI, Indonesian Socialist Party) founded in 1948 by followers of former Prime Minister Sutan Sjahrir. In 1950 it was rewarded with seventeen seats. One of its prominent members was the economist Sumitro Djojohadikusumo, who during the 1950s served in several cabinets. In the elections of 1955 the party ranked only eighth; up to that point, however, it had played a disproportionately large role in Indonesian political life.

The most radical variant of socialism was of course Partai Komunis Indonesia (PKI, Indonesian Communist Party), which was the single largest one outside the Communist bloc. PKI recovered from the suppression of the Madiun uprising in 1948 and obtained thirteen seats in the DPR at the allocation in 1950. From 1951 it was led by the charismatic D.N. Aidit. It maintained strong links with radical unionism, in particular through the, Sentral Organisasi Buruh Seluruh Indonesia (SOBSI, Central All-Indonesia Workers' Organization). The position of PKI as the nation's fourth largest political party, ranking immediately behind NU, was reaffirmed in the general elections of 1955, when it attracted 16 per cent of the votes. PKI became the most vocal opposition party in parliament, as it did not participate in any cabinet during the period of constitutional democracy.

After 1950 party politics were of far greater importance than they had been previously. Throughout the Indonesian Revolution, from August 1945 until December 1949, the struggle against the Dutch was unquestionably the main priority. At this time, the party political system itself was still very much in its infancy. Indonesia's first two prime ministers, Sjahrir and Amir Sjarifuddin, were both social democrats, but their cabinets also contained PNI and Masjumi members. The strongly leftist orientation of the cabinet was abandoned in early 1948, when Sukarno installed an emergency cabinet with Vice-President Moh. Hatta as its Prime Minister.

The inauguration of the provisional constitution on 17 August 1950 marked the beginning of genuine constitutional democracy with cabinets accountable to the DPR (Appendix 1; Ricklefs 1981:230-44; Moedjanto 1988, II:77-114). Since Masjumi was assumed to be the largest political party, its chairman Natsir, former Minister of Information, was invited to form a cabinet with as wide a parliamentary backing as possible. However, talks with PNI proved fruitless, and Natsir ended up heading a minority cabinet with Sjafruddin Prawiranegara (Masjumi) as Minister of Finance and Sumitro Djojohadikusumo (PSI) as Minister of Trade and Industry.

The Natsir cabinet was rather ineffectual. It lacked solid electoral support and came under increasing criticism from PNI and Sukarno and even from some Masjumi politicians. Natsir handed in his resignation in March 1951 after two of the smaller participants in the coalition, Persatuan Indonesia Raya (PIR, Unity of Great Indonesia) and Partai Sarikat Islam Indonesia (PSII, Indonesian Islamic Union Party) had withdrawn their cabinet ministers. Following lengthy deliberations Natsir's rival within the highest ranks of Masjumi, Sukiman, succeeded in forming a coalition based on cooperation with PNI. Jusuf Wibisono of Masjumi became Minister of Finance, and the Department of Trade and Industry was allotted to two PNI figures in succession, first Soejono Hadinoto, known for the slogan *dari ekonomi kolonial ke ekonomi nasional,* then Wilopo. The Sukiman cabinet was confronted by Darul Islam uprisings in West Java and South Sulawesi, and became notorious for its vigorous suppression of PKI. In February 1952, after ten months in office, the Sukiman cabinet fell due to its pro-Western foreign policy.

A new, tripartite coalition consisting of PNI, Masjumi and PSI was formed by Wilopo. Wilopo was succeeded at the helm of the Department of Economic Affairs, as it was henceforth labelled, by fellow PNI politician Sumanang, while Sumitro returned to the cabinet, this time as Minister of Finance. The most urgent issue during the Wilopo cabinet was the relationship between the government and the armed forces. The position of the latter in Indonesian society was strong, on account of the army having been the victor of the Indonesian Revolution and its alleged capability to provide stability in a society weakened by political strife. Plans for large demobilization entertained by the Wilopo cabinet met with resistance and an ineffectual display of force. Sukarno made several replacements in the central military hierarchy, including the suspension of Commander-in-Chief A.H. Nasution. At that moment, the army appeared to be weakened by the prospect of a demobilization which, however, was not carried out. Eventually the Wilopo cabinet succumbed to heavy criticism following the shooting of peasants occupying foreign-owned estate land at Tanjung Morawa, North Sumatra, in March 1953.

It took two months to form a new cabinet, the fourth one since the provisional constitution had come into effect three years earlier. PNI politician Ali Sastroamidjojo headed a coalition with NU and the far smaller PIR, which meant that Masjumi, just as PSI, was now excluded from participation. Minister of Finance was Ong Eng Die (PNI), an ethnic Chinese, which as such was highly unusual. The militant economic nationalist Iskaq Tjokrohadisurjo

(PNI) served as Minister of Economic Affairs until forced to resign due to alleged corruption. The (first) Ali Sastroamidjojo cabinet was faced with rebellion in Aceh, a spectacular growth in PKI membership, and a restoration of the strength of the armed forces. The international success of the Asia-Africa Conference in April 1955 in Bandung failed to save a cabinet already tarnished by corruption scandals and suffering from weak parliamentary support. It was brought down in mid-1955 by the departure of the NU cabinet members. Another round of complex negotiations among the political parties ensued.

The short-lived Burhanuddin Harahap cabinet, until March 1956, was based on an alliance between the country's two large Islamic parties, Masjumi and NU, which left out PNI but brought PSI and Sumitro back in. Within weeks of its inauguration, general elections were held showing that there were really only four political parties to be reckoned with in Indonesian politics, of which two, PNI and PKI, were now relegated to the opposition benches. The election results also highlighted a growing split between Java, the stronghold of PNI, and the Outer Islands, where Masjumi was by far the largest party except in non-Muslim areas (Cribb 2000:163-4). The Harahap cabinet came to terms with the army, and Nasution was rehabilitated and appointed Chief of Staff. The cabinet resigned after only seven months in office, following the departure of the NU cabinet members.

The (second) Ali Sastroamidjojo cabinet enjoyed broad electoral support as it included three of the four major political parties, all except PKI. Jusuf Wibisono returned as Minister of Finance and the non-parliamentarian Djuanda occupied a key position as Minister of Economic Planning. However, tensions were rising. Relations with the Netherlands deteriorated, the rivalry between the army and PKI grew fiercer, a coup attempt in North Sumatra failed. Confidence in the system of constitutional democracy was rapidly eroding. On 1 December 1956 Vice-President Hatta stepped down, paving the way for a resurgence of personalized presidential power at the expense of parliament. In February 1957 Sukarno presented the principles of his 'Guided Democracy' (*Demokrasi Terpimpin*), a form of government which in Sukarno's opinion was more suitable to the situation of a young developing nation such as Indonesia.

March 1957 saw the outbreak of the Permesta rebellion in Sulawesi, declaration of martial law throughout the nation, and the resignation of the second Ali Sastroamidjojo cabinet. The new cabinet was extra-parliamentary (*kabinet kerja*, working cabinet), with Djuanda as Prime Minister and most posts filled by PNI and NU representatives. The creation of a Dewan Nasional (National Council) in May 1957 underscored the waning power of parliament. In December 1957 tensions culminated with the take-over of Dutch business firms (see Chapter VIII). Shortly afterwards, in February 1958, the existence of Indonesia as a unitary state appeared to be threatened by a rebellion in West

Sumatra. The rebel government, Pemerintah Revolusioner Republik Indonesia (PRRI, Revolutionary Government of the Republic of Indonesia), in Bukittinggi counted among its supporters several prominent former cabinet ministers, including Natsir, Harahap and Sumitro, with Sjafruddin Prawiranegara actually serving as Prime Minister. At the same time the Permesta rebellion in Sulawesi flared up again. The regional rebellions were crushed and the unity of the nation prevailed. Sukarno asserted his power by replacing Djuanda as head of the extra-parliamentary cabinet in July 1959. He insisted upon a return to the original 1945 Constitution, thereby allowing the President more power, and formally inaugurated 'Guided Democracy' on 17 August 1959.

The general economic and political context of the 1950s was strongly affected by increasing militancy on the part of trade unions, in particular SOBSI, which was ideologically influenced by the PKI. Labour conflicts were especially rampant in 1950, 1953, and from 1955 up until the proclamation of martial law, which ruled out any strike activity (Appendix 4). Labour activism had important repercussions on the conditions under which remaining foreign, in particular Dutch, business firms operated in newly independent Indonesia.

The stage is now set for the story of this book. Economic decolonization in Indonesia entailed the eradication of the heritage of a colonial society and a colonial economy, and the construction of a national economy at a time of high expectations and much tension. It promised to be a dramatic operation.

CHAPTER III

Occupation and revolution

Young Kuntara, in the novel *Saksi mata*, while roaming the streets of Surabaya in 1944, sees how buildings of well-known Dutch enterprises have been taken over by the Japanese. The premises of the shipping concern Koninklijke Paketvaart Maatschappij (KPM, Royal Packet Company) are being used by the news agency Domei, Lindeteves serves as a repair shop for military vehicles, and the proud office of Internatio, like so many buildings in the city, has been painted a dark grey (Suparto Brata 2002:204, 283). Such tangible effects of fundamental change in Indonesia were immediately apparent to the eyes of a twelve year old. However, further dramatic changes were to follow, particularly after the Japanese occupation had come to an end and the newly proclaimed Indonesian Republic struggled to assert its independence in the face of Dutch attempts to restore colonial rule.

This chapter covers the tumultuous period from early 1942 to late 1949. It consists of four sections, the first two dealing with the Japanese occupation (March 1942-August 1945) and the latter two with the Indonesian Revolution (August 1945-December 1949). The dividing line is marked by the capitulation of the Japanese armed forces on 15 August 1945 and the proclamation of independence just two days later. Four themes are discussed. The first is the way the Japanese authorities reorganized the economy after the surrender of the Dutch colonial army. Attention then shifts to the role played by Indonesians in the country's economy after the internment of most Dutch managers and supervisors. The following two sections on the Indonesian Revolution reflect the effective partition of the archipelago into two countries, the newly proclaimed Republik Indonesia (RI, Republic of Indonesia) and the territories under the control of the returning Dutch colonial government. The chapter concludes with the terms under which the Netherlands acknowledged Indonesian independence, or, from another perspective, the price Indonesia had to pay for decolonization.

Nipponization

When the Koninklijk Nederlandsch-Indisch Leger (KNIL, Royal Netherlands Indies Army) capitulated to Lieutenant-General Hitoshi Imamura on 8 March 1942, the Japanese military authorities already had plans prepared for the economy. A rudimentary blueprint entitled 'Principles governing the administration of occupied Southern areas' had already been drawn up at Imperial headquarters in November 1941. The occupation forces were to promote 'the acquisition and development of resources vital to national defence', or more specifically, to secure access to Indonesian oil and other raw materials to be obtained from Indonesia (Kurasawa 1990:12-3). In accordance with another official document, 'Principles of economic counter-measures in the South', all oil installations were immediately put under the direct management of the armed forces, that is, the 16th Army in Java and Madura, the 25th Army in Sumatra, the Second Southern Army and the Navy in Kalimantan, Sulawesi, and the entire eastern part of the archipelago (*Japanese military administration* 1963:302-3). Within days, foreign banks, including the four Dutch banks, were closed down and their assets 'voluntarily' surrendered (Aziz 1955:191; Shibata 1997:181-2). Foreign-owned agricultural estates were confiscated as 'enemy property' (Prillwitz 1946; Iwatake 1995:157-60; Keppy 2006:116-8).

Occasionally the Japanese take-over of productive assets was hampered by the scorched-earth tactics applied by departing Dutch personnel, for instance at the BPM oil refinery in Balikpapan, East Kalimantan. Up until this day a hideous monument commemorates those who perished in the Japanese revenge attack (Lindblad 1988a:115; De Jong 2002:35). The take-over of a jute bag factory in Delanggu, near Yogyakarta, occurred in a less dramatic fashion. The Japanese commander simply ordered locals to plant hemp on tobacco fields in Klaten, Central Java, as a first step towards alleviating the shortage of jute bags (Yulianto 2005). Such a measure fitted with a general Japanese policy that encouraged self-sufficiency at each level of administration. This served the double purpose of economizing on imports and shipping space from Japan and preparing the area for a possible Allied attack (Thompson 1945-1946:202; Hikita 1997:139).

The Japanese authorities implemented a variety of strategies to safeguard production while staging a significant redirection of the economy at large. In the initial phase the rubber estates in Sumatra were managed directly by units of the 25th Army, which was also responsible for the occupied Malay Peninsula. After about two months management was taken over by officials arriving from Japan. The two main Dutch organizations of estate managers, Deli Planters Vereeniging (DPV, Deli Planters'Association) and Algemeene Vereeniging van Rubberplanters ter Oostkust van Sumatra (AVROS, General Association of Rubber Planters in East Sumatra), were merged with the corresponding organization in Malaya to form the Singapore Rubber Association. Observers with the 25th Army reported that estates in Sumatra formerly under the DPV flag covered 250,000 hectares and employed 40,000 labourers (Iwatake 1995:217-20). As the rubber industry had a vital military function, the army continued to exercise tight control after the establishment of the new producers' organization. The tapping of rubber trees was prohibited unless ordered by the local military commander (*Economisch Weekblad voor Nederlandsch-Indië* 6 July 1946).

Matters were different on Java's sugar plantations, which played a less direct role in the war economy. Dutch supervisors were ordered to stay on and continue managing the estates in anticipation of the arrival of Japanese officials. Continuity of operations was all the more important as the planting of the 1941-1942 harvest had just been completed and an output of no less than 1.3 million tons was forecast (Rodenburg 1946; Aziz 1955:190; Kurasawa 1990:12; Iwatake 1995:160-2). On 1 June 1942 the military administration took over the umbrella organization Nederlandsch-Indische Vereeniging voor de Afzet van Suiker (NIVAS, Netherlands Indies Association for Marketing of Sugar) as well as the industry's research laboratories and the 85 individual sugar factories still in operation in Java. Processing facilities were upgraded, an administrative office opened its doors in Surabaya, and Japanese inspectors toured Central and East Java searching for equipment hidden prior to the Japanese invasion. NIVAS itself was reorganized into the Surabaya Sugar Sale Union under direct military command (Osaka Mainichi Shimbun 5 July 1942; Postma et al. 1946:8-9; Iwatake 1995:162-3).

Reliance on retained Dutch administrators was common during the first few months of occupation. On occasion, Dutch managers were even freed from internment to resume their supervisory tasks. At the cement factory in Padang, for instance, the former Dutch manager, W.J. van Konijnenburg, was released to supervise operations in conjunction with an Indonesian employee, Dusun Malin Kajo, or 'Pak Dusun' ('Mister Dusun') , as he was affectionately known, who had worked for the factory since 1924. Their joint management lasted for about one year, until the Asano Cement Corporation in Tokyo sent Japanese officials.[1]

Reorganization was given a high priority by Japanese authorities, reflecting contemporary Japanese ideas about how an economy should be structured. On 5 July 1942 the Saibai Kigyô Kanri Kôdan (SKKK, Public Corporation for Management of Cultivation Enterprises) was established as an intermediary between the army and estates in key branches of agriculture such as rubber, tobacco, tea, and cinchona. Whenever possible, management was entrusted

1 PT Semen Padang, Indarung: report by H. Dusun Malin Kajo, 5-7-1986.

The cabinet of the Republic of Indonesia captured during the second Dutch military action in Indonesia, December 1948-January 1949 (KITLV 41591)

to owners or administrators, but production targets and results had to be reported in detail to the military authorities. Although sugar was excluded, the distribution apparatus in Surabaya and its tandem organization, the newly founded Sato Renggokai (Java Sugar Association), were both institutionally linked to the SKKK (*Osaka Mainichi Shimbun* 5 July 1942; *Osaka Asahi Shimbun* 18 July 1942; *Economisch Weekblad voor Nederlandsch-Indië* 6 July 1946; Iwatake 1995:163-5; Keppy 2006:124-6).

From the second half of 1942 there was a tendency to distinguish carefully between civilian and purely military tasks in matters concerning the economy. In August 1942 a separate administrative organization, Gunseikanbu, was created within the 16th Army with departments focusing on sectors of the economy such as finance (*zaimubu*), industry (*sangyobu*) and transportation (*kotsubu*) (Kurasawa 1990:9). The authorities now took a more active interest in services and manufacturing. The Algemeene Volkscredietbank (AVB, People's Credit Bank), the main institution for extending micro credit founded in 1912, was allowed to continue doing business. In October 1942 the AVB reopened as the Syomin Ginko (People's Bank), with seventy branches throughout Java (De Jong 2002:77). Non-Japanese commercial banks, including the four Dutch banks, were liquidated and their assets and activities taken over by the Yokohama Specie Bank and the Taiwan Bank, both already operating in Indonesia since before the war. In April 1943 Nanpo Kaihatsu Kinko (Southern Development Bank), founded one year earlier, was commissioned to function as the central bank in the occupied territory, with responsibility for the circulation of money. The Nanpo Bank accumulated very sizeable funds and eventually surpassed the Taiwan Bank.[2]

Textile manufacturing was especially important in terms of reducing import needs and achieving self-sufficiency (Sato 2003:279). A regulating agency, Balai Pengoeroes Peroesahaan Tenoen Priangan Shu (Office for Management of Textile Companies in Priangan Province), for Priangan in West Java was set up in November 1942 with its main office in Bandung and a branch in Majalaya, within easy reach of the majority of the textile mills in West Java. But the Japanese control of the textile industry proved a double-edged sword. In 1944 the factories in West Java were literally deprived of thousands of handlooms (Keppy 2001:87-94). The subsequent acute shortage of clothing became a lasting and painful memory for many Indonesians who lived through the Japanese occupation.

Japanese control over the economy gradually tightened. In November 1942 all Dutch-owned sugar estates were formally expropriated and distributed among six private Japanese companies. For the sake of convenience,

2 Bank Indonesia, Jakarta: DJB 128, 8-7-1948; Shibata 1997:187-9.

estates formerly run by the same managing agency were allocated to the same Japanese firm. The plantations under the administration of NHM consequently ended up under Dai Nippon Seito (later Nitto Kogyô), those of HVA under Taiwan Seito, those of Internatio under Meiji Seito, those of Tiedeman and Van Kerchem under Ensuiko Seito, those of the Koloniale Bank under Nanyo Kohatsu, and the rest under Okinawa Seito. A year and a half later, in May 1944, the sugar estates were rearranged into regional clusters and redistributed among the same six Japanese companies (Postma et al. 1946:9-12). These measures did not affect sugar factories with non-Dutch owners such as those held by Oei Tiong Ham in Semarang or by the Mangkunegaran court in Solo.

There was also a change in attitude towards the Dutch. Dutch managers were retained only until the supervision of day-to-day operations could be handed over to arriving Japanese or qualified Indonesians. From January 1943 Dutch staff members were dismissed and interned, in some cases reinterned (Postma et al. 1946:33). But this process proceeded slowly, held back by the waves of reorganization. In June 1943 the SKKK was replaced by the Saibai Kigyô Kôdan (SKK, Public Corporation of Cultivation Enterprises), an organization set up to prepare for the transfer of estates to private Japanese firms. In due course 22 private Japanese companies were designated to manage enemy-owned estates. One year later, in June 1944, the SKK was replaced in turn by a federation of Japanese-owned agricultural enterprises, including the six companies to which sugar estates had originally been entrusted. By July 1944 the process of weeding out Dutch supervisors was completed (*Asia Raya* 15 July 1944; Postma et al. 1946:11; Aziz 1955:190; Sutter 1959:219, 254-5; Iwatake 1995:168-72, 178; Keppy 2006:139-42). Predictably, the Japanese replacements gained notoriety among Dutch observers, who criticized their lack of professional knowledge (De Graaf, Joustra and Vromans 1960:256, 275).

Active involvement by leading Japanese firms was also a significant feature of the mining industry, which played a crucial role in the Japanese war economy. Mitsubishi ran the tin mines in Bangka and Belitung, Mitsui was involved in coal and bauxite mining, Sumitomo was assigned the nickel mines in Sulawesi (*Japanese military administration* 1963:304; Hikita 1997:141). Diamond cutting in Martapura, South Kalimantan, was controlled by Nomura, which had been present in the region for several years (Lindblad 1988a:75; Dick 1989:258). This more active participation by private Japanese enterprises was inexorably accompanied by a continued strict adherence to priorities as formulated by the armed forces. This is illustrated by the alternative uses to which some sugar factories of the Internatio group were put: distillation to obtain butane (the Tjomal estate), oil refining, and even munitions manufacturing

(Postma et al. 1946:appendix xxiii-v; De Jong 2002:254). The Japanese authorities were keen to maintain and expand facilities to manufacture military and related supplies. Vital trading links with Japan were maintained by more than 300 private Japanese firms (Bisuk Siahaan 1996:115; Hikita 1997:143).

Economic performance during the Japanese occupation was appalling. Sugar production fell to 600,000 tons in 1943 and 500,000 tons in 1944, less than one-third of the level in the late 1930s, when the industry had still not fully recovered from the Depression (Kurasawa 1990:12; Iwatake 1995:161-2). In 1945 only 51 sugar factories were in an operational condition. Another 62 could not be used at all, and 16 were in urgent need of repair.[3] The export trade was hampered by an acute shortage of shipping capacity, a problem which only worsened as the war progressed and Allied submarines wreaked havoc along the shipping lines of Southeast Asia. There was no market for Java sugar in Japan itself, as sufficient supplies of sugar could be obtained from the Japanese colony of Taiwan.

Elsewhere in export production results were at least as disappointing, if not more so, having been struck a staggering blow by the dramatic loss of market outlets. By 1943 rubber output in Sumatra and Java had dropped to one-fifth of what it had been in 1941. Only one-third of the tea estates were producing and the total planted area was halved. Consequently, in the 1945-1946 harvest year total output fell to less than one-tenth of what had been harvested in 1942-1943.[4] Not surprisingly, the greatest efforts at reconstruction were undertaken in the oil industry, where in 1943 production already approached the pre-war level. Almost half of the output was destined for Japan. However, in 1944 these deliveries declined sharply after massive Allied bombardments of refineries in Sumatra and an acceleration in naval warfare (De Jong 2002:236). By 1945 oil exports from the Indonesian archipelago had virtually come to a standstill.

This distressing downward trend also applied to food supplies. Rice production fell by one-third, output of cassava by more than one-half, and that of maize by two-thirds (Burger 1975, II:160-1). The Japanese policy of rice distribution failed dismally; the average daily intake of calories is estimated to have fallen from 2,000 kcal in 1940-1943 to 1,500 kcal in 1944-1945 (Van der Eng 1994:17-21, 27; Sato 1994:122; Kurasawa 1997:121-4; Dick et al. 2002:165-6). There were alarming food shortages and signs of impending famine. This desperate situation gave rise to a vigorous black market and a great upsurge in clandestine trading. The subsequent high inflation was reinforced by a continuous enlargement of the money supply, with the amount of bank notes

3 Bank Indonesia, Jakarta: DJB 126, 22-1-1948.

4 ANRI, Jakarta: Netherlands Forces Intelligence Service (NEFIS) 121, 20-3-1946; Prillwitz 1946; Voigt 1946; De Jong 2002:232.

allegedly rising sevenfold between 1942 and 1945 (De Jong 2002:235, 263-75).

Available statistics do not permit even a rough estimate of the decline in national income and standards of living in occupied Indonesia.[5] Initial speculations suggested a drop in national income to less than half of the level in 1941, but the author in question, economic historian Pierre van der Eng, would later withdraw this wild speculation (Van der Eng 1992:369, 2001:182). The one area in which the deterioration was less dramatic was in manufacturing, as import restrictions opened up new opportunities for local producers. The number of factories actually rose, from 340 in 1942 to 540 in 1945.[6] Despite this one positive point, the general picture remains very bleak, even without taking into account the suffering of some four million Indonesians who were subjected to forced labour by the Japanese (De Jong 2002:243).

Pioneering with Japanese consent

A disillusioned Dutch rubber planter, H.J.H. Alers, writes about the situation on his estate in West Java in the 1950s. One staff member is Surachman, who had retired after forty years of loyal service to the estate and was living in Tasikmalaya. During the Japanese occupation Surachman took control when the Dutch manager was interned. 'It was said that he saved the estate' (Alers 1958:58). Experienced Indonesian employees often assumed the responsibilities of estate management, working alongside Japanese superiors between January 1943 and July 1944, while Dutch supervisors were gradually removed and replaced by Japanese officials.

Indonesian participation in management was obviously only upon Japanese invitation, but it often proved a practical solution to problems of day-to-day operations. Senior Indonesians just below the top level of Dutch supervisors were likely to be far more knowledgeable about daily operations than administrators arriving from Japan. Up until the second half of 1944 this was coordinated with systematic efforts to increase active involvement in the Indonesian economy by private Japanese firms.

Japanese policy with respect to the role of Indonesians in their own economy was elaborated in April 1944 in an official document entitled 'Principles

5 Significantly, in all relevant statistical tables in an authoritative Japanese language economic history of Indonesia blanks are left for the Japanese occupation and for the Indonesian Revolution (Kano 2004).

6 Van Warmelo 1946. There is evidence that in 1944 the 16th Army command in Java compiled a comprehensive report on 'industry in Java' (*Gunseikoa Jawa sangyo sokan*). The third volume, on manufacturing, would have contained details on this development, but has not been located.

for the construction of a new economic system of the Javanese people'. It stated that the economic capacity of the Javanese was very weak (*sangat lemah*), as a result of 300 years of colonial exploitation, and that the Javanese had been 'deliberately kept stupid' (*dibiarkan soepaja tinggal bodoh*) (*Soeara Asia* 29 April 1944). Five objectives were formulated to address this 'shortcoming of history': 1. the inculcation of new economic ideas; 2. the appointment of Indonesian economic leaders; 3. the fostering of indigenous entrepreneurship; 4. the nurturing of cooperatives; and 5. the dissemination of a spirit of labour service and technological learning among the people (*Japanese military administration* 1963:306-8). It sounds like a blueprint for *Indonesianisasi*.

The Gunseikanbu set up a committee (*kikakukatyoo*) with a member of the Nomura clan as its chairman and no less than five subcommittees. In July and September 1944 the committee reported back. Apart from the inevitable rhetoric about the 'sacred' Greater Japanese Empire, its final report contained some concrete recommendations. The third subcommittee, dealing with 'Enterprise planning', advised that qualified indigenous individuals be selected and assigned to manage enemy-owned estates, to set up new enterprises in rubber processing and traditional home industries, and to serve as agencies for the Japanese army and private Japanese companies in local distribution networks. Other subcommittees urged a complete reorganization of agricultural cooperatives and money circulation. A later observer spoke of 'desk plans', adding that 'their execution was almost impossible' (*Japanese military administration* 1963:308-12; De Jong 2002:252). This may be a slightly simplistic judgement.

Final results may have been a far cry from the ambitions of the *kikakukatyoo*, but some tangible steps were indeed taken. In early August 1944 the Gunseikanbu established a new office, Kantor Perekonomian Rakjat (Office for the People's Economy), with three branches, one dealing with general affairs, one with enterprises, and another with cooperatives. It was headed by Ali Sastroamidjojo, who would later become Prime Minister. In September 1944 the intention was announced to entrust the management of 436 enemy-owned upland estates in Java to 'qualified' Indonesians, who were to receive financial support from the Syomin Ginko (Sutter 1959:213-4, 254-5; Iwatake 1995:178). Yet implementation was very slow. A committee for screening the subsequent flood of applications was not formally installed until May 1945. It had a long name, Panitia Pemilih Bangsa Indonesia Mendjadi Pengoeasa Keboen2 Milik Moesoeh ('Selection committee for Indonesians who want to become managers of enemy-owned estates'). Moh. Hatta was its chairman. The screening process was still not completed when the Japanese armed forces capitulated on 15 August 1945 (Sutter 1959:25, 220-1; Iwatake 1995:179).

Measures also included training. In March 1945 plans were formulated to set up a national training institute (*kenkoku-gakuin*), directly under the command of Major-General Otoshi Nishimura. Twelve Indonesian leaders, including Hatta, were asked to participate alongside ten Japanese professors and the Japanese administrators. Two months later a training institute for future leaders of cooperatives began, with 170 students. Despite such initiatives, embryonic *Indonesianisasi* under Japanese supervision did not really have a chance to spread its wings. In June 1945 General Nishimura reminded a newly established forum, Panitia Penjelidikan Perekonomian Rakjat (Committee for Research on the People's Economy), that its discussions were not supposed to venture beyond general concepts. Hatta accepted the restrictions; the committee identified a few global targets, and no results ever materialized (Sutter 1959:250-4).

Economic conditions during the Japanese occupation were extraordinary, for two very good reasons: the direct intervention by the military authorities and the vacuum which ensued when Dutch entrepreneurship vanished and economic activities by ethnic Chinese were stifled. Contacts with the Japanese, a keen sense for new opportunities, and sometimes sheer luck were determinants of success for pioneering Indonesian businessmen at this time.

One interesting example is presented by the Sumatran trader Agoes Moesin Dasaad, director of Malaya Import. In late 1941, just before the Japanese invasion, he had purchased the Kantjil Mas textile factory in Bangil near Pasuruan, East Java, which was put up for sale by the Netherlands Indies government. The latter had confiscated it from its German owners following Germany's invasion of the Netherlands in 1940. During the Japanese occupation Dasaad served as an advisor to the Japanese controlled Persatoean Perniagaan Indonesia (Association for Indonesian Commerce) (*Asia Raya* 11 September 1942; Post 1997:101, 106). In May 1944 Dasaad emerged as one of three spokesmen for ninety Javanese businessmen prepared to make a substantial financial contribution towards the purchase of aeroplanes to be put into service by both the Japanese authorities and the Indonesian defence forces Pembela Tanah Air (PETA, Protectors of the Fatherland) (*Soeara Asia* 2 May 1944). In the following year, shortly after the Japanese capitulation, Kantjil Mas, later to become the single largest textile factory in Indonesia, was incorporated with a paid-up equity of one million guilders. Simultaneously, Malaya Import became a separate firm with a capital of half a million (Sutter 1959:289).

Sumatra was also home to Bakrie and Bros., founded on 10 February 1942 as a general merchandise and trading commission agency in Telukbetung, Lampung, in southern Sumatra, by Achmad Bakrie and his brother Abujamin. Bakrie exchanged agricultural produce from Sumatra such as coffee, pepper, and cloves for textile products and sugar from Java. The firm was temporarily renamed Yasuma Shokai as a judicious adjustment to the changing conditions during the Japanese occupation, and Jakarta soon became the centre of its trading network (Syafruddin Pohan 1992:5-10; Nasir Tamara 1998:39-40).

Other examples include the merchant combination of Soelaiman Djohan and Perpatih Djohor, both related to Vice-President Hatta, as well as Raden Mas Soedarmo, who even managed to obtain Japanese funding for a rope and sack factory in Kalibata near Jakarta in 1945 (Sutter 1959:259). Little has been documented about the economic activities of ethnic Chinese during these years. Suffice it to say that in April 1945 Oei Tiong Ham in Semarang was invited by the Japanese authorities to join a 37-member fund-raising committee , Badan Pembangkit Fonds Perang dan Kemerdekaan (Body to Raise Funds for War Effort and Independence). This bears at least indirect testimony to the continued prominence of ethnic Chinese in the occupied economy (Sutter 1959:251).

Indonesians struggling to survive

'All foreign property other than that which the state needs to run itself, will be returned to its legal owners, and that seized by the government will be compensated as fairly as possible' (*Segala milik bangsa asing selain daripada jang diperlukan oleh negara kita untuk diusahakan oleh negara sendiri, dikembalikan pada jang berhak, serta jang diambil oleh negara akan dibajar kerugiannja dengan seadil-adilnja*) (*Pidato* 1949; Sutan Sjahrir 1956:20-1). This quotation from the Republican government's Manifesto Politik, proclaimed on 1 November 1945, was used again by Vice-President Hatta in his opening address at the Round Table Conference in The Hague on 23 August 1949.[7] It is indicative of the pragmatism of the Republican government when survival as a sovereign nation was accorded top priority and economic nationalism became subordinate to political aspirations. The Republican government's strategy was to accept the inevitable necessity of foreign control over large segments of the economy in order to secure political independence.

The Indonesian archipelago during the years of the Indonesian Revolution was for all intents and purposes divided into two countries. The territory controlled by the Republican government initially embraced almost all of Java and Sumatra. After the first Dutch military campaign, in 1947, the area under Republican jurisdiction was reduced to Banten in West Java, the eastern part of Central Java, the western part of East Java, and parts of Sumatra (Cribb 2000:157, 160; see also Map 1).

The economic situation was highly confusing, with no clear dividing lines between the officially registered economy and informal or illicit transactions. The Republican government, temporarily relocated to Yogyakarta in January

7 ANRI, Jakarta: Delegasi Indonesia 1217.

1946, had very limited sources of income but a great need for funds to build up a state apparatus and, above all, to wage a guerrilla war against returning Dutch colonial forces. The Republican government's budget deficit amounted to Rp. 1.6 billion in 1948 and Rp. 1.5 billion in 1949.[8] By the latter year, the Republic's accumulated public debt was estimated at almost Rp. 3.5 billion (DJB 1950:12). A roaring clandestine trade took place across the waters of the Straits of Malacca. Rubber, coffee, quinine, oil, and coal from Sumatra were exchanged for weapons and ammunition, with opium smugglers also trading freely (Cribb 1988:712-21; Kahin 1997:200-4; Yong 1997:233-8; Twang 1998:95-6, 199). The Republic's governor of South Sumatra even bragged that he was 'the biggest smuggler in Southeast Asia' (Cribb 2000:158).

Military involvement in economic life was absolutely crucial. A ready explanation for this is found in the authority vacuum arising between the capitulation of the Japanese armed forces and the arrival of Allied troops. In the early months after the proclamation of Indonesian independence various defence organizations reportedly became involved in the management of economic assets in Java which had been abandoned by the Japanese. These assets included power installations, transport companies, mines, factories, and even an occasional Dutch-owned tea estate (Bambang Purwanto 2005). Activities undertaken by local military units in Sumatra in 1946 allegedly had more to do with trading than with warfare; in Bukittinggi a separate organization, Oesaha Moeda (Young Effort), was created for young officers interested in trading (Mestika Zed 2003:361).

Although less important than rubber exports and smuggling, oil exports from Sumatra also served as a means of financing the Indonesian Revolution. Again, there was heavy military involvement. In 1947 Palembang housed a coordinating body for sales and distribution run by A.K. Gani, a former actor. The oil company Peroesahaan Minjak Republik Indonesia (Permiri, Oil Enterprise of the Republic of Indonesia) was said to be controlled by the army. In Pangkalan Brandan (North Sumatra) BPM's severely damaged installations were operated by the Indonesian government at a level far below pre-war capacity. The Republican government refused to return the installations to BPM, claiming that the Dutch owners had forfeited their rights by ordering the property to be destroyed in 1942. Nevertheless, other oil installations in Sumatra were gradually returned to their owners between October 1946 and mid-1947.

In 1948 what became known as 'Let Alone' agreements were concluded with the three large foreign oil producers, Anglo-Dutch BPM, American Stanvac and Caltex. The agreements were the outcome of negotiations which

8 Bank Indonesia, Jakarta: DJB 181, 5-9-1949.

had originally been entered into with the Dutch colonial authorities. The three giant oil firms pledged to repair damaged installations and resume production as soon as possible on condition that they would be exempted from government restrictions on access to foreign exchange and remittances of profits (Anspach 1969:160; Hunter 1971:259-62; Purnawan Basundoro 2004:179). It was a highly pragmatic solution. By respecting the rights of non-Dutch foreign ownership of vital economic assets, the Republican government hoped to drive a wedge between the Netherlands and other Western countries.

Bukittinggi in West Sumatra became a focal point for economic activity under the banner of revolution. In August 1948 the Central Trading Corporation (CTC) was founded here on the initiative of Vice-President Hatta, with two Acehnese as directors, Tengku Hamid Azwar and Tengku Moh. Daud. Its initial line of business was rubber exports to markets in Southeast Asia, and local armed forces were soon deeply involved in the firm's trading operations. After the Indonesian Revolution CTC moved to Jakarta and broadened its range of activities. Part of the equity continued to be held by the Indonesian state, and an ethnic Chinese named Koo Liong Bing was appointed the company's third director. CTC was widely perceived as an Indonesian challenge to the leading Dutch trading firms (*Antara* 6 August 1956; Thee Kian Wie 2003:256). The company later became PT Panca Niaga.

The position of the ethnic Chinese was extremely precarious throughout the Indonesian Revolution. Widespread violence was reported in places such as Banten, West Java, in early 1946 and in Palembang in January 1947. Many people were kidnapped or murdered and houses and shops were set ablaze.[9] Occasionally tensions between ethnic Chinese and Indonesian nationalists led to outbursts of violence. Possibly the most heated confrontation took place in Bagan Si Api Api in eastern Sumatra. This coastal town was known as the world's second largest centre of maritime fisheries. It had a large Chinese majority, with five out of six inhabitants being of Chinese descent. On 12 March 1946 the death of Sun Yat-sen was commemorated by hoisting the Chinese instead of the Indonesian flag, which instantly sparked further violence. A delegation of local Chinese businessmen departed for Singapore to request that the Dutch reoccupy the town. Several months later a large-scale counterattack by nationalists, assisted by 'long-haired terrorists', resulted in numerous deaths and forced many ethnic Chinese to seek refuge abroad. Contingents of Chinese guerrilla fighters began pouring in from Malaya. At long last, in October 1946, an armistice was concluded which placed Bagan Si Api Api under a mixed Indonesian-Chinese administration.[10]

9 ANRI, Jakarta: Algemeene Secretarie: 147-8.

10 ANRI, Jakarta: NEFIS 75; Somers Heidhues 1988.

Even under the extraordinary conditions of the times, plans for cooperative ventures were forged between ethnic Chinese businessmen and military units, notably in the textile industry in West Java. Here the 32nd/Garuda Hitam Battalion, under the command of Lieutenant-Colonel Moh. Rivai, cooperated closely with Chinese owners of weaving and spinning factories in determined efforts to revitalize production (Keppy 2001:100, 288).

Indigenous Indonesian business flourished during the guerrilla warfare, and attempts were continually made to gain international recognition and improve external relations. Dasaad became a major supplier to the Republican army of weapons, ammunition, tyres, and medicines, most of which he procured from Singapore. He developed a close personal friendship with Sukarno and travelled around the world setting up agencies in Adelaide, New York, and Brussels (Sutter 1959:503).

Hasjim Ning also came from Sumatra, where he had been born in Padang in 1916. He was a nephew of Hatta and in 1946-1947 became personal assistant to the Vice-President. Following this he concentrated on nurturing his private business, in particular the assembly and import of motor cars. In 1950 he ran an assembly plant in Telukbetung, Lampung (where he had once worked together with Achmad Bakrie), as well as two car service stations in Jakarta, one of which catered specifically to military customers. He eventually became founder and director of the Indonesian Service Company (ISC), a highly successful car importing firm (Robison 1986:54-5).

It paid off to have close personal contacts with the political leadership. Other examples include Soetan Sjahsam, younger brother of Sutan Sjahrir, and Burhanuddin Muh. Diah, founder of the newspaper *Merdeka*, who became Minister of Information and later served as Indonesian Ambassador in London (Data Consult 1991:453-6). In August 1947 a former Volksraad member, Sosrohadikoesoemo, founded the trading firm Indonesian Trading and Transport Company (Intraport), which soon ranked among the three leading private Indonesian commercial concerns (Sutter 1959:631).

The emphasis shifted to trading and shipping as opportunities opened up to local businessmen in the vacuum created by KPM's inability to restore its one-time near-monopoly in inter-island shipping. Less attention was paid to manufacturing, but there were exceptions. In 1949 Ivan Tanodjo of the Kattuari family established the Wing soap factory in Surabaya, which became one of the leading business groups in East Java (Data Consult 1991:754). Sometimes the Republican government itself was actively involved in manufacturing. In Yogyakarta, the temporary capital of the Republic, it operated a cigar factory, Negresco, through a newly established agency. The Dutch owners were unable to reach the factory located in the Republic's very capital and therefore offered to sell half of the equity. Decisions about the deal were shelved (Sutter 1959:799).

The large agricultural export sector was effectively split between Republican and Dutch-controlled territories. In North Sumatra the rubber and palm oil estates were neatly divided between the two political authorities. The situation in the tobacco industry was completely different. All Deli estates lay in Dutch-controlled areas and all Dutch-owned plantations in East Java were operated by Indonesians.[11]

In May 1946 the Republican government created two agencies for the management of agricultural estates, one specifically for the sugar industry, Badan Penjelenggaraan Peroesahaan Goela Negara (Body for Management of State Sugar Companies), and a more general one entrusted with responsibility for all other state-owned plantations, Poesat Perkeboenan Negara (PPN, Centre for State Estates). An ambitious production plan was drawn up and the problem of a shortage of supervisory personnel was solved by recruiting the most qualified managers from technical departments in the two government bodies. Experienced senior Indonesian employees were entrusted with the supervision of daily operations at about 900 enterprises in Java and 300 enterprises in Sumatra. The same procedure was also applied outside agriculture. In 1947 Java's largest oil refinery, in Cepu, East Java, was reportedly under complete Indonesian management and fully operational.[12]

Assessments vary on the performance of enterprises under all-Indonesian management. Dutch observers insisted that there had been no improvement since the Japanese occupation. Rarely, if ever, is mention made of those enterprises which indeed were fully operational (Burger 1975:184; Van Doorn 1994:289; Wasino 2004). A case in point is the cement factory at Padang, which operated for almost two full years, from October 1945 until August 1947, under a new name, Kilang Semen Indarung. The Indonesian directorate included 'Pak Dusun', whom we already came across during the Japanese occupation. Pak Dusun was assisted by four technical advisors, none of them Dutch. Historians of West Sumatra claim that in 1946 production reached 80,000 tons, or almost half of pre-war capacity (Mestika Zed, Hasril Chaniago and Khairul Jasmi 2001:122-6). By contrast, the factory's Dutch owners were convinced that production would come to a virtual standstill when run by its employees.[13] It is safe to conclude that more was achieved towards recovery than Dutch observers were inclined to admit, although full potentials were far from realized.

In few areas was the confusion as great as in money circulation. Scores of new currencies were introduced, none of which was accepted by banks in the

11 ANRI, Jakarta: Algemeene Secretarie 763.

12 ANRI, Jakarta: Kementerian Perburuhan dan Sosial 69, 6-9-1947.

13 PT Semen Padang, Indarung: report by H. Dusun Malin Kajo, 5-7-1986; Nederlandsch-Indische Padang 1949.

Dutch-controlled territories. The Oeang Republik Indonesia (ORI, Republic of Indonesia [RI] Currency), issued on various occasions in Yogyakarta, was followed by Propinsi Sumatera (ORIPS, RI Currency for Sumatra Province) in Bukittinggi, ORIDAST (RI Curency for the East Sumatra Region), ORITA (RI Currency for Tapanuli), ORIPSU (RI Currency for the North Sumatra Province) in Aceh and, finally, ORIDAB (RI Currency for the Banten Region) after the westernmost part of Java had been cut off from the the Republican territory in Java. Estimates of the volume of ORI in circulation varied between Rp. 2.5 and 6 billion, possibly including a large amount of counterfeit money.[14] The newly founded Republican central bank had the arduous task of bringing order to this chaotic situation.

The Bank Negara Indonesia (BNI, State Bank of Indonesia) was established in September 1946, a year after a cabinet decision had been made to set up a central bank. The President-Director was Margono Djojohadikusumo; the initial operating capital, about Rp. ten million, had been amassed by a physician named Soeharto, not the later president. Suitable premises were found at the Yogyakarta branch office of the Java Bank, which also provided some staff members. BNI was entrusted with the issue and circulation of the Republic's currency. Minister of Finance A.A. Maramis authorized the issue of new ORI bank notes to replace existing Japanese money on 30 October 1946, a day remembered ever since as *hari keuangan* ('Day of Finance').[15] The BNI is occasionally credited with having played an important role in helping finance the struggle against the Dutch (Widigdo Sukarman 2005:49). However, a solid financial basis for the Republic never really materialized. The directors of the Java Bank doubted whether the BNI directors fully understood the difficulties lying ahead of them.[16]

After agreement had been reached with the Dutch to work towards a federal state, including all Dutch-controlled territories, it still remained to be decided what the future monetary system would look like. Representatives of the Republican government met in April 1948 with the Dutch authorities at Kaliurang near Yogyakarta to negotiate. After a year and a half in operation, BNI was prepared to relinquish its right to serve as central bank. The acknowledgement that the Java Bank was better qualified, with 120 years of experience in this role, is yet another illustration of the pragmatic approach adopted by the Republican government during the Indonesian Revolution. BNI's wish to remain a bankers' bank and to handle foreign exchange was swept from

14 Bank Indonesia, Jakarta: DJB 126, 22-11-1948; 3352, no. 5. There were even more currencies in circulation, for instance Netherlands Indies Civil Administration (NICA) money and *gunpyo*, a currency introduced by the Japanese military authorities (Cribb 1981).

15 ANRI, Jakarta: Sekretariat Negara 375, 5-7-1946, 378, 29-10-1946.

16 Bank Indonesia, Jakarta: DJB 125, 3-10-1946.

the table.[17] Not everybody rejoiced at the outcome of the talks at Kaliurang. Sumitro Djojohadikusumo, son of Margono, already at the age of 31 a well-known figure in Indonesian economics, equated this to allowing the KNIL, the colonial army, rather than the Republic's own army, Tentara Nasional Indonesia (TNI, National Army of Indonesia) to serve as the foundation for the nation's armed forces (Thee Kian Wie 2003:58-9).

The realization of an extreme shortage of Indonesians with banking skills prompted an unusual initiative. In November 1949 some members of the Indonesian delegation at the Round Table Conference in The Hague went to Amsterdam to meet the directors of the Amsterdam/Incasso Bank and discuss facilities for training young Indonesians in banking. This group included Vice-President Hatta, Minister Djuanda, Margono, his son Sumitro, and Dasaad. The Dutch bankers were apprehensive, but were reproached by the Dutch Minister of Finance, Pieter Lieftinck, who urged them to adopt a more cooperative attitude (*Het Parool* 11 November 1949; Lindblad 2005a:18). It is worth noting that the Dutch banks operating in Indonesia at the time had not been approached at all. In any case, nothing ever came of this initiative.[18]

In December 1949 BNI ceased to be the central bank of Indonesia and in January 1950 its name was changed to Bank Negara untuk Pembangunan (State Bank for Development), bestowed with a new primary task. Henceforth, it was to extend credit to Indonesian importers linked with the Gabungan Importir Indonesia (Gabindo, Union of Indonesian Importers). From March 1950 it handled the affairs of the Algemeene Import Organisatie (General Organization for Imports) which had just been liquidated. The fate of BNI is symptomatic of the dilemma between far-reaching nationalist aspirations and practical limitations in short-term implementation, characterizing the formative years of the Indonesian Republic. The dilemma called for unconventional solutions such as the one taken in the case of BNI, which continued to work towards *Indonesianisasi*, albeit in a different way.

Towards the end of the 1940s two new trends emerged, both paving the way for developments a decade later. One related to the fate of Dutch-owned enterprises, the other to the institutionalization of participation by the armed forces in economic life. Pressure was increasing from newly established trade unions to nationalize Dutch-owned enterprises which in practice were already being managed by Indonesian employees. In April 1948 the printing workers' union submitted a request to this effect to the Republican government. In October 1948, shortly after the suppression of the Communist uprising in Madiun, Central Java, several government bodies for economic management

17 Bank Indonesia, Jakarta: DJB 1584.
18 Bank Indonesia, Jakarta: DJB 1583, 2-12-1949.

were placed under military supervision in order to guarantee security of operations. They included PPN, the umbrella organization for estates, as well as its pendant in the sugar industry and similar agencies for the management of daily operations in forestry, textile factories, oil installations, printing presses, public utilities, telecommunications, and railways.[19]

Pragmatism, priorities in warfare, and new opportunities under unusual circumstances – these words epitomize economic life during the formative years of the Indonesian Republic in the second half of the 1940s. But this was just one side of the coin. The other was the attempt to restore Dutch colonial rule in the archipelago.

Dutch struggling to return

In September 1946 one of the directors of the Dutch central bank, the Java Bank, on his return from a journey to Yogyakarta and Malang reported that 'the idea of *Medeka* [*Merdeka*, Independence] is solidly anchored in all layers of the population, intellectuals as well as others'. Ten months later, in July 1947, his closest colleagues at the Java Bank claimed that the unwillingness of Indonesians to fight during the military action, then at full force, 'most clearly' (*ten duidelijkste*) demonstrated how weak the authority of the Republic really was.[20] Such contradictory statements by supposedly well-informed observers tell us how difficult it was for returning Dutch people to fully grasp the situation. Chin Yuan, a journalist publishing in Republican territory, nurtured no illusions. Very soon after the Indonesian proclamation of independence he dismissed the Dutch belief that '90 per cent of the population stood behind Her Majesty [Queen Wilhelmina]', describing it as 'a mere tragi-comical bluff' (*hanyalah suatu tragische komieke bluf*) (*Soeara Merdeka* 22 November 1945).

Initially the Dutch-controlled territory in the archipelago was virtually confined to the islands outside Java and Sumatra. However, following two military campaigns it grew considerably and in early 1949 the Dutch claimed authority of the entire Republican territory in Java as well as over large parts of Sumatra (Cribb 2000:156-8, 161; see also Map 2). The constitutional structure took the form of a federation, consisting of a bewildering array of units. It eventually encompassed six nominally independent states (*negara*): Indonesia Timoer (December 1946), Soematra Timur (December 1947), Madoera (February 1948), Pasoendan (February 1948), Soematra Selatan (September 1948), and Djawa Timoer (November 1948). In addition, there

19 ANRI, Jakarta: Sekretaris Negara: 781, 24-4-1948, 21-9-1948, 25-10-1948.

20 Bank Indonesia, Jakarta: DJB 125, 3-10-1946, 1581, 26-7-1947.

were nine autonomous constitutional units (Daerah Istimewa Kalimantan Barat, Federasi Kalimantan Timur, Dajak Besar, Daerah Bandjar, Kalimantan Tenggara, Bangka, Billiton, Riau, and Djawa Tengah), not to mention other units such as the Jakarta municipal district, the vast region of western New Guinea, the municipality of Padang, the port of Sabang (Aceh), and the indigenous statelet Kota Waringin in southern Kalimantan (Cribb 2000:160).

The apparatus for export production was in a shambles when the Dutch staff of private firms resumed their responsibilities in 1946 and 1947. Export volumes were at a fraction of pre-war levels: 12 per cent for oil, 5 per cent for estate rubber, less than 1 per cent for sugar and palm oil (Booth 1998:49-51). Estates were in a deplorable condition, with many having been unproductive for several years. Although conditions were better among smallholders, whose modest production facilities had remained largely intact, their exports also remained far below pre-war levels, as they were severely hampered by the slow recovery of transport and trading networks in 1946 and 1947.

Foreign trade in the Dutch-controlled territories expanded dramatically during the years 1947-1949, but we must bear in mind that the starting point was very low. The pre-war level of export revenue, approximately one billion guilders, was not regained until 1948. However, the official trade figures cover only trade registered in the Dutch-controlled Federation. By one estimate, 15 per cent needs to be added to the Federal figure in order to obtain a total for the entire archipelago.[21] Yet this upward revision appears improbably low in light of the widespread smuggling taking place despite the Dutch naval blockade of Java and Sumatra as of January 1947.

The recovery of exports was affected by military fortunes. The potential for export production from Dutch-controlled regions was considerably enlarged as a result of the two military campaigns which in both the Dutch and the international literature are euphemistically referred to as 'police actions', thus implying a purely domestic matter. In Indonesian historiography they are invariably referred to as acts of aggression. The first Dutch military campaign (*agresi pertama*) was undertaken between 21 July and 5 August 1947. It went under the code name 'Operation Product' (*Operatie Produkt*), which betrays the underlying economic rationale. Although the campaign did not restore peace and security, economic effects were soon forthcoming, as production areas came under Dutch control and the Dutch naval blockade continued to be enforced (Keppy 2006:69-70). Exports from rubber estates climbed to more than 100 million guilders in 1948, as opposed to 20 million in 1947. Palm oil estates in North Sumatra similarly made a giant leap in their contribution to

21 ANRI, Jakarta: NEFIS 29, 18-5-1949. Exports from the Republic were inferred from the trade statistics of Malaya and Singapore.

export revenues, from three million guilders in 1947 to forty million guilders in 1948.[22]

These were only the direct effects. An indirect effect of the Dutch military campaign was the overall improvement in economic conditions throughout Dutch-controlled territory. Oil installations were back on track after massive investment in reconstruction, and the value of their export production rose fivefold. The tin mines in Bangka and Belitung, as well as indigenous copra producers in Sulawesi, doubled their export earnings, and smallholder rubber exporters in Kalimantan and Sumatra raised the value of their export production by as much as 100 million guilders.[23] Although we cannot calculate exactly how much of the threefold increase in total value of exports between 1947 and 1948 may be attributed to the Dutch military campaign, it is highly likely that direct and indirect effects taken together were responsible for most of the recovery.

The second military campaign (*agresi kedua*), from 19 December 1948 to 5 January 1949, was a military success but a political failure from the Dutch point of view. The Republic's scorched-earth guerrilla tactics could not prevent vast production areas from being brought under Dutch control. However, within the international community Dutch prestige fell as fast as Indonesian prestige rose. Areas planted with rubber, oil palm, and, tea in North Sumatra and West Java doubled in size, and the number of agricultural enterprises in the Dutch-controlled territory increased from about 650 to 750. Dutch observers projected that after the military campaign total export production capacity had risen by 250 million guilders. This corresponded to half of the increase in total export revenue from 1948 to 1949.[24]

Two new trends became visible in the second half of the 1940s, both forming a marked contrast to patterns prevailing in late-colonial Indonesia, only a decade earlier. One trend related to the commodity base of export expansion, the other to the relationship between export earnings and expenditure on imports from abroad. An increasingly narrow range of export goods now accounted for a very large proportion of total export revenue. Three products alone – rubber, oil, and copra – made up more than 60 per cent of total export earnings recorded in the Dutch-controlled ports.[25] Rubber ranked first in 1946, copra in 1947, oil in 1949. However, such abrupt changes in the composition of exports must be interpreted with caution. Sumatra's rubber trade was a particularly important bone of contention between the Dutch and the Republic. Total export volumes may in reality have been more stable than the short-

22 Bank Indonesia, Jakarta: DJB 181, 5-9-1949.
23 ANRI, Jakarta: NEFIS 29, 18-5-1949.
24 ANRI, Jakarta: NEFIS 29, 18-5-1949; Bank Indonesia, Jakarta: DJB 181, 5-9-1949.
25 ANRI, Jakarta: Algemeene Secretarie 806, 10-12-1948.

term fluctuations suggest. In any case, previously important export products such as sugar, tobacco, coffee or tea scarcely played a role in the immediate post-war economic recovery. Export earnings were not sufficient to finance expenditure on imports, as a result of which the deficit in the balance of trade increased rapidly in 1946 and 1947. There was, however, a marked improvement in 1948 and 1949, owing to the accelerated expansion of exports.

Demands on scarce resources were heavy for the returning Netherlands Indies administration. The 1947 budget listed total expenditure of nearly 2.9 billion guilders, with government income barely exceeding one billion. In other words, a deficit of 1.9 billion guilders was projected, even larger than the deficit incurred by the Republican government in Yogyakarta at the same time. But the Netherlands Indies budget deficit was highly artificial, as about two-thirds of it were attributable to the costs of the war against the Republic. The only way to cover this huge deficit was through loans from the home government in the Netherlands. Projections made in September 1948 with an eye to similar predicaments in public finance in the budget year 1949 explicitly mentioned Marshall aid to the Netherlands as a possible source of funding.[26] A direct link could thus be perceived between American financial aid to the Netherlands and Dutch warfare against the Republic in Indonesia. Sumitro Djojohadikusumo certainly saw things this way when he served as a representative of Indonesia at the United Nations in New York in December 1948. Sumitro's one-man action, enhanced by its carefully scheduled publicity, was decisive in prompting intervention by the United States government bringing the second military campaign to a halt (Lindblad 2001:136).

A Dutch-controlled bureaucracy had to be re-established in order to administer what was now Federal territory. One statistic illustrates the scope of the ambitions fostered. Total staff at the various agencies of the Department of Finance numbered 900 in 1947, only one year later there were more than 1,500.[27] The bureaucracies of all the hastily constructed puppet units and statelets of the Federation were increasingly being staffed by Indonesians, who to some extent believed in a future cooperation with the Dutch. In East Sumatra in January 1948, for instance, the cabinet director and two of the four department heads were Sumatrans.[28] This can be seen as an accelerated *Indonesianisasi* of the civil service born of political necessity.

The Dutch authorities in the Federal areas faced a multitude of tasks in restoring operations and reforming the economy. Dutch-owned firms were in

26 Van der Eng 1987:208-16; Bank Indonesia, Jakarta: DJB 128, 15-10-1948 and 31-12-1948. Lower estimates of the government budget deficit, 1.2 and 1.5 billion guilders for 1947 and 1948 respectively, are quoted in the secondary literature (Tervooren 1957:104-5).

27 ANRI, Jakarta: Algemeene Secretarie 373.

28 ANRI, Jakarta: Algemeene Secretarie 1283.

urgent need of reconstruction. In early 1947 the Java Bank conducted a survey among Dutch firms to find out the amount of corporate funds available for reconstruction. The 740 firms surveyed held deposits and government bonds worth 466 million guilders, but another 120 firms had accrued debts totalling 47 million guilders. After subtracting the required transfers to the Netherlands, 284 million guilders were available for reconstruction in Indonesia.[29] Although this may appear an impressive amount, it works out to no more than 330,000 guilders per individual enterprise, hardly sufficient.

Existing credit and banking facilities were not commensurate with demand. The Java Bank began to function as the central bank in 1946 and was determined to continue its traditional dual function of regulating money supply and providing credit to solvent private firms. Still, its credit policy continued to be conservative. By March 1948 115 companies had borrowed a total of 8.7 million guilders, a tiny proportion of the corporate funds reportedly available for the reconstruction of Dutch firms. Interestingly, 76 out of the 115 companies had Chinese names, whereas only 22 of the companies were European. Only three indigenous enterprises were on the list: Dasaad's Kantjil Mas, the Sumatran trading firm Djohan and Djohor, and *kretek* cigarette manufacturer Nitisemito in Kudus. Their combined debt amounted to 400,000 guilders, less than 5 per cent of the total.[30]

Credit shortages prompted immediate and far-reaching intervention by the Netherlands Indies authorities, in particular in foreign trading. A government body for the state regulation of exports and imports (NIGIEO, Nederlandsch-Indische Gouvernements Import- en Export-Organisatie) was established in 1946 in close cooperation with major Dutch trading firms and entrusted with monopoly rights. During the first eight months of its existence it handled foreign trade transactions worth almost 230 million guilders.[31] Later the authorities switched to extending credits and guaranteeing possible losses in the private import trade. In April 1949 guarantees already granted were reported to add up to a total liability of 120 million guilders, far more than the initial estimate of 40 million guilders, while at the same time certain European trading houses reported high profit rates. Throughout 1949 the authorities kept wavering between withdrawing such guarantees and strengthening support

29 Bank Indonesia, Jakarta: DJB 126, 5-5-1947. Of the 742 firms with a positive balance, 360 reported assets of 352 million guilders, and liabilities of 138 million payable to the Netherlands. A similar payable proportion (39 per cent) was applied to the assets of 114 million guilders (466-352) held by firms not giving details on liabilities. This calculation produced two figures on available corporate funds, an actual one, 214 million (352-138), and an imputed one, 70 million (61 per cent of 114), together 284 million guilders.

30 Bank Indonesia, Jakarta: DJB 128, 8-7-1948.

31 ANRI, Jakarta: Algemeene Secretarie 799, 31-8-1946; Keppy 2001:104.

mechanisms through a more rigid institutionalization.[32]

The promotion of Indonesian participation in the economy was another professed priority, although the idea was slow in gaining acceptance. The proposal in January 1946 by the Department of Finance to set up a Reconstructieraad (Council of Reconstruction) was reminiscent of the pre-war Volksraad in providing for the representation of private Indonesian businessmen, alongside their European and ethnic Chinese counterparts.[33] AVB, catering in particular to small-scale indigenous enterprises, successively reopened local branches of the Syomin Ginko throughout 1947 and 1948, adding another fifteen offices in early 1949 in newly conquered areas of Java and Sumatra. Total outstanding credits climbed from seven million guilders in December 1947 to more than 28 million guilders by March 1949. Borrowers included the fisheries in Bagan Si Api Api, the *kretek* industry in Kudus and Pati, and the batik industry in Solo.[34]

In 1947 suggestions that lending conditions for Indonesian traders be eased were still met with stern resistance from the Java Bank directors, who argued that this would be 'doomed to fail'. The Java Bank insisted that extension of credit to foster Indonesian entrepreneurship remained a purely political aim; they claimed never to lose sight of the commercial soundness of the borrower. In fact, as the transfer of sovereignty drew nearer, the situation gradually improved. Between April and August 1949 three loans of more than 200,000 guilders each were awarded to indigenous Indonesian businessmen, a textile importer in Bandung, a rice trader in Pare-Pare (Central Sulawesi) and, again, Djohan and Djohor.[35]

Production by Indonesian smallholders contributed substantially to the recovery of exports originating from the Dutch-controlled area in 1948 and 1949. In 1948 nearly three-fifths of all rubber exported came from smallholders in Sumatra and Kalimantan, and virtually all copra exports from Sulawesi consisted of deliveries from indigenous cultivators. Support of Indonesian-style export production served the double purpose of transforming smuggling into an official export trade and stimulating indigenous entrepreneurship. A shrewd system of export inducement for smallholder rubber had already been introduced in West Kalimantan, where smuggling had reached unprecedented levels by early 1947. The system was eventually applied throughout the archipelago to almost all commodities produced by smallholders. It began with a voucher entitling the exporter to purchase 10 kilograms of rice at a price below market level for every ton of rubber export-

32 ANRI, Jakarta: Algemeene Secretarie 789, 26-4-1949, 27-9-1949.
33 ANRI, Jakarta: Algemeene Secretarie 763.
34 Bank Indonesia, Jakarta: DJB 181, 5-9-1949.
35 Bank Indonesia, Jakarta: DJB 126, 22-1-1948, 129, 3352, no. 4.

ed. A larger quantity of rice was added a few months later, and then textiles could be imported too. The system became extremely complex, with rates of exchange varying according to commodity, region of supply, and even destination. A lively trade in vouchers evolved, and ethnic Chinese intermediaries were said to 'get rich effortlessly' (*slapend rijk*) because of the sheer complexity of the system.[36] Such interventions in the market mechanism were precursors to policies pursued by the Indonesian government in the 1950s.

One seemingly easy way to support Indonesian business was to grant certain privileges to indigenous traders in a situation plagued by an acute shortage of foreign exchange and excessive regulation. In December 1947 a system was introduced in North Sumatra allowing Indonesian importers to buy imports on credit lasting 45 days, whereas European importers had to pay cash. The assumption was that indigenous importers would be able to sell the merchandise within the 45-day period and that European importers were fortunate enough to be more solvent. In reality, this special provision failed to benefit those intended, since the commodities arrived in Medan too late.[37] In more than one respect this regulation paved the way for the policy of positive discrimination applied in Indonesia during the 1950s.

New enterprises were set up by indigenous Indonesians under the aegis of Dutch rule, albeit few in number. Examples include several trading corporations in Makassar and Medan (Sutter 1959:630). In March 1947 six Ambonese businessmen took the initiative of establishing Bank Rakjat Maloekoe, with an initial capital of 500,000 guilders. The explicit aim of the bank was to enable locals to start small-scale enterprises in agriculture and fisheries without having to rely on high-interest loans from ethnic Chinese or Arab moneylenders.[38]

Dutch protection proved particularly useful in the West Java textile industry. Dutch authorities in Negara Pasoendan stimulated the construction of new textile mills. The number of Indonesian-owned weaving enterprises tripled between April 1948 and April 1949, which was a far steeper increase than was seen in factories owned by ethnic Chinese. However, Chinese-owned factories tended to be larger in size. This led to a dramatic revival of the Majalaya weaving industry (Keppy 2001:109).

Apart from the boom in weaving in West Java not much progress was made in industrialization during the second half of the 1940s. The number of rice-mills, ice factories, rubber-remilling plants, and metal foundries remained virtually the same in 1949 as it had been in early 1942. Although there were more cigarette factories and more printing presses than before the Pacific War,

36 Bank Indonesia, Jakarta: DJB 181, 5-9-1949, 1584, 4-2-1950.
37 ANRI, Jakarta: Algemeene Secretarie 538.
38 ANRI, Jakarta: Algemeene Secretarie 482.

industrial development at large was awaiting a new impetus in the form of active support to be rendered under more favourable circumstances.[39]

A final word needs to be said about the position of firms owned by ethnic Chinese in the Dutch-controlled Federation. There was increasing competition in manufacturing with indigenous producers, notably in the West Java textile industry, while cooperation with Dutch enterprises intensified. In mid-1948 it was publicly stated that 60 per cent of assets of ethnic Chinese traders in the Dutch-controlled territory had effectively been transferred to Dutch trading firms (*Antara* 1 July 1948). Such an assertion does not easily lend itself to verification.

Nonetheless, there was a growing understanding that Dutch acknowledgement of Indonesian independence could not be put off much longer. Perhaps this was realized at an earlier stage among Dutch businessmen working in Indonesia than within government circles, let alone among politicians in the faraway Netherlands. Signs throughout 1949 indicated that among Dutch officials there was a new willingness to be accommodating towards the Indonesians. A. Oudt, Acting Treasurer-General at the Department of Finance, put forward the idea of nationalizing the central bank after the transfer of sovereignty. Lengthy considerations led him to conclude that nationalization was not needed, provided the influence of the Republican government was strengthened. Inclusion of Indonesians in the top management of the bank was 'imperative and should be done to as great an extent as possible' (*Het opnemen van Indonesiërs in de leiding – waar zulks maar enigszins mogelijk is – is noodzakelijk*).[40] Oudt later served as a general advisor to Indonesia's Department of Finance.

At the Java Bank the ambitions of the Republican government were regarded with apprehension. Foreign capital was indispensable to structural economic change, including industrialization, as the bank directors asserted, and any action that might scare away foreign investors would be detrimental to Indonesia's own progress. Since 1948 two of the five members of the Board of Trustees had been Indonesian: Darmawan Mangoenkoesoemo from Solo, pre-war consultant in the colonial Department of Economic Affairs, and the Ambonese J.F.A. Hendrik, former employee of the Escompto Bank and Internatio. None of the directors were Indonesian. Caution remained the hallmark of the Java Bank, sometimes verging on the extreme, as in September 1949 when, after the untimely death of President-Director R.E. Smits, one candidate for the vacant post was feared to be unacceptable to Indonesians simply for being a great-grandson of Governor-General Johannes van den Bosch, who

39 ANRI, Jakarta: Algemeene Secretarie 776.
40 ANRI, Jakarta: Algemeene Secretarie 474.

in 1830 had introduced the widely despised Cultivation System in Java.[41]

At long last, on 23 August 1949, negotiations commenced in The Hague to settle the terms under which the Netherlands would acknowledge Indonesian independence. Three parties were present: the hosting Dutch delegation chaired by the Minister of Overseas Territories, J.H. van Maarseveen, the delegation of the Republic of Indonesia headed by Vice-President Hatta, and a delegation representing the Dutch-controlled Federation chaired by Sultan Hamid II of Pontianak. The tone of this Round Table Conference was set by Hatta's opening address, in which he explicitly promised that seized Dutch corporate assets would be returned to their legal owners. In a formal sense, this was a reiteration of article 14 of the Linggadjati Agreement concluded between the Republic of Indonesia and the Netherlands government on 25 March 1947 (*Ronde Tafel Conferentie* 1949:105). Why did Hatta find it so important to make this statement? Was he prompted by sheer pragmatism, to secure Dutch cooperation at almost any cost, akin to Sukarno's acceptance of the short-lived and rather awkward union construction in constitutional arrangements? Or did Hatta's unequivocal standpoint reflect a genuine conviction that the Indonesian economy could not yet do without Dutch capital, technology, and management know-how? Or, yet another possibility, was it a message to other nations, in particular the United States, that Indonesia was a trustworthy partner for the Western world, that is, did it intend to purvey a similar message to the one sent out by the heavy-handed crushing of the Communist uprising in Madiun in September 1948?

Two financial and economic matters would receive a great deal of attention during the Round Table Conference (RTC or KMB, Konferensi Meja Bundar, KMB). These were the debt taken over by the Republic from the colonial government and the position of the Dutch private firms that would continue to operate in Indonesia. Both issues had potential consequences for the actual degree of autonomy in future Indonesian financial and economic policy. The Dutch government insisted on safeguards to guarantee the repayment of the debt in the form of a say in policy making in Jakarta whenever Dutch interests were at stake. The Dutch firms above all wished to continue to do business as usual.

This proposed degree of intervention by the former colonial mother country in the former colony's economic policy making emerged as one of the most serious points of disagreement during the negotiations in The Hague. After three weeks the RTC committee for financial and economic affairs concluded that there was a 'fundamental difference of opinion with respect to the guarantees considered necessary regarding Indonesia's liabilities to the

41 Bank Indonesia, Jakarta: DJB 128, 31-12-1948, 1583, 2-12-1949.

Netherlands'. The Republican delegation insisted that any intervention that was too far-reaching was incompatible with the status of Indonesia as a sovereign nation. Eventually, the realization dawned on Indonesian delegates that there was also a difference of opinion within the Dutch delegation. The committee's chairman, W.J. Cator, author of a book on the Chinese in Indonesia, was described as a man with wide international experience and a broad outlook. But he was 'hampered by old colonial officials wishing to maintain the present structure of "cooperation"'.[42] It was not the last time that official Indonesian representatives were to complain about a want of mental decolonization among the Dutch.

On 2 November 1949, the final day of the RTC, the parties signed a financial and economic agreement known as Finec (Financieele en Economische Overeenkomst). Article 1 ordered the full restoration of legal rights as laid down under colonial rule, with article 3 offering guarantees against nationalization, unless deemed to be in the public interest, in which case adequate compensation had to be paid. Under article 5 Dutch enterprises promised to participate in economically viable (*zakelijk verantwoorde*) joint ventures with Indonesian capital, and under article 12(d) they agreed 'to include as soon as possible capable Indonesians in the management (including boards of directors) and staff positions of companies' with the intention 'that within a reasonable time frame the majority of the supervisory personnel would consist of Indonesian citizens' (*het zo spoedig mogelijk opnemen van daartoe geschikte Indonesiërs in de leiding (ook directies) en staven der bedrijven* [...] *er op gericht om na zekere redelijke termijn het overwegende deel van het leidend stafpersoneel der bedrijven te doen bestaan uit Indonesische staatsburgers*).[43] Article 19 stipulated the obligation of the Indonesian government to consult the Dutch government on matters of financial and economic policy with a bearing on Dutch interests. These stipulations were all to prove important during the continued process of decolonization following the transfer of sovereignty.

Responses to the Finec Agreement varied. According to economic nationalists more outspoken than Hatta, too many concessions had been made, although little open criticism was voiced. The Dutch Minister of Domestic Affairs, F. Teulings, congratulated himself on having obtained maximum protection of Dutch business interests (Baudet and Fennema et al. 1983:21-3; Meijer 1994:46-7). Even before the Finec Agreement had been signed, the proverbially cautious directors at the Java Bank pointed out that article 19 could

42 ANRI, Jakarta: Delegasi Indonesia 1251.

43 *Ronde Tafel Conferentie* 1949:24-9; see also *Round Table Conference* 1950. The text is virtually identical to the proposal discussed in the committee for financial and economic affairs at the Round Table Conference (ANRI, Jakarta: Muh. Yamin 72).

easily become a 'dead letter' should the Indonesian government so wish it.[44]

The size of the debt to be taken over from the colonial government was a matter of profound disagreement. The origin of the debt lay in the financial separation of the Netherlands and the Netherlands Indies governments back in 1867. As a consequence, budget deficits of the colonial government were covered by loans from the Dutch state. Accumulated debt to the Netherlands rose from 2.6 billion guilders in March 1942 to 3.2 billion guilders in December 1945. By March 1947 the colonial government's internal debt to the Netherlands amounted to a massive four billion guilders, and this sum would be further increased by deficit spending in 1947 to cover the costs of the first military campaign. The final estimate of the colonial debt, as of September 1949, reached a staggering 5.9 billion guilders. Negotiations during the RTC reduced this sum to three billion guilders, although another 1.5 billion guilders was added from the external debt of the Netherlands Indies government.[45] The Republican government was thus saddled with a debt burden unprecedented in the history of decolonization. Indonesia paid a high price for its independence, quite apart from the physical damage and loss of human lives during the Revolution. Indonesia's large inherited debt was the crucial difference with neighbouring decolonizing nations such as Malaysia and the Philippines (Dick et al. 2002:171).

In 1949 Suparto Brata's hero Kuntara would have been seventeen, a young adult looking for a job in Surabaya or possibly planning to enrol as a student at the newly opened Gadjah Mada University in Yogyakarta. It is not at all certain that he would have paid much heed to the news about the solemn transfer of sovereignty taking place in The Hague on 27 December. The ceremony signified Dutch acceptance of a historical reality already in existence for over four years. Political decolonization had arguably run its course. Amalgamating the Dutch-controlled territories of the Federation into the Republic and dissolving the union were now only a formality, accomplished within less than a year.

44 Bank Indonesia, Jakarta: DJB 1583, 18-10-1949.

45 Clerx 1992:65; ANRI, Jakarta: Algemeene Secretarie 258. There is a stubborn misconception in the historiography that Indonesia itself had to pay for the military actions taken against it in 1947 and 1948-49. Such an arrangement was apparently attempted by Dutch negotiators but the Indonesians flatly refused.

CHAPTER IV

A new dawn in business

In a novel set in Jakarta in the 1950s Mochtar Lubis contrasts the fate of two young men, a poor man named Saimun and the privileged Surjono. Saimun comes to the big city from the countryside, finds a low-paid job as a garbage collector, and is continuously haunted by his debts. Surjono has returned to independent Indonesia from abroad; he leads a life of luxury and begins a secret relationship with his young stepmother. Surjono's father is Raden Kaslan, a former Javanese civil servant who had, when the Dutch acknowledged Indonesian independence, gone into private business, sensing that unique opportunities would be opening up in the new Republic. His trading firm, Bumi Aju (literally 'Beautiful Earth'), is highly successful owing to close contacts with the 'Indonesian Party', easily recognizable as the novelist's representation of PNI. Raden Kaslan meets the party chairman, Husin Limbara, behind closed doors, and is told that the party needs money for the forthcoming election campaign. Raden Kaslan has an idea:

> Of all the economic sectors, the easiest from which to get money is certainly the import sector [...] We're just going to sell the import licences which we obtain. I suggest that we make two plans. One for quick results, that is via the import sector of business. And the other, a permanent plan, for establishing banks, industries and so forth (Mochtar Lubis 1963:70-1).

Husin Limbara is delighted. Raden Kaslan truly lives up to his reputation as an expert economist (*benar kata orang saudara Raden Kaslan ahli ekonomi*) (Mochtar Lubis 1964:62). They settle on a 50/50 split of profits between the private firm and the party. However, things do not work out quite as smoothly as they expected. One month later the newspaper *Suluh Merdeka*, clearly named after two existing daily newspapers (*Merdeka* and *Suluh Indonesia*), exposes the close personal links between private business and party politics under the headline 'This is how the leaders of the Indonesian party enrich themselves (*Djadi Kaja*)' (Mochtar Lubis 1963:85, 1964:76).

Several features of this episode are relevant to my account of economic decolonization in Indonesia. The nexus between private business and party politics had real-life parallels in Indonesia during the 1950s. The long-term strategy refers to the ambitious aim of the Indonesian government to radically transform the economy and generate rapid economic growth. The background to such an aim was, of course, poverty, represented in Mochtar Lubis's novel by Saimun and his colleagues in garbage collection. Democracy and openness characterized these times of new challenges, so an exposure of corruption and nepotism as was reported in the fictional newspaper *Suluh Merdeka* could very well have really happened.

This chapter picks up the thread of profound change in the Indonesian economy during the 1950s, hinted at by Raden Kaslan in Mochtar Lubis's novel. A great deal more was happening than what may be gleaned from the highly publicized scandals about businessmen involved in politics and politicians involved in business. Fresh initiatives, especially the setting up and development of new business enterprises, significantly altered patterns of participation in the country's economy by the various ethnic groups. The resulting reshuffling of these groups had a more lasting impact than the short-term ups and downs in political and economic fortune.

The new spirit in business needs to be considered in a wider context, with two matters warranting extra attention. The first concerns structural change in the economy at large, more specifically the quest for industrialization, which was widely perceived as the key to the transition from a traditional to a modern economy. The second is the critical need for credit when embarking on new business ventures. This brings us to the banking sector, which was itself at the time undergoing a rapid transformation. The newly established business firms were of two main categories, and it is instructive to consider them separately. The first consists of small-scale firms which on the whole have remained anonymous in Indonesian business history. In the second category we encounter large, well-known conglomerates which were highly visible to the public and often politically well-connected. At this juncture it is useful to introduce a further distinction, namely between large business groups run by indigenous Indonesians and those owned by ethnic Chinese. Although both had a great impact on the process of economic decolonization, the former adhered more closely to the ideals of *Indonesianisasi*.

Industrialization

Bruynzeel Dajak Houtbedrijven had been operating a large sawmill in Sampit in South Kalimantan during the late-colonial period. This industry represented one of the few inroads into manufacturing in a region otherwise characterized by swidden agriculture, smallholder rubber cultivation, and the collection of forest products. In 1951 it was transformed into a joint venture with 51 per cent of equity held by the state industrial bank (BIN, Bank Industri Negara), a proportion soon to be increased to 85 per cent. Immediate new investment amounted to Rp. 10 million, of which the Dutch owners, Bruynzeel, provided two-thirds and BIN the rest. All technical staff remained Dutch.

Losses during the first few years of the joint venture, 1951-1953, were reported at Rp. 12 million and complaints about the company's management were rife. Dutch observers described the firm as being in 'a big financial chaos' (*op financieel gebied een grote chaos*), but others attributed the poor financial results to 'the staff taking lengthy holidays in the Netherlands' (*rojalnja pegawai2 pergi tjuti ke Belanda*).[1] Such experiences in wood processing on the South Kalimantan coast epitomize the pitfalls on the path to rapid industrialization in Indonesia during the 1950s. This section offers a brief macroeconomic background before discussing some policy issues in detail.

There was widespread consensus among Indonesian policy makers and foreign economic advisors that industrialization should be given top priority in restructuring the economy. Towards the very end of effective Dutch colonial rule a start had been made, if not belated, in anticipation of important changes in the structure of the economy. Although using different methodologies, two independent calculations show a shift in the composition of national income in favour of manufacturing. Van der Eng claims that the share of the secondary sector in gross value added rose from 15 per cent in 1930 to 20 per cent in 1940. Booth's more conservative estimate suggests an increase from 8 to 12 per cent during the same period (Booth 1998:88; Van der Eng 2002:171-2). It appears that Indonesia once again had a real chance to achieve self-sustained economic growth, driven by industrialization. However, the momentum was lost due to the Japanese occupation and subsequent turmoil (Dick 1993a:138; Dick et al. 2002:162).

A new start was made as soon as factories had been made fully operational, following the withdrawal of the Japanese and the conclusion of the Indonesian Revolution. Nevertheless, by one estimate, it was not until 1954 that value added in manufacturing, Rp. 295 million at 1938 prices, exceeded the 1939 level, Rp. 280 million. The upward trend continued and by 1957 the manufacturing sector contributed a value added of Rp. 380 million, again expressed in 1938 prices (Suhadi Mangkusuwondo 1976:34-5). However, that was still only 35 per cent more than what had been accomplished eighteen years previously. Progress was being made, albeit at a slow pace.

According to the 1961 census 72 per cent of Indonesia's labour force were still engaged in agriculture, whereas only 7.5 per cent were involved in manufacturing – leaving 9 per cent involved in trading and transport and 11.5 per cent in other services, including government. This occupational distribution is

1 Bank Indonesia, Jakarta: DJB 3322; *Antara* 14-5-1954.

The Menteng Theatre in Jakarta in 1955 (KITLV 41591)

typical of a highly traditional economy and suggests that the industrialization effort did little to change the economy's structure. After having been recorded at 61 per cent in 1953 the share of agriculture in the total labour force had even increased to the 72 per cent quoted in 1961; proportions of manufacturing and services had both dropped from a level of around 13 per cent in 1953 (Suhadi Mangkusuwondo 1976:30).

As mentioned before, the tendency to back away from modernization of the economy has been labelled structural retrogression (Booth 1998:70). This characterization fits with the rising share of peasant agriculture in national income during the mid-1950s and a share of manufacturing which at any rate did not exceed that of the late 1930s (Robison 1986:64). Yet the case for structural retrogression becomes more dubious when we consider the sectoral composition of net domestic product at factor cost in the 1950s. The share of agriculture averaged 57 per cent in 1952-1954, but then gradually declined to 53 per cent in 1957. The manufacturing share saw the reverse, increasing from 8.5 per cent in 1952-1954 to 12 per cent in 1957. By 1958 agriculture accounted for slightly over 50 per cent, manufacturing for 13.5 per cent, and services for 32 per cent of national income.[2] Whether a temporary structural retrogression occurred in the 1950s or not, the true setback to economic development in Indonesia came with the overall stagnation of the economy in the early 1960s, accompanied by a steep decline in the contribution of manufacturing to national income (World Bank 1976:122).

Still, employing 1.8 million workers in 1961, manufacturing in Indonesia had definitely passed beyond an embryonic stage. Two features in particular suggest that there was considerable scope for further expansion. One characteristic of the sector was its largely rural character. Fewer than 700,000 of the sector's labourers, barely more than one-third of the total, were registered in urban areas. By implication, most manufacturing production was small-scale, using simple technology and catering to local demand. The other conspicuous characteristic was an uneven distribution across regions. Java and Madura, with two-thirds of the nation's population and labour force, had a disproportionately large share, almost 80 per cent, of all employees in manufacturing. Jakarta alone – a metropolitan agglomeration with three million inhabitants – had almost 150,000 workers in manufacturing. In Sumatra and Kalimantan the share of manufacturing in the regional labour force was significantly lower than the national average, a mere 3 per cent (Thomas and Panglaykim 1973:27).

Structural change in any economy always takes its toll. As a rule of thumb,

2 Bank Indonesia 1966:3; Suhadi Mangkusuwondo 1975:13. The remainder, 4.5 per cent, was in mining and construction, listed separately in the 1958 statistics.

in the 1950s and 1960s less developed countries were assumed to have to invest at least 10 per cent of GDP in order to achieve self-sustained economic growth. However, money for investment in new industries in Indonesia was always in short supply. Gross domestic capital formation was unimpressive, with barely 9 per cent of GDP during the first half of the 1950s and falling to scarcely more than 5 per cent of GDP in the second half of the decade (Suhadi Mangkusuwondo 1976:327). After reopening in June 1952 the Jakarta Stock Exchange did not become the vehicle for mobilizing private investment capital that had been hoped (Charlesworth 1959:170). It became increasingly clear that a sizeable proportion of the funds for fresh investment would have to come from the government. The ambitious five-year plan for 1956-1960 envisaged a total investment of Rp. 30 billion, of which the government would contribute Rp. 12.5 billion in the optimistic hope that private investors and village cooperatives would provide the rest.[3]

In March 1951 a committee for industrialization was appointed by Sumitro, then Minister of Trade and Industry, with Khouw Bian Tie of the Java Bank as its chairman. The committee's recommendations were rather general, notably government leadership in an industrialization effort designed to create a more balanced economic structure (Sutter 1959:778). Its work was effectively superseded by an Economic Urgency Plan, prepared in Sumitro's department in April 1951. This became the blueprint for further industrialization during the following years. It is instructive to take a closer look at the Sumitro Plan, as it was occasionally called.

The point of departure was Indonesia's largely agrarian economy, which was highly vulnerable to international business cycles and hence unstable. Only industrialization could offer a greater measure of stability. Import-substituting manufacturing at home would enable Indonesia to import more capital goods. Industrialization would also solve problems such as underemployment and lack of mechanization in rural production. The plan targeted three business arenas: one reserved exclusively for initiatives by Indonesians (*bangsa Indonesia*), a second for joint ventures between Indonesian firms and foreign investors, and a third for state-controlled enterprises. Although the first category did not explicitly rule out ethnic Chinese, references to the 'economically weak' suggest that indigenous Indonesians were to be given preferential treatment. Foreign capital, appearing in the second category, was expected to play a more active role. Foreign investors, however, were required to include Indonesians in management positions and pave the way for full Indonesian control of future operations. Foreign management could also be acquired on a contract basis. The government, finally, was to monitor the

3 Bank Mandiri, Jakarta: Jaarverslag NHM Factorij 1956, I:42-3; *Antara* 9-10-1956.

entire process and also assume direct responsibility for certain key industries (defence-related, chemicals, cement, public utilities, and transport). The plan was a blend of industrialization and *Indonesianisasi*, reinforced by more state involvement.

The Sumitro Plan was very ambitious. Total outlays during the first two years were set at Rp. 920 million. The largest slice of the planned outlays, Rp. 522 million or 57 per cent, was earmarked for nine huge long-term industrial projects, including three new plants in Surabaya (glass manufacture, caustic soda, and fertilizer) and an aluminium smelter at Asahan in North Sumatra. The second largest category of investment, amounting to Rp. 179 million (19 per cent), comprised a wide range of short-term projects in diverse undertakings such as printing, rubber remilling, textiles, and tyres. One of the projects was a second cement factory to be built in Gresik near Surabaya. Investment in the third largest category, making up another 14 per cent (Rp. 126 million) of the grand total, was destined for the mechanization and technological upgrading of small-scale industry in rural areas. Strikingly little funding, only Rp. 27 million (3 per cent), went into production centres (*induk*, literally 'mother') available to small and medium-sized industrial firms.[4]

Results were disappointing. None of the major projects were completed within the allotted two-year time frame. A few printing presses were acquired by private Indonesian firms using state credits, and the government itself financed five rubber remilling plants, all much less than what private investors of their own accord had accomplished in the meantime. Difficulties in finding qualified Indonesian personnel were widely reported to have forced newly established factories to delay the start of operations (Sutter 1959:777). Targets were reformulated in the context of a full-scale five-year investment plan for the years 1956-1960. This included priority financial support to three major industrial projects already in an advanced stage of completion, namely the Gresik cement factory, a caustic soda factory in nearby Waru, and a cotton spinning plant in Cilacap on the south coast of Java.

The cement factory in Gresik was the single largest industrial project completed in Indonesia in the 1950s. It was largely financed by credit from the American Exim Bank, offered by the United States government shortly after the transfer of sovereignty (Higgins 1957:74; Dick 2003:291). The newly established *induk* were probably the most tangible outcome of the entire policy. Over a period of six years the government agency responsible for supervision in manufacturing, Lembaga Penjelenggara Perusahaan-Perusahaan Industri (LP3I, Management Authority for Industrial Firms), channelled a total of Rp. 150 million into thirty *induk* already in operation and another 32

4 Bank Indonesia, Jakarta: DJB 3352, no. 55.

under construction (*Antara* 9 October 1956, 7 October 1957).

BIN was the chief financial instrument in the implementation of industrial policy. The bank had been established in April 1951, with the government as sole shareholder and a nominal equity capital of Rp. 500 million which was paid up gradually. BIN was modelled after the Herstel Bank (Bank of Reconstruction) which had been planned by the Dutch authorities in 1948 but had never begun operations. The President-Director of BIN was Margono Djojohadikusumo, who at the time still held the same position at BNI. At the top management level Margono was seconded by an Indonesian economist, Sukasno, and E.T. Kuiper, the Dutch director of the foreign exchange agency Lembaga Alat-Alat Pembajaran Luar Negri (LAAPLN, Regulating Body for Foreign Payments), while the Board of Trustees included Treasurer-General Soetikno Slamet and Moh. Sediono from the Department of Finance. The investment budget for 1952 amounted to Rp. 290 million, of which one-quarter was reserved for the reconstruction of sugar factories. More than half of the capital was available for investment in BIN's 'own' firms, that is companies in which the bank had a permanent influence on decision- making.[5]

Margono remained BIN's President-Director until 1953. His strategy of steady expansion was continued under Sumanang, who became Executive Vice-President after having stepped down as Minister of Economic Affairs in the Wilopo cabinet. Outstanding credits climbed from Rp. 260 million at the end of 1952 to Rp. 350 million at the end of 1953 and to Rp. 530 million by 31 December 1955, all expressed in current prices and subject to inflation.[6] But these commitments constituted only 17 or 18 per cent of all loans extended in 1953 and 1954 to private companies and individuals by the three state banks (BI, BNI, and BIN) (Bank Indonesia 1955:73). The financing of new investment in manufacturing was constrained by the many demands on credit facilities in the Indonesian economy. This even applied to BIN itself, as a large chunk of its total credit volume consisted of financial support to agricultural enterprises, particularly sugar factories.

BIN was actively involved in a wide range of manufacturing enterprises, the two largest being the cement factory in Gresik and a large paper-mill in Aceh, both projected for a long-term investment commitment of about Rp. 200 million. In both cases BIN sought cooperation with non-Dutch foreign suppliers of technology and capital. The Gresik factory sent technicians to the United States for training, and an American management firm, Morris and Knudsen, was in charge of operations until management could be transferred to BIN's own subsidiary, Usaha Industri Indonesia (Usindo, Indonesian Industrial

5 Bank Indonesia, Jakarta: DJB 3322, 13-12-1951.
6 Bank Indonesia, Jakarta: DJB 3322, 13-8-1953.

Enterprise). Meanwhile at the Aceh plant auxiliary logging operations in the local river were designed by a Swedish expert with many years of experience in his own country. There were other examples. West German technology was used in the Seranite hardboard factory in Banyuwangi, East Java, which was run as a joint venture by BIN and an ethnic Chinese factory manager. French capital participated in the new glass factory in Surabaya; Japanese capital in the cotton spinning plant in Cilacap, and Italian capital in a large new paper factory in Gowa, South Sulawesi (*Antara* 18 May 1955, 3 November 1956, 16 January and 8 November 1957; *Warta Niaga dan Perusahaan* 6 and 13 December 1958).

Diversification became the most distinguishing feature of BIN's investment ventures. Indonesia's largest sack factory was founded in Ngagel near Surabaya in 1952 as a joint venture with three partners. BIN provided initial investment capital, Rp. 20 million; the Dutch managing agency Tiedeman and Van Kerchem built the factory; and two estates, Pandji Tandjungsari and Tani Mulja, in Jombang, East Java, supplied the fibres used in production. Other examples include the Djantra spinning factory in Semarang, the paper factory Takengon built on a Swedish model, and the caustic soda plant in Waru. In 1956 BIN even ventured into the hotel business, when it pledged to support the construction of the five star Hotel Indonesia in downtown Jakarta, an investment undertaken by the Natour (National Hotel and Tourist Corporation) which was initially estimated to cost Rp. 70 million but in the end was far more expensive. BIN's Executive Vice-President Sumanang sometimes likened the bank's simultaneous targeting of a great variety of enterprises to the highly successful industrial policies pursued by Taiwan. One wonders, however, whether a bit more focus would not have made the investment effort more effective (*Antara* 8 March, 4 April and 6 July 1956; Sutter 1959:788-90; Dick 2003:292).

The efforts did, however, bear fruit. In 1955 large and medium-sized firms employed more than half a million labourers. The number of firms with at least ten employees climbed above 10,000 in 1957, while more than 3,000 establishments employed over fifty people, including 28 very large companies with 1,000 or more labourers each. Textile and cigarette factories were by far the largest branches of manufacturing, together accounting for almost 40 per cent of total employment in large and medium-sized manufacturing enterprises (Bank Indonesia 1955:150; BPS 1959:4-5; Suhadi Mangkusuwondo 1976:203, 223).

Industrial production also increased, albeit not consistently. In 1952 prewar production capacity had been restored in manufacturing branches such as breweries, cement, copra oil, *kretek* cigarettes, spinning of yarn, and tyres. Yet it was still lagging behind in the weaving of sarongs and the fabrication of paint and soap (*Dunia Ekonomi* 19 December 1953). The same uneven pattern is seen in indicators of production trends in the mid-1950s. Registered production capacity gains were the largest in textiles, with spinning recorded in 1956 at 80 per cent above the 1953 level. Progress was considerably less impressive in cigarette manufacturing and printing, where the increase from 1953 to 1956 amounted to less than 15 per cent. Curiously, imports of paper for printing increased more rapidly than imports of cotton for weaving, a statistical discrepancy suggesting that some factories were not operating at full capacity (Bank Indonesia 1955:150-1, 1957:199, 202, 1958:203).

Conventional wisdom at the time gave high priority to the development of a domestic textile industry due to its great potential for import substitution. This branch of manufacturing enjoyed special attention and was sometimes unofficially referred to as the 'favourite child' (*anak mas*) of the Indonesian government. This preferential treatment had arisen towards the end of Dutch colonial rule. Majalaya in West Java would remain the heart of the industry. In the late 1940s and early 1950s the number of handlooms in that region rose dramatically. The chief distributor of yarn and one of the main operators of the equipment was a cooperative association of Indonesian weaving-mills, Gabungan Pertenunan Indonesia (Gaperti, Union of Indonesian Textile Manufacturers), established in 1949 (Antlöv and Svensson 1991:117). In 1951 Gaperti already had about 600 members in Majalaya alone, who between them owned some 5,700 weaving looms, the vast majority of which were hand-operated. In the course of the 1950s the number of members affiliated with Gaperti rose from 600 to 1,000, primarily in Majalaya and Bandung, while at the same time increasing numbers of power looms were put into production.

Gaperti was hailed as a successful example of cooperation among indigenous producers. It also functioned as a subcontractor to Pretex, the local association of ethnic Chinese employers. The government was involved in the background through its regulation of imports of vital raw materials, thus forging a 'triple alliance' between indigenous entrepreneurs, ethnic Chinese industrialists, and the state (Keppy 2001:143-4, 158-61).

There was a correlation between technological sophistication in production and ethnicity in management and ownership. A survey of the textile industry in 1951 listed 2,500 individual firms, of which 2,350 used handlooms, 50 power looms, and 100 a mixture of the two. The indigenous share in the non-mechanized factory plants, the vast majority, amounted to 75 per cent, while 75 per cent of the fully mechanized enterprises were run by ethnic Chinese and European employers. Another survey, in the Bandung area, showed that Gaperti-affiliated plants often operated far below capacity.[7] In East Java

[7] Bank Indonesia, Jakarta: DJB 183, 24-3-1952, 184, 19-9-1952.

ethnic Chinese owned more than half of the weaving mills, three-quarters of the printing presses, and all of the mechanized cigarette factories (Anspach 1969:182; see also Palmer 1972).

Government intervention became increasingly important to the industrialization effort, so much so that by the late 1950s Gaperti's influence was waning in the textile industry of West Java. Indigenous textile producers were also supported through import regulations and financing. In very few cases, however, did government involvement go as far as it did in the emerging batik industry of West and Central Java. In 1952, wishing to strengthen its control over supplies of cambric, the indispensable raw material, the government assigned an import monopoly to one firm, the Batik Trading Company. When it became known that batik cooperatives in Yogyakarta, Solo, and Pekalongan were excluded this led to vehement protests. A few years later, in 1955, government funding supported the establishment of two cambric factories in Central Java with a total planned investment of Rp. 100 million. Here again, an ethnic factor was lurking in the background, as the government support did not alleviate the dependence of numerous indigenous producers on local suppliers of advance credit, often ethnic Chinese. A complaint commonly heard from Javanese batik producers was that 'profits were pocketed by another side' (*keuntungannja diambil pihak lain*) (*Berita Indonesia* 17 July 1952; *Antara* 21 April, 7 September 1955).

All in all there was little disagreement about the urgency of industrialization, and the Indonesian government took up the formidable challenge with seriousness and determination. Results were forthcoming but mostly in fits and starts; the process clearly did not proceed as rapidly as policy makers wanted. Implementation was arguably hampered by the extreme diversification, or lack of focus, in financing and the matter was further complicated by the simultaneous aims of more industrial production and more indigenous Indonesian participation. Efforts to combine industrialization with *Indonesianisasi* did not make matters any easier.

Banking in a state of flux

As the tenth anniversary of BNI drew near in mid-1956, Director Abdul Karim proudly depicted his bank as a symbol of national entrepreneurship. He emphasized that lending to domestic firms with little capital of their own had been particularly important in 1950 and 1951. He refrained from giving details on the amount of defaulting in repayment of debts. Total credit extended by BNI had risen to Rp. 500 million, despite the bank not having been permitted to take over the commercial arm of the central bank in 1949, when it was decided that the Java Bank, later Bank Indonesia, was to henceforth serve as

Indonesia's central bank (*Antara* 2 May 1954, 4 July 1956). Lending practices at the central bank itself were undergoing rapid change at that time under the leadership of its first Indonesian president, Sjafruddin Prawiranegara (Chapter V). BNI and Bank Indonesia were increasingly fishing in the same pond for creditworthy clients. The simultaneous changes in both banks underscore that the entire banking sector was in the midst of a transformation during the 1950s.

At that time the banking sector – essential for the growth of new business in Indonesia – consisted of three types: government, foreign, and private domestic banks. The total number of banks increased from 31 in 1952 to 107 in 1957. This is a spectacular development by any standard. However, in terms of the number of institutions the expansion was confined to private domestic banks (96 by 1957), with numbers of banks in the two other categories remaining constant (Charlesworth 1959:1; Bank Indonesia 1966:55). Despite their increased numbers only nineteen private domestic banks had capital in excess of Rp. 100 million; almost half (42) were indigenously owned, responsible for only 11 per cent of all outstanding domestic credit (*Antara* 25 May 1956; Robison 1986:42). Consequently, a skewed structure evolved in the banking sector, where a small number of large government and foreign-owned banks competed with a great many small private domestic banks. The three state-owned investment banks were the central bank, BNI and BIN.

BIN kept targeting industrial development although its total commitments were modest compared to those of Bank Indonesia and BNI. The fourth state-owned bank, Bank Rakjat Indonesia (BRI, the Indonesian People's Bank), was essentially a savings bank, the successor to the Dutch-controlled AVB, or Syomin Ginko (People's Bank), as it was called during the Japanese occupation. The total volume of extended credit reached a magnitude comparable with that of BNI, approaching Rp. 500 million by the end of 1954. Lending at BRI was geared primarily towards smoothing current accounts for shopkeepers and other small-scale entrepreneurs in the services sector rather than facilitating the founding of new trading and manufacturing enterprises.[8]

In 1950 seven foreign banks were operating in Indonesia; this number would remain unchanged during the decade. Nationalist opposition to the idea of new foreign banks entering Indonesia was repeatedly voiced in Parliament (*Antara* 9 March 1957). The existing seven included three Dutch banks: NHM, the Handelsbank (Trading Bank; formerly Nederlandsch-Indische Handelsbank), and the Escompto Bank (formerly the Nederlandsch-Indische Escompto-Maatschappij). The other four were the Chartered Bank, the Hongkong-

8 Bank Indonesia, Jakarta: 184, 30-9-1953; Bank Indonesia 1958:103. The term used here by Bank Indonesia, 'middle class', is an erroneous translation of the original Dutch term 'middenstand'.

Shanghai Banking Corporation (HSBC), the Bank of China, and the Overseas Chinese Bank. Their combined equity amounted to Rp. 650 million in 1956, 75 per cent of which was Dutch (*Antara* 22 March 1956). Since colonial days they had been united in the Perhimpoenan Bank-Bank Devisen (Association of Foreign Exchange Banks), which now admitted BNI as a member and chose Abdul Karim as its chairman.

The volume of credit extended by foreign banks rose from Rp. 900 million in 1953 to almost Rp. 1.8 billion in 1956, a 100 per cent increase in just three years, which is impressive even when corrected for inflation. The foreign banks' total started to decline only in 1957, hitting Rp. 1.4 billion at the end of the year and Rp. 1.2 billion in 1958. Meanwhile, the volume of credit supplied by the six foremost domestic banks rose from Rp. 1.3 billion in 1953 to Rp. 2.1 billion in 1957, and even to Rp. 3.9 billion in 1958.[9] Such statistics demonstrate that foreign banking continued to play a key role in facilitating Indonesian entrepreneurship up until the late 1950s.

In May 1952 the Indonesian government determined to promote 'national' banking by establishing a separate organization, Perhimpunan Bank-Bank Nasional (Perbana, Association of National Banks). Initially it consisted of sixteen members: three government banks (Bank Indonesia, BNI, and BIN) and thirteen private domestic banks, including the veteran Bank Nasional in Bukittinggi. One of the organization's tasks was to promote the development of skills among Indonesian banking staff. This was accomplished through the Jajasan Pendidikan Kader Bank (Foundation for Education of Banking Staff). By 1957 almost 340 bank employees had completed their training. Perbana was meant to represent all private domestic banking in the country but its membership was slow to increase, from 17 in 1955 to 25 in 1957, and 27 in 1959. At the end of the decade three out of four private domestic banks still remained outside this organization. Those outside Perbana included banks run by ethnic Chinese, for instance Bank Indonesia Raja (Great Indonesia Bank), acquired in 1955 from a Sumatran businessman by Atang Latief (Lauw Tjin Ho), who was later to become an associate of Salim (*Antara* 28 June 1953, 25 April 1954, 29 March and 11 June 1955, 11 September 1957; Charlesworth 1959:146-8; Data Consult 1991:109).

Nowhere was the link between business and politics more visible than in banking. Bank Indonesia and BIN were especially close to the ruling party PNI, whereas BNI under Margono maintained a special relationship with the socialist party, PSI. Bank Umum Nasional (BUN, National Public Bank), was

9 Charlesworth 1959:87; Runturambi 1959:30. The six largest domestic banks were those authorized to handle foreign exchange, namely Bank Indonesia, BNI, BIN and three private domestic banks.

founded in November 1952 by three prominent members of PNI, the party Deputy Chairman Soewirjo, Ong Eng Die, and Iskaq Tjokrohadisurjo. Less than a year later the latter two were members of the (first) Ali Sastroamidjojo cabinet as Ministers of Finance and Economic Affairs respectively. BUN welcomed deposits by government agencies and developed particularly close ties with the importers' umbrella organization, Ikatan Importir Nasional Indonesia (Ikini, Association of Indonesian National Importers), which held the import licences of indigenous importers lacking sufficient funds to make the required advance deposits. The director of BUN and chairman of Ikini was Mohamad Tabrani, a businessman chairing PNI at the time, who was involved in setting up joint ventures with ethnic Chinese businessmen. Of the 47 members of Parliament for PNI during the first half of the 1950s, 28 (60 per cent) were said to have direct business interests, primarily in banking (Sutter 1959:791-8, 1311; Robison 1986:49).

Small-scale entrepreneurship

Life was often gay in Indonesia during the 1950s, in the original sense of the word. Popular culture blossomed in the wake of decolonization. A young generation of Indonesian writers emerged. Humour played a vital role in the press, for instance in the shape of what were known as *podjok* (literally 'corner'), witty columns poking fun at everyone and everything. Cinemas opened their doors in the most diverse locations. The small town of Magelang in Central Java, for instance, was enriched by three new cinemas in 1953-1954 alone. More examples from the same region are: Tjahaja Koening ('The Yellow Light') in Purwodadi and Pusaka in Purworejo in 1953, Raja in Semarang in 1954, Orion in Banyumas and Capitol and Elita in Purwokerto in 1955, City in Rembang in 1956, Ardjuna in Muntilan and Gloria in Pekalongan in 1957. Such small-scale enterprises targeting local clients may be seen as symptomatic of the widespread enthusiasm prevailing in the Indonesian economy during the 1950s. This section focuses on small-scale entrepreneurs, many of them indigenous and many, as was the case with cinemas, ethnic Chinese.

Enthusiasm to launch a new business welled up immediately following the transfer of sovereignty. Sutter, the first to study *Indonesianisasi*, claims that about 500 new firms per year were founded in 1951 and in 1953, and that indigenous businessmen were responsible for 40 per cent of the new firms (Sutter 1959:1307). One may reasonably conjecture that this estimate is valid for the first half of the 1950s as a whole. Assuming for the sake of argument that all these new firms were in either manufacturing or trading and that they were all legally incorporated, then the wave of new business establishments would account for a substantial proportion, one-third or more, of the 4,200 incorporated companies listed in a national business directory compiled in 1953.[10]

Although the information given in the individual entries of the business directory is scant, the firm's name and that of its owner or manager permit us to assign ethnicity in almost all cases with a reasonable degree of accuracy. Explicit references to nationalist ideology or Islam are not likely to turn up in the name of a foreign-owned firm, nor would Chinese names be used by businessmen other than ethnic Chinese.[11] Judging by such criteria, 40 per cent of the trading firms and 33 per cent of the manufacturing enterprises were found to be indigenous (Lindblad 2002:62-5). This corroborates the estimate given by Sutter. In addition, the small difference in indigenous share between manufacturing and trading, only 7 per cent, is worth noting as positive discrimination applied only to the latter sector. One might have expected the indigenous share in trading to be inflated by the use of strawmen in trading but not in manufacturing. Despite this, the majority of enterprises registered as indigenous in Central Java during the 1950s seem to have reflected genuine participation in new business undertakings by Javanese.

Participation by indigenous businessmen was bolstered by the opening up of sectors of economic activity previously closed to them. Of more than 1,500 newly established private firms in the province of Central Java (excluding Yogyakarta) between 1950 and 1960 52 per cent had Javanese owners and/or managers. Slightly fewer than one-third of all new firms (31.5 per cent) could be designated as being exclusively controlled by ethnic Chinese. Joint ventures of Javanese and Chinese businessmen played an important role, figuring in almost 10 per cent of all cases; only 40 per cent of these were found in trading, where strawman constructions might have been expected to predominate.[12]

10 This assumption is not as far-fetched as it may seem. Other new establishments would include agricultural estates, mines, and banks, but their numbers would be marginal in comparison to the many trading and manufacturing firms. In addition, the estimates given in the literature of new establishments between 1951 and 1953 by definition refer to firms that in one way or another had been registered. This also applies to the legally incorporated companies included in the business directory of 1953. The directory is comprehensive in the sense that it covers all branches of manufacturing and trading as well as all major locations in Indonesia. No source offers a statistical representation of business enterprises which were not registered or legally incorporated.

11 The designation of ethnicity on the basis of company and personal names permits only a global differentiation between three broad categories: indigenous Indonesians, ethnic Chinese, and others. No distinction can be made between Dutchmen operating as foreign investors and Indo-Europeans domiciled in Indonesia and in possession of an Indonesian passport.

12 Lindblad 2004a:93-4. The source is an unpublished manuscript entitled *Direktori perusahaan. Wilajah Jawa Tengah dan DIY* (although the Daerah Istimewa Yogyakarta (DIY, Special Region of Yogyakarta), is not actually included). There is no guarantee that this survey of newly established companies is exhaustive, but it likely offers a reasonably good approximation of new business initiatives taken in what was one of the largest provinces of Indonesia. The data were collected at

The vast majority of the 1,500 new firms were each established by a different person; only 55 individuals are recorded as founding more than one business during that decade, including seven people who appear three times in the list of new firms. This small group among the region's most active entrepreneurs was composed of four ethnic Chinese and three indigenous businessmen. The ethnic Chinese were Go Sing Bik, Liem Kok Lien, and Lauw Tedjakusuma, all three in Semarang, and Go Joe Han in Pekalongan. The indigenous businessmen were Djajusman and Kawi Oemarjanto, both in Semarang, and Iskandar Said in Pekalongan. The large number of businessmen involved in setting up new enterprises in Central Java during the 1950s, almost 1,400, suggests how small the new firms must have been.

Patterns of ethnicity in founding new businesses changed over time. The first few years up until 1954 witnessed a greater than average participation by ethnic Chinese. As of 1957, however, this was reversed. Javanese businessmen were then responsible for establishing as many as two-thirds or three-quarters of all new firms. The year 1956, when anti-Chinese sentiments were running high, stands out in the history of new establishments in Central Java. Founding activities fell to an unprecedented low, but the share of joint ventures between ethnic Chinese and Javanese was higher than at almost any other time during the decade (Lindblad 2004a:94). For ethnic Chinese, caution and cooperation served as a safeguard against discriminatory practices. From their point of view such joint ventures may have also served to guarantee more even-handed treatment by the government.

Javanese entrepreneurship was particularly strong in construction and transport, with exclusively indigenous firms accounting for respectively four-fifths and two-thirds of all new firms. Local transport was a sector which lent itself particularly well to cooperation between Javanese and ethnic Chinese. However, trading was especially favoured by ethnic Chinese, whose commercial enterprises, excluding those operated in conjunction with Javanese partners, made up 42 per cent of all trading firms and corresponded to half of all companies with an exclusively ethnic Chinese ownership. Other traditional strongholds of Chinese Indonesian business in Central Java included the chemical industry in Semarang and *kretek* manufacturing in Kudus.[13]

Yogyakarta continued to draw on a strong local tradition of indigenous entrepreneurship even following the Indonesian government's return to Jakarta. Activities of small family businesses were especially lively in Kotagede

---

Gadjah Mada University, Yogyakarta, and I am grateful to Bambang Purwanto for gaining access to this source.

13 Lindblad 2004a:96-7. It must be noted that the designations of firms by economic sector are no more than global approximations, since several alternative targets were sometimes specified in the intentions of the newly established enterprise.

and Moyudan. Silver handicraft revived, but fell short of returning to pre-war production levels. Consequently, Kotagede became an impoverished town with large numbers of day labourers and peddlers (Nakamura 1976:110-7; Hersumpana 2005).

Support from the local authorities was often crucial to the development of indigenous entrepreneurship. Yogyakarta is a case in point. Sultan Hamengku Buwono IX, former Minister of Defence in the Natsir cabinet, was not only head of the Daerah Istimewa Yogyakarta (DIY, Special Region of Yogyakarta) but also an entrepreneur in his own right, albeit with limited success. In 1954 he financed a tobacco plantation to serve as a vehicle for professionalization in peasant agriculture (Vak Organisasi Tani Primer, Professional Organization of Outstanding Peasants), but apparently it failed as a consequence of mismanagement, corruption, and political conflict. The Sultan's foundation, Jakti, proved a lame duck as an intermediary between the project and local peasants (Bambang Purwanto 2003). In early 1955 Jakti purchased a sugar factory in the village of Padokan near Yogyakarta for Rp. 88 million from its Dutch owner, the Vereenigde Vorstenlandsche Cultuur-Maatschappij (United Principalities Cultivation Company) in Amsterdam. The Sultan himself was director of this company and invited technical advisors from East Germany. It still took the sugar factory several years to operate at capacity, primarily due to problems in management and financial administration (Selosoemardjan 1962:318; *Antara* 4 February 1955, 2 February 1957, 30 May and 8 July 1958).

Additional information is available with regard to some 500 manufacturing companies in Java in the early 1950s, primarily in rice-milling, weaving, printing, and the remilling of rubber. A survey, conducted in 1953, showed a balanced distribution in ethnicity of ownership, with 235 indigenous Indonesians compared to 240 'other', presumably mostly ethnic Chinese (*Antara* 12 June 1954). A similar survey in Kalimantan a couple of years later contrasted a solid indigenous Indonesian domination in six popular branches of manufacturing (rubber smoking, rice-milling, footwear, copra oil, car and bicycle servicing, ice production) in South Kalimantan, with a largely undisputed stronghold of ethnic Chinese businessmen in East and West Kalimantan (*Antara* 6 July 1956).

Companies of small size were also favoured in the official ideology about the preferred future shape of the national economy. Vice-President Hatta seized every opportunity to promote the cooperative movement in Indonesia, emphasizing its vital role in economic development. On 11 July 1954, a day still celebrated as *hari koperasi* ('Day of the Cooperative'), looking back on the achievements of the preceding few years, he concluded: 'Though gratifying progress has been made, we are still at the beginning of the road.' The total number of cooperatives had indeed risen, from scarcely more than 600 in the colonial period to 5,800 at the end of 1952 and 8,600 at the end of 1953, with total membership approaching 1.5 million people (Hatta 1957:77, 108-9; *Antara* 11 July 1956). According to Hatta, progress up until the end of 1953 had been the most impressive for credit cooperatives (2,400 societies), reasonable for production cooperatives (1,500 units), and poor for consumer cooperatives (900 associations). Curiously, he left out the largest of them all, the *desa* cooperatives, catering to village needs and numbering 2,700 by 1953. Five years later, in 1958, Indonesia had 4,700 *desa* cooperatives, 4,700 credit cooperatives, and 1,800 production cooperatives, but fewer than 900 consumer cooperatives (Bank Indonesia 1955:167, 1959:285).

Production cooperatives offered the best alternative to private family enterprises due to the additional advantage of shared centralized facilities. This was particularly valuable when cooperatives entered into competition in the export market. Examples include rubber in Aceh, tea in West Java, and copra in Manado, North Sulawesi; the last of which could count on special support from the central government, including sizeable credits from Bank Indonesia.[14] The most controversial production cooperatives were in batik manufacturing. The leading Gabungan Koperasi Batik Indonesia (GKBI, Association of Indonesian Batik Cooperatives), even provoked heated debates in Parliament due to the special protection it enjoyed. GKBI, established in 1948 in Yogyakarta by local batik associations, obtained an import monopoly for unbleached cambric and would eventually establish a factory of its own (*Antara* 14 January 1955; Bambang Purwanto 2003).

Indigenous conglomerates

Under Soeharto Indonesia acquired a notorious reputation for the cosy relationship between large private business concerns and the apex of political power. This relationship is depicted as an almost incestuous nexus facilitating corruption, collusion, and nepotism. Much has been written about the most flagrant cases, often in the form of anecdotal evidence (Robison 1986; MacIntyre 1990; Backman 1999:255-99). Strikingly little use has been made of available statistical and historical data compiled on the country's largest conglomerates.[15] I draw on such systematic data here to assess the 1950s from the

[14] Bank Indonesia, Jakarta: DJB 183, 24-3-1952; *Antara* 21-8-1956.

[15] Most reports on Indonesia's top 200 conglomerates were prepared at the end of the 1980s and during the 1990s, primarily by the Jakarta-based market research firm PT Data Consult. The printed reports are prohibitively expensive and scarcely, if ever, found in library collections, although excerpts have appeared in the Indonesian press on various occasions. Elsewhere I have used this type of information to discuss Indonesian conglomerates in historical perspective in greater detail (Lindblad 2007).

vantage point of 1990. This perspective serves as an organizing principle in the presentation of the data. It also permits an assessment of the long-term viability of major enterprises. As indicated at the outset of this chapter, it is useful to consider indigenous Indonesian conglomerates separately from those owned by ethnic Chinese. First, however, we need a brief general overview of these conglomerates.

Around 1990 about 40, or one in five, of the 200 largest business concerns listed in Indonesia had been in operation since the 1950s (CISI 1990; Data Consult 1991). This group of old-timers consisted of just as many firms owned by indigenous Indonesians as by ethnic Chinese, whereas for the conglomerates existing in 1990 the ratio was 60-40 in favour of the ethnic Chinese. Even these simple statistics reveal two interesting points. First, there was, and still is, an unmistakable longevity in big business in Indonesia; companies that rose to prominence at an early stage were likely to endure. Second, the Sukarno period was more conducive to the development of indigenous big business than the Soeharto period, although the development of ethnic Chinese business does not appear to have been significantly hindered under Sukarno.

The true old-timers among the top conglomerates included two indigenous businesses dating from the colonial period. The oldest was the Javanese life insurance company Bumiputera 1912, but the most successful of the two was Bakrie and Bros., founded on the eve of the Japanese occupation. Achmad Bakrie, later described as 'a fantastic indigenous example [for others]' (*contoh pribumi hebat*), in 1952 transformed his trading corporation into a limited liability company. During the next few years he became the sole agent for imports of a variety of consumer goods such as radios, motorcycles, and sewing machines, all imported from Europe but none from the Netherlands. In 1957 he ventured into manufacturing by buying a small factory in Jakarta from its Dutch owners. With the aid of a generous loan from Bank Indonesia the plant was converted into a modern pipe factory and became the foundation for a dramatic expansion of activities. In 1991 Bakrie and Bros. employed 11,000 Indonesians and in 1994 it was listed as Indonesia's second largest indigenous conglomerate in terms of sales (CISI 1990:48-60; Data Consult 1991:96-100; *Eksekutif* August 1995; Nasir Tamara 1998:40-2, 51, 96). Achmad Bakrie died in 1988, aged 72. In 2004 his second son, Aburizal, became Coordinating Minister for Economy and Finance under President Susilo Bambang Yudhoyono; the following year he was appointed head of the Department of People's Welfare.

Four of the indigenous old-timers had risen to prominence before the Indonesian Revolution. The most public figure among them was Hasjim Ning, who was introduced previously. Through the Indonesian Service Company (ISC) Hasjim Ning held the sole agency for imports of General Motors cars, and in the press was often referred to as the 'Henry Ford of Indonesia'. As a nephew of Vice-President Hatta he was very well-connected, with easy access to credit and lucrative contracts. He played a leading role in Jakarta's Chamber of Commerce, eventually becoming its chairman (Navis 1986:337-63; CISI 1990:202-4). The three other old-timers were Burhanuddin Muh. Diah, owner of the daily newspaper *Merdeka*, the Wartono family with their Sukun concern centred around a large *kretek* cigarette factory in Kudus, and Kentjana Widjaja, who ran the Galva business group along with various family members (CISI 1990:297-8, 452-3; Data Consult 1991:668-9).

Three other prominent indigenous conglomerates emerged soon after the transfer of sovereignty. Their owners all came to play a leading role in the business community of several major cities for decades to come. In Jakarta Soedarpo Sastrosatomo reputedly became the single most successful indigenous capitalist of the Sukarno period. He was of Javanese origin but grew up in Pangkalan Susu, North Sumatra, pursued medical studies in Yogyakarta, and entered the Indonesian diplomatic service at the critical time of the Dutch military campaigns in the late 1940s. After a brief spell working with Hasjim Ning, in 1952 he set up his own company in Jakarta. He benefited a great deal from ready access to import licences and contracts for military vehicles. In 1953 he borrowed money from Sultan Hamengku Buwono IX of Yogyakarta to purchase 75 per cent of the equity in the Indonesian Shipping and Transport Agency (ISTA) from the Dutch trading concern Jacobson van den Berg, which combined divestment with retaining operations in Indonesia. ISTA obtained lucrative sole agencies for German and Japanese shipping lines. In 1956 Soedarpo benefited from regulations to accelerate *Indonesianisasi* when he acquired the Dutch-owned stevedoring firm Stroohoeden Veem in Surabaya. In 1966 ISTA was integrated into the shipping line Samudra Indonesia, which formed the core of Soedarpo's business empire. Soedarpo was very well-connected, through both the Sultan and one of his brothers, chairman of the PSI faction in Parliament. It is worth noting that his business conglomerate continued to expand even after the days of protection had ended (Robison 1986:55-6, 93, 339; Data Consult 1991:613-4; Thee Kian Wie 2003:148-57).

Haji Kalla played a role in Makassar akin to that of Soedarpo in Jakarta. Spectacular expansion of Haji Kalla's small business concern began in 1952, after having shifted from the distribution of cars and equipment to the manufacturing of electrical and vehicle parts under the brand name Bukaka (CISI 1990:189-91; Data Consult 1991:295-7). The founder's son, Yusuf Kalla, was elected Vice-President of Indonesia in 2004.

If Haji Kalla personified indigenous business success in South Sulawesi, the same can be said about T.D. Pardede for North Sumatra. Tumpul Dorianus Pardede was a Protestant from a small village on the shores of Lake Toba. After a military career fighting the Dutch in North Sumatra, where he was imprisoned for several months, he became engaged in organizing the transport of passengers and goods between Medan and Tapanuli. In 1953 he founded a knitting factory, Pardedetex, in downtown Medan. This factory was allegedly one of the first to attach a label reading 'Made in Indonesia' to textile goods destined for foreign markets. Pardedetex produced shirts, towels, socks, and blankets. Within ten years he was employing some 3,000 workers. Pardede boasted that he was capable of supplying one-third of domestic demand for singlets. His ambitions soon transcended Medan: he served as vice-chairman of two bodies at the national level of economic policy making, first the Madjelis Industri Indonesia (MII, Advisory Council for Indonesian Industry), then the Dewan Ekonomi Indonesia (DEI, Council for the Economy of Indonesia). In 1965 he was appointed an honorary unpaid member of the cabinet, responsible for regulating economic self-reliance (*Urusan Berdikari*). He also represented the PNI in Parliament, ran a hotel chain in Medan, and founded his own local university, Darma Agung. He died in 1991, aged 75 (*Antara* 26 June 1957; Tridah Bangun 1983:75-98, 269-74, 1987; CISI 1990:342-4; Data Consult 1991:524-6).

The mid-1950s saw the establishment of two indigenous conglomerates, Gobel and Indrapura, which have since both developed into high-profile business groups in Indonesia. Thayeb Muh. Gobel was a technical engineer who in 1954 set up a transistor radio factory in Indonesia. He borrowed Rp. 5 million, adding another million from his own savings, and began production in downtown Jakarta with 55 workers. These were the beginnings of the highly successful National Gobel conglomerate, which at a later stage would benefit substantially from a joint venture with the electronics concern Matsushita (*Antara* 29 September 1958; Data Consult 1991:485-6). Indrapura, also focusing on commercial services, was founded by the Ambonese Julius Tahija, who cooperated closely with Soedarpo. The core of the conglomerate was the insurance company Indrapura, one of the five largest in Indonesia in the mid-1950s. In 1955 Tahija founded Bank Niaga, which later became Indonesia's third largest private bank. Tahija himself eventually became a national public figure when serving as chairman of the board of Freeport Indonesia and Caltex Pacific (*Antara* 4 December 1956; Data Consult 1991:341-2).

Two other indigenous conglomerates emerging towards the end of the decade also illustrate the importance of exclusive rights and political connections in setting up new businesses in Sukarno's Indonesia. Pioneer Trading was founded in 1958 in Jakarta by Paul Hamid Njotokusumo and Hans Mahendra; Poleko Trading was established in 1959 in Makassar by Arnold Baramuli, at the time Governor of South Sulawesi. The former firm benefited from being the sole agency for Yanmar diesel engines and the latter was linked to the apex of political power in the region (Robison 1986:359-60; Data Consult 1991 538, 543-4).

The thirteen indigenous conglomerates described above – Bumiputera 1912, Bakrie, Merdeka, Sukun, Galva, Hasjim Ning, Soedarpo, Haji Kalla,

Pardede, Gobel, Indrapura, Pioneer Trading, and Poleko – all conducted business activities at one stage or another during the process of economic decolonization. They were all capable of maintaining their place in the top echelons of Indonesian conglomerates up until the early 1990s, and sometimes beyond. The same holds true for another seven indigenous conglomerates which can only be mentioned in passing here, namely Djawa Indah, Panatraco (an Ambonese firm), Sahid (a Javanese hotel chain), Sukabumi, Tehnik Umum (run by Eddy Kowara, a national figure), Tunggal, and Wirontono (CISI 1990; Data Consult 1991).

The evidence from these twenty business groups suggests a long-term continuity in indigenous big business. But that is not the whole story. It is also necessary to compare contemporary qualitative information with the detailed systematic data collected several decades later. Of 21 prominent indigenous businessmen in the 1950s only five were ranked in the top 200 conglomerates around 1990: Hasjim Ning, Soedarpo, Pardede, Eddy Kowara, and Fritz Eman with his business group Udatin.[16] Such an unimpressive score reflects the high degree of vulnerability of indigenous business to changes in the political regime. This is borne out by examples from the group of sixteen pioneers enjoying business success in Indonesia in the 1950s but who have since fallen from the top ranks.

In 1947 the Musin Dasaad concern was reconstituted as a conglomerate of six separate enterprises. At the core was the Malaya Import Company, Dasaad's original creation. The concern also embraced Indonesia's largest textile factory Kantjil Mas, a plant for radio manufacturing in Semarang, and a warehouse, Negara Veem – all testified to the founder's inclination to continuous diversification. In the first half of the 1950s 1,900 workers were employed and average annual turnover was Rp. 15 million. Dasaad obtained a range of sole agencies for imports such as Westinghouse and Lockheed, and also for Fiat motor cars. Musin Dasaad survived as a leading conglomerate into the Soeharto era, although not for long. In the 1970s all lucrative sole agencies expired or were sold; the only remnant of the once extensive assets was a minority equity holding in timber in Palembang (*Antara* 30 December 1954, 2 January 1955; Robison 1986:51-4, 330-1).

Like Dasaad, five other Sumatran traders with roots in the late-colonial period had ascended to the level of the national economy by the 1950s. One of them was the highly active trading combination of Djohan and Djohor, another was Rachman Tamin, who purchased a Dutch printing press in Surabaya and invested Rp. 35 million in a large textile factory, Ratatex, in East

[16] Robison 1986:51; Data Consult 1991:3-12. The list also includes one production cooperative (GKBI), but strangely leaves out Nitisemito, owner of the large *kretek* cigarette factory Nodjorono in Kudus.

Java. Incidentally, when buying equipment for Ratatex, he deliberately opted for German rather than Dutch machinery. Abdul Ghany Aziz from Palembang expanded his company Masayu from distributing railway rolling stock to general trading and secured the sole agency for International Harvester. Omar Tusin became a leading figure in the organization of economists, Kongres Ekonomi Nasional Seluruh Indonesia (KENSI, All-Indonesia Congress of National Economy), and Haji Sukar Sjamsuddin, a factory owner, played a leading role in the national organization of Indonesian textile manufacturers (*Antara* 19 February 1956; Robison 1986:51-3, 337; Data Consult 1991:41).

Another ten indigenous entrepreneurs belonged to the private business elite in Sukarno's Indonesia, including three Javanese who deserve special mention. Sosrohadikoesoemo, an engineer by training, led the Intraport trading company to the forefront of domestic distribution of consumer goods such as electrical appliances from the Philips factory at Bandung. Koesmoeljono was of illustrious *priyayi* (Javanese aristocractic) lineage and had read law in the Netherlands before the war. During the Japanese occupation he was the administrator of a coconut plantation in Tegal and in 1945 he founded Bank Perniagaan (Trading Bank) in Yogyakarta, winning support from both Dasaad and Hasjim Ning. In 1951 he founded Indoplano for manufacturing pencils and pumps, and later secured contracts to supply government agencies through a personal link with the then Prime Minister Wilopo. Wahab Affan's connections were even better, as he was a relative of Sukarno's second official wife, Fatmawati, and it appears that Sukarno himself even participated as a shareholder in some shipping and trading firms set up by Wahab in conjunction with Sukar Sjamsuddin. Wahab joined the board of KENSI in August 1956 (*Antara* 10 March 1955, 6 August 1956; Robison 1986:54, 332-4). The remaining seven on the list of prominent indigenous businessmen can only be mentioned in passing. They were Herling Laoh, Mardanus, Rudjito, Soetan Sjahsam (Sutan Sjahrir's brother), Moh. Tabrani, Sidi Tando, and Usman Zahiruddin (Robison 1986:51).

Lists compiled long afterwards are not likely to be complete, especially not when relying on qualitative and circumstantial evidence. There are striking omissions in the list of 21 prominent indigenous businesses cited here, for instance Bakrie and Bros. At the time, in the 1950s, there was much talk of the 'Big Four' picking up the challenge laid down by the Dutch 'Big Five'. Of these four trading firms only Musin Dasaad and Intraport figure among prominent indigenous enterprises; Djamaludin Malik, yet another Sumatran, and Birokorpi are both left out. With BIN and aided by Japanese credit, Birokorpi participated in a large-scale investment effort to erect the soda factory in Waru near Surabaya (*Antara* 19 July 1956; Muhaimin 1990:227-33).

Other examples of possibly important omissions are the ABC concern, which grew out of Tjandra Djojonegoro's rice wine distillery and was later known for its dry cell batteries, and the Sukun conglomerate based around Wartono's *kretek* cigarette factory, dating from 1947. Wing Soap in Surabaya also started out in the late 1940s, eventually evolving into a leading business group in East Java controlled by the Kattuari family (CISI 1990:452-3; Data Consult 1991:295-7, 668-9, 754).

An important aspect of indigenous big business concerned its relationship with the military. Cooperative links had been forged during the Indonesian Revolution (Chapter III) and direct military involvement in business operations was strongly boosted in the aftermath of the take-over and nationalization of Dutch companies as of December 1957 (Chapter VIII). Here it must suffice to mention in passing the basic continuity in business endeavours undertaken by military units. In Yogyakarta Soeharto, later to become President, set up a separate organization for this purpose, the YPTE, the Jajasan (Yayasan) Pembangunan Teritorium Empat (YPTE, Foundation for Development in Territory 4), which by 1957 had accumulated investment funds amounting to Rp. 16 million destined for enterprises in Yogyakarta, Solo and, Salatiga (Elson 2001:62). Shortly following the Permesta rebellion in South Sulawesi in March 1957, Sulawesi's copra trade is said to have been monopolized by a newly established agency, Badan Urusan Kopra (Body for Regulating the Copra Business) which stood under the direct command of the region's military governor (Bambang Purwanto 2005).

Chinese conglomerates

On 10 July 1961 all assets belonging to the Kian Gwan Indonesia trading company of the Oei Tiong Ham concern were expropriated by order of the judiciary represented by Pengadilan Ekonomi (Court for Economic Offence). The Kian Gwan company was charged with being involved in large-scale smuggling of copra from Sulawesi. At the time several of Oei Tiong Ham's sons were at odds with one another and were living abroad. Therefore they could offer little resistance in the conflict with the Indonesian authorities which reached its climax in July 1961. The wider context included a court case in the Netherlands initiated by Kian Gwan Indonesia to gain access to shares held in custody by the Indonesian central bank as well as to contest allegations of cooperating too closely with leading Dutch trading houses in the past. The take-over of Kian Gwan Indonesia marked the conclusion of operations by the Oei Tiong Ham concern in Indonesia, once the country's most brilliant example of ethnic Chinese entrepreneurship (Yoshihara 1989). This final section of my survey of new businesses in Indonesia in the 1950s focuses on ethnic Chinese entrepreneurship in a time of positive discrimination favouring indigenous business and a new dynamism in indigenous economic life.

Again it is useful to review the situation in the 1950s, making use of the systematic data on big business in Indonesia compiled around 1990. Half of the forty-odd top conglomerates pre-dating the New Order regime were controlled by ethnic Chinese. During the Soeharto period this numerical balance changed in their favour. Moreover, ethnic Chinese conglomerates accounted for two-thirds of total sales and assets of the top 200 business groups and held almost all of the top ten places (Lindblad 2007:74, 78). Clearly, the ethnic Chinese conglomerates were far more successful than indigenous big businesses after the Sukarno period had ended. However, such a facile observation makes it easy to forget that the seeds of success had in several cases been planted during the 1950s.

Oldest among the ethnic Chinese conglomerates to later gain prominence was the Sampoerna cigarette company, established in 1913 by Liem Seng Tee in Surabaya. The rest originated after 1945, including five companies emerging very soon after the transfer of sovereignty. Djarum was founded in 1950 in Kudus by Oei Wie Soan, later known as Hartono, and over time developed into the country's second largest producer of *kretek* cigarettes. In 1951 Bentoel followed in Malang with Budhiwidjaja Kusumanegara (Tjioe Yan Hwie) at the helm. Originally a printing press, it soon switched to *kretek* and became the country's third largest producer. Lautan Luas was set up in 1951 by Ng Adjansjah Masrin (Ng Kee Chun) and made steady progress in marketing chemical products. Gayah Tunggal, founded in the same year, was run by Sjamsul Nursalim (Lim Tek Siong), who later became the owner of the originally indigenous Bank Dagang Nasional Indonesia (BDNI, National Indonesian Trading Bank) in Medan. The combination of printing and cigarette manufacturing was also tried by the Sumatra Tobacco Trading Company (STTC) in Pematang Siantar, North Sumatra, a business operated from 1952 by Ng Chin Ton with the assistance of his three sons (CISI 1990:386-8; Data Consult 1991:137, 223-4, 255-6, 402-3).

A cluster of three ethnic Chinese conglomerates originated in the mid-1950s. Foremost among them was Astra International, founded in 1954 by William Soerjadjaja (Tjia Kian Liong). This business group evolved from a distributor of construction materials called Leperansir Indonesia (Lepindo, Indonesian Suppliers). From the start Soerjadjaja engaged two indigenous managers, Simatupang and Nainggolan. Rapid expansion occurred in the 1970s when Astra entered into joint ventures with Toyota, Honda, and Komatsu for the assembly of motor cars, motorcycles, and tractors, respectively. In the late 1980s and early 1990s Astra International consisted of several hundred firms; the concern ranked second among Indonesia's conglomerates, surpassed only by the Salim group. Astra became Indonesia's most conspicuous partner in joint ventures with Japanese multinationals. The company's early policy of active *Indonesianisasi* of management remained a hallmark throughout the years (CISI 1990:40-2; Data Consult 1991:79-93; Amir Husin Daulay 1993; Suryadinata 1997:42-4; Lindblad 2005b:209).

Moh. Saleh Kurnia (Wu Lai Chang) opened a small all-purpose shop in an alley in West Jakarta at about the same time as William Soerjadjaja started out. At the end of the 1950s he began importing consumer goods from Singapore. As an ethnic Chinese, he did not benefit from priority access to import licences. Still his store grew to become Indonesia's first supermarket chain, Hero. Another trading firm in Jakarta at the time, Mansur, specializing in agricultural products, became the nucleus of the Dharmala corporation. Its initial capital was furnished by Soehargo Gondokusumo (Go Ka Him) and his family, plus five business partners, all ethnic Chinese (Data Consult 1991:210-2, 308-9).

The period when Dutch private firms were taken over proved highly conducive to the establishment of new ethnic Chinese business ventures. The most famous of all was the Salim group, founded in 1957, when Liem Sioe Liong purchased Bank Central Asia (BCA), which eventually became a leading conglomerate in its own right. In later years Salim towered above all other conglomerates in Indonesia in every ranking. The group was composed of several hundred subsidiaries and had at least 135,000 employees. The story of Salim has been told many times and need not be repeated here (Robison 1986:296-315; Suryadinata 1997:38-40; Backman 1999:113-7; Schwarz 1999:112-3). It will suffice to draw attention to Liem's early and highly beneficial association with Soeharto in connection with business dealings with the military, as well as to the company's high managerial quality which impressed observers (Elson 2001:62; Dieleman 2007:44-6).

In 1958 the trading firm Mantrust was founded in Bandung by Tegoeh Soetantjo (Tan Kiong Liep), who managed to acquire some of the assets of the Dutch trading concerns Borsumij and Geo. Wehry when they were nationalized. A similar history is recorded for Dwi Satrja Utama, established in 1958 by Gunawan Tjiptobiantoro (Tjoa To Hing) as a continuation of the Dutch construction firm (*bouwmaatschappij*) Maria. In 1959 Tan Siong Kie started his general trading company, Rodamas, in Jakarta; in the same year the newly founded Bank Internasional Indonesia (BII), together with the cooking oil factory Sinar Mas Tunggal, provided the foundation for the Sinar Mas conglomerate belonging to Eka Tjipta Widjaja (Oei Ek Tjhong) (*Antara* 16 October 1958, 26 March 1959; Data Consult 1991:231, 430-1, 579-81, 643-4).

Several other successful ethnic Chinese enterprises also began operations at this time. In 1959 Eugene Trismitor (Tjoe Mo Tjiang) founded the Mugi cosmetics factory in Jakarta, followed the next year by Ferry Teguh Santosa (Kang Sum Tjhiang) with his Ometraco concern and Susanto Lyman (Lie An Djian) who, with family and friends, ran the trading company Satya Djaya Raya (Data Consult 1991:472, 503-5, 627-8). Other examples from the 1950s include Gunung Agung, managed by its founder Tjio Wie Thay, who changed his name to Masagung and converted to Islam. Rankings of the top 200 conglomerates later list the names of ethnic Chinese firms such as Sinar Sahabat, Khong Guan, Dumaco, Konimex, and Parit Padang, all claiming to have been launched in the 1950s.

The fragmentary evidence presented here demonstrates that the development of ethnic Chinese business was not seriously hindered by the economic nationalism and preference for indigenous entrepreneurship prevailing throughout the 1950s. On the contrary, this was a period during which ethnic Chinese conglomerates were emerging.

Economic decolonization implied a new beginning, both on the macro level of economic structural change and on the micro level of new private business ventures. Efforts in the direction of promoting industrialization received greater attention than ever before, although this was only the initial stage of a long path of development and immediate results fell short of expectations not least due to bottlenecks in financing new investment arising from the simultaneous transformation of the banking sector. The new dynamism in private business was reflected in the large number of newly established small firms, set up by indigenous Indonesians and ethnic Chinese and combinations of the two, as well as the beginnings of numerous conglomerates. Empire builders such as Hasjim Ning, Soedarpo Sastrosatomo, Agoes Moesin Dasaad, Achmad Bakrie, T.D. Pardede, and Haji Kalla maintained a high profile and were at the centre stage of national economic policy. Yet ethnic Chinese were emerging as strong rivals. They tended to show a greater adaptability to changing business conditions after the Sukarno period had ended.

CHAPTER V

Voluntary nationalization

The novel *Sesuai petang* ('At the end of the afternoon') vividly depicts the radically changed conditions under which Dutch enterprises were operating in Indonesia immediately after the transfer of sovereignty. One chapter relates events occurring at the fictitious coffee and rubber estate Kali Musang in East Java. The estate manager and his assistant, both Dutch, meet two representatives of the local labour union to discuss a complaint about a corrupt *mandur* (overseer). The administrator Blim, the older of the two Dutchmen, calmly asserts that such matters are not part of his duties. His assistant Flacon, who with this novelist's characteristic humour has been assigned the nickname *Bola Madu* (literally 'round concubine') after the fly sitting on his private parts, a highly conspicuous figure in his tight shorts, haughtily disputes the authority of the two Indonesians to speak for the labourers. The younger of the union leaders gets angry and retorts: 'Be careful, sir. There is no longer any place for people like you in the world of independent Indonesia' (*Tuan harap hati-hati. Untuk orang macam tuan tidak ada tempat lagi dalam Indonesia merdeka*) (Jacob 1986:75). This anecdote illustrates the new assertiveness in Indonesia during the early 1950s, which at a national level translated into a comprehensive strategy to wrest control from the Dutch and establish state control over vital sectors of the economy.

The most radical instrument with which to achieve economic decolonization was nationalization. The hostile take-overs of Dutch firms in 1957-1958 were preceded by acts of nationalization of a different kind which have received far less attention in the literature. Such measures are the focus of this chapter, which also considers achievements in *Indonesianisasi* with regards to the personnel of the nationalized companies. The first case is that of the Java Bank, the nation's central bank which in 1953 became Bank Indonesia. The discussion then shifts to aviation and inter-island shipping, areas of economic activity which are both of highly symbolic value for a newly sovereign nation. The chapter's final section focuses on government enterprises such as public utilities, railways, and port facilities, and also touches on the state's increasing participation in commercial production.

A symbol of sovereignty

'A central bank in the hands of foreigners contradicts the status of a sovereign nation' (*suatu bank sentral dalam tangan bangsa asing bertentangan dengan kedudukan negara jang berdaulat*). This is how the draft of the law providing for the nationalization of the Java Bank begins.[1] The legal document then goes on to specify the procedure by which the Java Bank, as it was still called at the time, would become the property of the Indonesian state. Ownership was transferred in accordance with an old regulation, dating from 1928, on expropriation by a voluntary surrender of property rights in return for adequate compensation (*onteigeningsordonnantie*). Ironically, the transition of the central bank from a symbol of colonial legacy to a symbol of national sovereignty was carried out according to a procedure inherited from colonial legislation. The transition was achieved in two consecutive stages, the actual nationalization of the Java Bank, followed by its transformation into Bank Indonesia. Both stages are discussed in some detail here and the position of Indonesians in the bank's hierarchy is scrutinized.

Since its establishment in 1828 the Java Bank had performed a dual function in the colonial economy. Its public function was to regulate the money supply, while its commercial function was to extend credit to private businesses with the intention of making profits for its shareholders. In its former capacity, the bank grew increasingly independent of the central bank in the Netherlands; in its latter capacity it acquired a reputation for being highly conservative. Dutchmen dominated managerial and supervisory positions, with only 2 per cent of the staff being of recognizably non-European origin during the 1920s and 1930s. The first post-war survey of the bank's personnel, which curiously combined the situation in 1946 with that of 1941, shows that all supervisors, 80 per cent of the administrative staff, and more than half of the lower administrative ranks were Europeans, while almost all of the cashiers were ethnic Chinese.[2] Few enterprises in independent Indonesia offered such a wide scope for *Indonesianisasi*, in the sense of achieving an all-Indonesian staff, as the nation's central bank.

Between September 1946 and December 1949 the Java Bank had functioned as one of two central banks in operation in the divided country, being the counterpart of BNI in Republican territory. As branch offices reopened throughout Dutch-controlled territory there was little appreciation among the Java Bank directors that the changing conditions would require some adjustment with regard to the bank's personnel. Neither was it considered necessary to change

1 ANRI, Jakarta: Peraturan Pemerintah Pengganti Undang-Undang 32, 6-12-1951.
2 Bank Indonesia, Jakarta: 125, 21-11-1946.

the bank's name. However, two vacant trustee posts were eventually filled by Indonesians. One of them was the Ambonese J.F.A. Hendrik, who had worked for major Dutch firms and had been interned by the Japanese. The Javanese Darmawan Mangoenkoesoemo was the other, a one-time advisor to the colonial government and at the time of his appointment as trustee, in April 1947, the Republic's Minister of Economic Affairs. At first Prime Minister Sutan Sjahrir refused to give Darmawan permission to take this position, arguing that the Republican government would prefer the Java Bank to merge with BNI.[3] Not until March 1948 did Darmawan actually join the Java Bank's Board of Trustees. His appointment was a rare example of the cautiously cooperative attitude displayed by the two rival central banks.

The final choice of the Java Bank over BNI as the central bank of a future independent Indonesia was made in April 1948 during negotiations at Kaliurang; it reflected Hatta's conviction that the Java Bank was far better equipped to take on this responsibility, an argument conveniently omitted from the official history of Bank Indonesia (Dawam Rahardjo et al. 1995:54-5). The Java Bank expanded its scope of operations in anticipation of its future tasks, with the total number of personnel climbing from 350 in 1947 to 500 in 1949. Despite this expansion the stratification along ethnic lines remained intact, with almost all management positions filled by Dutchmen. A Javanese deputy head of the foreign exchange section at the head office, a bookkeeper in Padang, and a Chinese chief cashier in Banjarmasin formed the sole exceptions to the rule.[4]

The failure to implement *Indonesianisasi* with respect to the rank and file of the bank's staff stood in stark contrast to the expectation that the institution as a whole would, in due course, be brought under Indonesian control. As early as September 1949, even before the Java Bank had begun functioning as the central bank for the entire nation, the Dutch directors foresaw the replacement of the bank's president and a majority of its directors by Indonesian citizens, with some Dutch officials staying on in the background as advisors. In December of the same year the national congress of Masjumi passed a resolution pressing for nationalization. In January and early February 1950 a change of name was considered by a joint committee of representatives from the Department of Finance and BNI, dismissing alternatives such as Bank Djawa and Bank Sirkulasi Indonesia as unsuitable for international communication. Rumours of a pending nationalization repeatedly stirred up unrest among the staff; Herrie Teunissen, the last Dutch director, later admitted that for some time he had known that the day

3 Bank Indonesia, Jakarta: 197, 21-4-1947, 1581, 24-4-1947.
4 Bank Indonesia, Jakarta: 126, 3-4-1947, 128, 16-4-1948, 7-4-1949.

Sjafruddin Prawiranegara, first Indonesian president of the nation's central bank, the Java Bank, later Bank Indonesia, around 1950 (KITLV 41410)

would come when he would have to step down.[5]

The relationship between a Dutch-owned central bank managed by Dutchmen on the one hand and an increasingly assertive Indonesian government on the other was, understandably, a delicate one. The position of the Dutch directors was reinforced by the obligation of the Indonesian government under the Finec Agreement to consult the Dutch government in matters of economic policy as long as Indonesia's debt to the Netherlands had not been paid off. Board meetings at the Java Bank were conducted in Dutch and witnesses were struck by the sometimes condescending attitude of the Dutch directors towards representatives of the Indonesian authorities, even at the level of cabinet minister.

The Indonesian government was dependent on the central bank for funds to cover budget deficits. The scope of credit available was enlarged from 1.3 billion guilders in October 1950 to 3.2 billion guilders in March 1951. In addition, the Java Bank handled all transactions of state-run commercial enterprises, including the agricultural estates under the umbrella of PPN, set up in 1946 to succeed the Dutch-style Gouvernementsbedrijven (State Enterprises).[6] All board meetings were attended by a government representative. The lawyer Loekman Hakim held this position in 1950 but in January 1951 he was appointed a bank director alongside another Indonesian, Indra Kasoema. Loekman was succeeded as government representative by Sumitro Djojohadikusumo, at that moment Minister of Trade and Industry.

Interaction between the government and the central bank gradually intensified, but the relationship was often strained. Matters did not improve in November 1950, when one of the bank's Dutch directors, Paul Spies, was arrested and detained for several days without charge. Sultan Hamengku Buwono IX of Yogyakarta, then Deputy Prime Minister, had to intervene personally to have the Dutchman released.[7]

In early 1951 the Java Bank's top management consisted of two five-member bodies, each with the smallest possible majority of Dutchmen. A. Houwink, who had succeeded Smits as president in 1949, chaired a team of directors composed of two Dutchmen, Spies and Teunissen, and two Indonesians, Loekman Hakim and Indra Kasoema. The Board of Trustees traditionally included representatives of the shipping company KPM, the sugar industry, and the insurance companies, all three of them Dutchmen. Among the Indonesian trustees Darmawan was replaced by Sarsito Mangoenkoesoemo, superintendent of a controversial foundation of the Mangkunegara court in Solo, which was

5 Bank Indonesia, Jakarta: DJB 198, 30-6-1953, 1583, 24-9-1949.

6 Bank Indonesia, Jakarta: DJB 130, 15-3-1951; Bank Mandiri, Jakarta: Jaarverslag NHM Factorij 1950-51, I:77-8.

7 Bank Indonesia, Jakarta: DJB 131, 9-5-1951.

engaged in a drawn-out conflict with the government. The other Indonesian trustee post was held first by the Ambonese M.A. Pellaupessy, then by Wilopo, the later Prime Minister. Only ten out of almost 100 supervisors and managers were recognizably non-European, including six ethnic Chinese.[8]

In April 1951 Jusuf Wibisono became Minister of Finance in the Sukiman cabinet. He was intent on carrying out the central bank's nationalization which his political party, Masjumi, had so insistently demanded. He announced his intention in a sensational newspaper interview, adding that *Indonesianisasi* (awkwardly rendered as *indonesiatie*) of the personnel was not so important as long as the reins of power ended up in the hands of the Department of Finance (*Nieuwsblad van Indonesië* 30 April 1951). President Houwink learnt of the government's intentions for the bank from his morning paper and angrily handed in his resignation. He was succeeded by Sjafruddin Prawiranegara, also from Masjumi and one-time head of state,[9] a moderate and highly pragmatic politician who had just stepped down as Minister of Finance in the preceding Natsir cabinet.

Nationalization was prepared by a committee installed by Jusuf Wibisono in early July 1951. This committee was chaired by Moh. Sediono, Secretary-General in the Department of Finance, and had five other members, including Sumitro, Treasurer-General Soetikno Slamet, and even one Dutchman, Oudt, senior advisor to the Minister of Finance. The committee quickly agreed upon a procedure by which the Indonesian government would purchase all shares in the Java Bank held by the public. Towards the end of the month a two-man delegation, Secretary-General M. Saubari from the Department of Finance and Khouw Bian Tie from the Department of Economic Affairs, travelled to Amsterdam to negotiate the price to be offered by the Indonesian government for privately held shares. Their opening offer was 115 per cent of the nominal share value. The representatives of the Amsterdam Stock Exchange were disappointed and even inquired discreetly, when the two Indonesians were briefly outside the room, whether the Netherlands central bank could not intervene and block the entire transaction. The officials from the Dutch bank wisely did not commit themselves. Saubari and Khouw were then authorized to raise the offer to 120 per cent, which was accepted. At the prevailing official exchange rate, the offer amounted to 360 per cent in rupiahs for Indonesian nationals, but foreign citizens living in Indonesia were disadvantaged and

8 Bank Indonesia, Jakarta: DJB 131, 6-4-1951. Personnel lists at DJB did not differentiate by ethnic origin. This therefore had to be obtained from surnames, allowing a rough distinction between Europeans, ethnic Chinese, and indigenous Indonesians.

9 Sjafruddin Prawiranegara served for several months as designated Head of State of the Republic of Indonesia after President Sukarno and Vice-President Hatta had been taken prisoner during the second military campaign of the Dutch in December 1948-January 1949.

would get only 240 per cent. Shareholders were informed via announcements in the Indonesian and Dutch press on 4 August 1951. The offer was valid until 1 November 1951.[10]

Reactions among stockbrokers in Amsterdam were enthusiastic. One firm, Van der Werff and Hubrecht, published a special issue of its news bulletin which sold out almost immediately. The brokers argued against judging the transaction solely from a Dutch perspective and asked readers to take into account the nationalistic Indonesian point of view. Their final assessment of the Indonesian government's offer for the shares was that it was 'proper, fair and just' (*behoorlijk, fair en billijk*). 'We are satisfied', the brokers concluded 'and await future nationalizations with confidence' (Van der Werff and Hubrecht 1951; Lindblad 2004b:33-6, 2005a:19-21).

Total equity in the Java Bank amounted to nine million guilders. Major shareholders allegedly included 'rich Armenian families in Java' and 'some Chinese'. The controversial Mangkunegara foundation in Solo figured on the list of minor shareholders, as did several Dutch families with a Jakarta address. By 15 October 1951 the Indonesian government had already acquired 97 per cent of total equity (8.8 million guilders) and on 6 December 1951 the law nationalizing the Java Bank was passed in Parliament.[11]

Nationalization was only the first step. Shares were in fact still changing hands when a lively discussion began about restructuring the central bank. The directors' suggestion for a new name, Bank Sentral Indonesia, was rejected by advisors of the Departments of Economic Affairs and Finance, Khouw and Oudt, respectively. Their preference, 'Bank Indonesia', was to prevail. They also wished to enlarge the bank's equity, from 9 to 25 million guilders, although this would virtually exhaust accumulated reserves. Another proposal was to replace the Board of Trustees by a Dewan Moneter (Monetary Council), consisting of one of the bank's governors (instead of the president of the bank) and the Ministers of Finance and Economic Affairs. Such an arrangement would effectively subordinate the central bank's activities to the cabinet's economic policy. The most controversial issue concerned the bank's dual function. Should it retain its commercial credit facility in addition to the regulation of money supply which by definition should fall under responsibility of a central bank? A committee, Panitia Nasionalisasi (Committee for Nationalization), was formed to draw up a blueprint for the future Bank Indonesia.

A meeting in January 1952 brought to light the difference of opinion between the Panitia Nasionalisasi and the Board of Directors. The committee

10 Bank Indonesia, Jakarta: DJB 3234. See also Thee Kian Wie 2003:71-2.

11 ANRI, Jakarta: Peraturan Pemerintah Pengganti Undang-Undang 32, 6-12-1951 Bank Indonesia, Jakarta: DJB 3234.

accepted the Khouw-Oudt idea of a Dewan Moneter and proposed that the bank should continue only as a bankers' bank, that is without its commercial function, which could be more usefully transferred to BNI. The directors, led by Sjafruddin, objected vehemently, especially to the surrender of the bank's credit arm. Sjafruddin even drew on the rhetoric of a nineteenth-century French philosopher, Jean-Baptiste Lacordaire, citing him as saying 'La liberté du fort c'est l'oppression du faible' (The freedom of the strong is the oppression of the weak). 'The weak in Indonesia are our own nationals. They need to be protected and be accorded the necessary support', Sjafruddin argued.[12] He wished to retain the bank's dual function, albeit with its commercial function adjusted so as to better serve the pressing needs of Indonesia at that moment.

The first two years of Sjafruddin's rule at the Java Bank, as it was still named, saw a rapid expansion in its activities. Sjafruddin seized every opportunity to point out that the bank was already functioning in a way very different from popular perception and previous practice. In early 1953, on the occasion of the 125th anniversary of the founding of the Java Bank, he stated, 'DJB [De Javasche Bank, Java Bank] is our bank' (*DJB adalah bank kita*). He emphasized that despite the views of outsiders, the bank was now offering important support to indigenous newcomers in the economy (*mungkin berlainan dengan dugaan diluar, memberi bantuan jang penting guna kemadjuan golongan newcomers kita*). Outstanding credit to private individuals amounted to Rp. 108 million, half of which had gone to indigenous Indonesians (*Antara* 24 January 1953).

The number of staff was increased to keep pace with activities. Total personnel rose by more than 40 per cent, from 516 in 1951 to 734 in 1953. Although the proportion of Europeans, including Indo-Europeans, did decline, it still remained by far the largest, 45 per cent of the total. There was a slight shift in favour of indigenous Indonesians over ethnic Chinese, with the former's share rising from 16 to 20 per cent and the latter declining from 37 to 35 per cent. For the first time in the bank's history two major branch offices, those in Medan and Surabaya, were now headed by non-European managers.[13]

The five-member directorate had had an Indonesian majority ever since Sjafruddin took office. From May 1952 the same applied to the Board of

12 Bank Indonesia, Jakarta: DJB 1581, 30-8-1951, 3233, 3236. See also DJB 1953. One of the foremost advocates of moving the credit function from the Java Bank to BNI was the Dutchman E.T. Kuiper, director of the foreign exchange bureau Lembaga Alat-Alat Pembajaran Luar Negri (LAAPLN).

13 Bank Indonesia, Jakarta: DJB 131, 6-4-1951, 132, 4-4-1952, 133, 8-4-1953. These figures are based on annual surveys of personnel with a permanent affiliation with the bank. In addition, about 500 employees, mostly Indonesians, worked for the bank in various capacities. Bank Indonesia, Jakarta: DJB 3353, no. 17; Dawam Rahardjo et al. 1995:94.

Trustees, where the Dutch representative of the international insurance business, D. Bijl, was replaced by a Javanese, Niti Soemantri. Shortly before that, Wilopo had become Prime Minister and was replaced on the board by yet another Javanese, Raden Ng S. Sosrohadikoesoemo. *Indonesianisasi* was generally referred to as a laudable aim, but remained confined to the highly visible positions at the very top.

The bill on the future Bank Indonesia had been in preparation for quite some time before finally being discussed at length in Parliament in late March and early April 1953. The ever-active delegate Siauw Giok Tjhan inquired whether, in accordance with the Finec Agreement, the Indonesian government had consulted the Dutch government about this matter. Minister of Finance Sumitro explained that he had informed representatives of the Dutch government of impending changes (*kita mau mengadakan perubahan-perubahan*) but without giving details. He assured Parliament that government policy had not been influenced by the Dutch in any way whatsoever. Another issue related to what was known as the escape clause, allowing a non-Indonesian citizen to become a bank director in exceptional cases. Jusuf Wibisono, now voicing his opinion from the opposition benches rather than a cabinet post, did not approve of this clause, claiming that even if a foreign citizen were selected, it need not be a Dutchman with a colonial past (*tidak berarti harus mengambil seorang Belanda kolonial*). Sumitro emphasized that there were Indonesian candidates with sufficient qualifications and reaffirmed that ultimate responsibility for the bank's policy should rest with Indonesians.[14] On 10 April 1953 the DPR passed the law, on 30 June the Java Bank ceased to exist, and on 1 July 1953 Bank Indonesia came into being (Lindblad 2004b:37-40, 2005a:23-5).

The transformation of the central bank was hailed with enthusiasm by economic nationalists, who saw Bank Indonesia as 'a symbol of sovereignty in monetary and economic respects'. This opinion was shared by figures such as Abdul Karim, director at the 'rival' BNI, who habitually referred to the Java Bank as 'a colonial instrument of colonial power' (Oey Beng To 1991:251, 255). Others, including foreign observers, were less impressed, arguing that the transformation amounted to little more than a name change and a reorganization. Sjafruddin himself adopted a middle position, characterizing Bank Indonesia as 'a happy compromise between theoretical desiderata and historical fact, between lofty ideals on the one hand and practical possibilities on the other' (Ali Wardhana 1964:40-4; DJB 1953:12). The transformation of the privately owned Java Bank into the state-owned Bank Indonesia seems to have gone far beyond a mere reorganization. The reorientation in lending

14 Bank Indonesia, Jakarta: 3235. Interestingly, Sumitro himself had insisted on Indonesian citizenship as a precondition for becoming a director of Bank Indonesia when the draft bill was discussed in the cabinet in August 1952. ANRI, Jakarta: Kementerian Keuangan 313, 22-3-1952.

activities in alignment with national economic policy signified a fundamental break with past practices.

The foremost obstacle in promoting Indonesian nationals to managerial and supervisory posts at the central bank remained the lack of candidates with sufficient qualifications. Training programmes in banking for Indonesian personnel had been running since 1950; such activities were intensified after 1 July 1953. By December 1954 33 Indonesian nationals on the staff had completed one-year courses, with another eight still enrolled. The share of Indonesian citizens in total personnel had risen to 40 per cent, compared to 10 per cent in 1951 (Lindblad 2004b:45-6). Indonesian heads were appointed at four branch offices – in Yogyakarta, Cirebon, Makassar, and Manado – while two of the twelve Dutch department heads at the main office in Jakarta were replaced by Indonesians. Khouw took charge of the Amsterdam branch office. In the five-member directorate the last two Dutchmen, Spies and Teunissen, were succeeded by Indonesians: Darmawan Mangoenkoesoemo, returning to the bank after a few years with the Department of Economic Affairs, and T.R.B. Sabaruddin, the first Indonesian director of the foreign exchange agency, LAAPLN. A Dewan Penasehat (Council of Advisors) was installed to replace the Board of Trustees; one of the nine members was Jusuf Wibisono. In August 1954 it was with considerable indignation that Sjafruddin refuted allegations made by the local labour union that *Indonesianisasi* of the bank was not proceeding fast enough.[15]

Bank Indonesia is a prime example of nationalization without any preceding *Indonesianisasi* of the personnel. Was the former necessary because the latter lagged behind? This remains difficult to ascertain due to the key position of the central bank in national economic policy making and its concomitant symbolic function in society. At any rate, the case study of Bank Indonesia gives rise to two concluding observations. The first concerns the nationalization procedure. In 1955 Ong Eng Die, Minister of Finance in the (first) Ali Sastroamidjojo cabinet, asserted that future nationalizations should follow the example set by Bank Indonesia, a standpoint strikingly similar to that advocated by Amsterdam stockbrokers in 1951 (*Antara* 15 June 1955). The second observation refers to the process of *Indonesianisasi* within the organization. This process only got underway after the establishment of full Indonesian control. The plan was to gradually phase out all remaining Dutch employees before 1960. In the event, only 23 remained by late 1957, down from more than 300 in 1953, and their contracts were discontinued as of 1 January 1958 in the light of a general take-over of Dutch firms (*Merdeka* 31 December 1957).

15 Bank Indonesia: DJB, 3353, no. 17.

Flying the national flag

Every self-respecting nation wants to have its own airline.[16] In a huge archipelago such as Indonesia it is equally important that shipping be state-run as this constitutes the main form of inter-island passenger transport. This section contrasts the different strategies chosen to enhance Indonesian control over national aviation and inter-island shipping. The chief actors were the national carrier Garuda and the shipping company Pelajaran Nasional Indonesia (PELNI, Indonesian National Shipping Company), of which the latter was intended to challenge KPM supremacy in Indonesian waters. Once again the process of *Indonesianisasi* of personnel within these organizations is an important theme.

On 28 December 1949, one day after the transfer of sovereignty, two aircraft belonging to the Dutch airline Koninklijke Luchtvaart Maatschappij (KLM, Royal Dutch Airlines) were painted with the now familiar logo of the legendary eagle *garuda*. The Republic actually did possess a small airline of its own, Indonesian Airways, set up in January 1949, but its resources were insufficient to provide a comprehensive domestic network, let alone international flights. For the time being cooperation with the Dutch was the pragmatic option.

Garuda Indonesian Airways (GIA) was established on 31 March 1950 as a joint venture between KLM and the Indonesian government, with the former holding 51 per cent of equity and the latter 49 per cent. KLM promised to safeguard a transition to majority Indonesian ownership within ten years. A management contract was concluded with KLM, which included responsibility for training Indonesian airline staff. Garuda started off with a fleet of 27 airplanes serving 34 domestic lines and two neighbouring international destinations (Singapore and Manila). The staff was rapidly enlarged and soon amounted to more than 1,000 people, including 400 from KLM. The President-Director was KLM executive E. van Konijnenburg, and the Board of Trustees was composed of three Dutchmen and two Indonesians.[17]

Almost immediately discontent was voiced about the conspicuously high Dutch presence in Garuda. In October 1950 the Indonesian Parliament proposed a change in the ownership ratio to provide an Indonesian majority, but Djuanda, Minister of Communications in the Natsir cabinet, retorted that a ten-year trajectory of *Indonesianisasi* was necessary before full national control could be obtained. At the moment, Djuanda added, no fewer than 335 Garuda personnel were being trained so that they might replace KLM staff. Nevertheless, there was a growing sentiment in Parliament that nationalization

16 A notable exception is Scandinavian Airlines System (SAS), set up in 1946 as a joint venture by the governments of Denmark, Norway, and Sweden.

17 ANRI, Jakarta: Muh. Yamin 89; Kabinet Presiden 18, 3-11-1951; Abriyanto 1995:35-6.

of the airline could not wait for ten years, especially since virtually all management positions were still occupied by foreign nationals (Sutter 1959:894-9).

The contract with KLM was renewed in early 1952, but in May 1953 negotiations were again underway about the terms of cooperation. Complaints were voiced about the way in which KLM managed Garuda, even if customers jokingly read the airline's name as 'Good And Reliable Under Dutch Administration'. An external observer, E.L. Barton, head of a mission from the International Civil Aviation Organization (ICAO), criticized the KLM managers for turning a blind eye (*bersikap buta*) to Indonesian interests, an attitude he described as 'highly unrealistic and in violation of the meaning and wisdom of the airline business' (*bertentangan dengan arti dan hikmat usaha penerbangan*) (*Antara* 12 May 1953). Shortly afterwards a conflict with the local labour union relating to pay and working-hours soured relations even further. In August 1953 Prime Minister Ali Sastroamidjojo announced the government's intention to buy KLM out. Although no longer in office, Djuanda asserted publicly that 'nothing had been done' to implement *Indonesianisasi* in Garuda. Apparently, he was now a great deal less optimistic about the situation at Garuda than he had been only three years before (*Times of Indonesia* 10 September 1953).

Negotiations on the transfer of ownership and the terms of future cooperation commenced in January 1954, with GIA trustee Professor Soepomo heading the Indonesian delegation. In March 1954 KLM agreed to sell its shares in GIA and to withdraw from all management activities. The Dutch airline would provide only technical assistance for a period of six years, up until 1960. The Indonesian government paid Rp. 16.5 million for the shares held by KLM, which corresponded to only 18 per cent of nominal value of equity expressed in rupiahs at the prevailing official rate of exchange (*Antara* 24 March, 8 June and 11 August 1954). It is only possible to speculate about how the Indonesian government was able to acquire half of GIA so cheaply, especially in comparison with what had been paid for the purchase of the Java Bank in 1951. In the case of GIA there was only one other holder of equity, KLM, which was also under pressure from the Netherlands government, whereas in the case of the Java Bank the Indonesian government had to deal with a large group of private shareholders, including many in Indonesia. Furthermore, the (first) Ali Sastroamidjojo cabinet probably had tougher bargaining skills than the Sukiman cabinet, reflecting PNI's more militant economic nationalism. Sukiman's Masjumi, by contrast, was on occasion praised by Dutch observers for its 'nationalism with a greater sense of realism' (*groter realiteitsbesef*).[18]

Van Konijnenburg stepped down in July 1954; he was succeeded by the engineer Soetoto, Secretary-General in the Department of Communications.

18 Bank Mandiri, Jakarta: Jaarverslag NHM Factorij 1954, I:19.

The government appointed a new Board of Trustees consisting of twelve members, ten of whom representing the factions in Parliament that supported the (first) Ali Sastroamidjojo cabinet (Abriyanto 1995:41). At that time Garuda possessed 44 aircraft flown by 92 pilots, of whom eighteen were Indonesians who had only recently received their wings. Young pilots were trained by foreign instructors, some of whom from Asian countries such as India, at Garuda's flight training schools in Jakarta (*Antara* 6 January 1954; *Times of Indonesia* 7 October 1954; Bank Indonesia 1955:158).

Total employment at Garuda increased from 3,400 in 1954 to almost 3,600 in 1955, and then to 3,900 in 1956. In the same period the number of personnel supplied by KLM fell from 393 to 350 and then to 340. By 1956 Garuda training facilities had supplied more than 500 technical, operational, and commercial personnel. *Indonesianisasi* was gradually achieved. Yet there were still almost 300 KLM employees, including 65 pilots, working for Garuda in December 1957, when open conflict between Indonesia and the Netherlands brought the collaboration to an abrupt conclusion (*Antara* 31 March 1956, 30 March and 3 December 1957; Bank Indonesia 1957:207, 1958:209).

The arrangement with Garuda was expected to also serve as a model for future Dutch-Indonesian cooperation in inter-island shipping. A proposal for a joint venture, named the Indonesian Steamship Company, was presented to KPM by the Indonesian government in April 1950, only three weeks after the establishment of Garuda. However, subsequent negotiations failed. The main point of disagreement concerned the majority equity holding. KPM wanted the company to remain fully Dutch, to which the Indonesian government responded by demanding 51 per cent of equity. The ensuing highly emotional debate involved issues such as which flag should be flown in Indonesian waters. In Dutch eyes KPM had a symbolic connotation, epitomizing the necessity of a continued Dutch presence in independent Indonesia. But to Indonesians it represented the legacy of the colonial past, and they were also very mindful of the fact that KPM had played an active role in the attempts to restore Dutch colonial rule in the late 1940s. Persistent resistance on the part of KPM precluded a compromise solution (Dick 1987a:14-5; Van de Kerkhof 2005c:129-32). Even relatively minor concessions such as the appointment of two Indonesian nationals to the Board of Trustees or an increase of Indonesians in senior administrative and nautical positions were rejected by KPM directors (A Campo 1998:21). When, at long last, KPM was prepared to discuss a 50-50 division of equity, measures were already being taken to build up a rival state-owned shipping fleet.

The first initiatives undertaken by the Indonesian government to create an alternative to KPM dated from 1947, but none of the subsequent firms proved viable. Against this background in 1951 Minister of Communications Djuanda proposed a *modus vivendi* by which KPM would be allowed to continue the operation of major shipping lines in the archipelago, thus preventing any hiatus in services, while the Indonesian government would simultaneously set up a shipping company of its own with time to get up to speed before eventually taking over (Sutter 1959:504-5, 932-5). The core for such a national shipping company was the recently established foundation Penguasaan Pusat Kapal-Kapal (PEPUSKA, Central Shipping Authority). At its commencement in September 1950 PEPUSKA possessed a fleet of nine small coasters once owned by the colonial government. The foundation proceeded to purchase six larger ships from Germany and Italy at a total cost of Rp. 48 million, with funding obtained from the government. Since PEPUSKA was unauthorized to undertake commercial operations of its own accord, the foundation's ships were chartered out to private shipping firms, often with good political connections (Dick 1987a:15-7; Singgih Tri Sulistiyono 2005:87).

PELNI was founded on 1 May 1952 as a fully government-owned enterprise with a total nominal equity of Rp. 200 million. The company began with a fleet of twelve ships, all bequeathed by PEPUSKA, which also provided 500 personnel. Unlike PEPUSKA, PELNI was permitted to operate its ships on a commercial basis. During the first two years of its existence, up until 1954, the Indonesian government spent Rp. 225 million on purchasing 45 ships from Germany, Italy, and Belgium. These acquisitions were financed with a loan from the Exim Bank. The professed objective for PELNI was to wrest control of inter-island shipping from KPM. In 1954 PELNI became more closely associated with two state-owned ocean lines, Djakarta Lloyd and the Indonesian Navigation Company (INACO) (*Berita Indonesia* 2 May 1952; *Antara* 6 January, 10 April and 7 October 1954). Although PELNI was growing fast, it was not in a position to seriously challenge KPM.

KPM was known to be a highly profitable company which traditionally paid dividends to its shareholders in the range of 8-9 per cent; this level was sustained up until the mid-1950s.[19] PELNI, by contrast, was plagued by losses almost immediately. In September 1954 Minister of Public Works Roosseno ordered an investigation into PELNI's accounts after allegations in the press that accumulated losses in the current financial year would reach Rp. 30 million, corresponding to 15 per cent of equity. The investigation confirmed that PELNI indeed had not made any profit, although losses had been vastly exaggerated; Roosseno cited a lower estimate of Rp. 7.8 million. Accounting procedures were described as 'less than adequate' (*kurang beres*) and the staff were accused of behaving as if they were civil servants (*merasakan sebagai pegawai negeri*). It later transpired that Roosseno had painted too rosy a picture of

19 ANRI, Jakarta: Algemeene Secretarie 808; *Antara* 18 June 1957, 9 October 1958; A Campo 1998:39.

the financial results. In 1952 and 1953 actual losses at PELNI amounted to Rp. 20 million per year and they did indeed climb to Rp. 30 million in 1954, while 1955 added yet another huge loss of Rp. 33 million (*Antara* 16 September and 15 October 1954, 10 November 1956; Bank Indonesia 1955:157). There were serious bottlenecks in operations, in part attributable to the lack of qualified personnel. It was even reported that 30 per cent of PELNI ships were lying idle at any given time (Bank Indonesia 1956:179; Dick 1987a:87-93).

In 1954 PELNI owned 39 vessels with a displacement of 23,000 tons compared to KPM's fleet of 105 ships totalling 190,000 tons. The average KPM ship was three times as large as the average PELNI vessel. Three years later, in 1957, the PELNI fleet was reported to consist of 53 vessels totalling 35,000 tons. A range of private Indonesian shipping companies supplemented the PELNI fleet with another 40,000 tons of capacity, which still brought the overall Indonesian aggregate to barely more than one-third of the KPM fleet's capacity. PELNI employed about 3,100 people, including 1,100 sailors, which was slightly more than half of KPM's labour force (Bank Indonesia 1955:157, 1958:207; *Antara* 12 September 1956; *Suluh Indonesia* 22 November 1958; *Pos Indonesia* 14 March 1960; Singgih Tri Sulitiyono 2005:89). By and large, Dutch supremacy in inter-island Indonesian shipping remained intact.

In June 1956 Vice-President Hatta conceded that Indonesia had to continue to rely on foreign skills in inter-island shipping. Some months later the PELNI management denied rumours of a pending nationalization of KPM by referring to the financial predicaments in which the government found itself at the time, an admission which incidentally reveals that compensation was assumed (*Antara* 19 June and 12 September 1956). The government's attitude towards KPM remained ambivalent. Indubitably, it authorized routes and set fares so as not to disadvantage customers, but all the while it hoped its own shipping company could compete. The 'protection' allegedly given to KPM was seen as the main obstacle to the development of a national alternative. Any attempt to compete with KPM was likened to 'suicide' (*berarti bunuh diri*) (Merdeka 19 December 1957).

A more militant attitude was discernible in 1957. In January the government announced a five-year investment plan for PELNI with the target of increasing total capacity to 150,000 tons in order to be able to compete more effectively with KPM (*Antara* 4 January 1957; Bank Indonesia 1957:205-6). The extra-parliamentary cabinet headed by Djuanda, installed in March 1957, included Indonesia's first Minister of Shipping, Budiardjo, former director of an educational institution in shipping and commerce, Akademi Pelajaran Niaga (Academy for Maritime Trading). Budiardjo captured the headlines by proclaiming that he saw the liquidation of KPM as his foremost task. In the newly founded ministry he was soon replaced by Commodore Nazir, who urged the formulation of a national shipping policy based on a government-owned fleet and facilities run by Indonesian citizens using 'national capital'. By that time, November 1957, KPM was already quietly moving its vessels out of Indonesian waters (*Antara* 9 April and 19 November 1957; *Merdeka* 25 September 1957).

The crucial difference between national aviation and inter-island shipping with regard to *Indonesianisasi* lay in the attitude of the Dutch rivals. Where cooperation and nationalization with proper compensation paved the way for a fairly smooth transition to national control in aviation, conflict and competition hampered progress in inter-island shipping. KPM policy was a double-edged sword designed to keep the company running for as long as possible while preparing for departure through a major restructuring (*omschakeling*). Since 1951 KPM had not invested in new vessels for inter-island shipping. Worn-out ships were replaced by chartered vessels (Dick 1987a:15).

In the end the Indonesian government had to pay a price, whether by purchasing shares in GIA from KLM or by covering losses incurred by PELNI. In the process KPM was transformed into a symbol, not simply of the burdensome heritage of colonialism but also of PELNI's failure to stand up to and vanquish its formidable rival. It seems more than a coincidence that seizures of Dutch corporate assets in Indonesia began, in early December 1957, at the KPM office in Jakarta.

More state involvement

In the 1950s most Indonesians did not line up to board passenger ships or queue up in front of the central bank, let alone travel by plane. Their most immediate contact with Dutch-controlled economic institutions was through public utilities such as electricity and gas companies, and local transport. A wide range of economic activities had already become eligible for take-over by the Indonesian government before the widely publicized final seizure of Dutch firms in December 1957. In the process, the role of the state in the national economy grew considerably, as may be demonstrated by examples from utilities, public transport, port facilities, and mining.

Electricity and gas were generally provided to households and industry by numerous local private firms with Dutch shareholders and management, which continued operations as usual even after the transfer of sovereignty. In November 1951 a committee in Parliament proposed that all public utilities be nationalized, starting with the Overzeese Gas- en Electriciteits-Maatschappij (OGEM, Overseas Gas and Electricity Company), the predominant provider in the Jakarta area. A resolution to this effect was passed by Parliament in August 1953. Newly launched electricity companies, for instance in Den Pasar (Bali), were reminded that nationalization was definitely on the cards. Dutch firms were urged to appoint Indonesians to management positions, as this was still a rare event. One leading supplier, Algemeene Nederlandsch-Indische Electriciteits-Maatschappij (ANIEM, General Netherlands Indies Electricity Company), reported that in 1951 just one Indonesian with a tertiary degree and working experience had been recruited.[20]

The (first) Ali Sastroamidjojo cabinet did not tarry long after having been authorized by the resolution of August 1953 to take action. In the next year the government took over the networks of four electricity firms. The largest was the OGEM network in Greater Jakarta and Cirebon, which changed ownership on 1 January 1954 (Sluyterman 2003:220). The other three were the Central and East Java branches of ANIEM and smaller companies in Balikpapan (East Kalimantan) and Ambon. Some discussion about the price preceded the acquisition of the OGEM assets. The Dutch owners asked Rp. 52 million but eventually received Rp. 15 million, described by observers as 'a fair compensation, taking into account the present condition of the properties'.[21] In the case of ANIEM nationalization of a large part of the network implied the dismissal of 300 Dutch employees working in Central and East Java. Electra, another major provider in East Java, was later taken over applying a similar procedure (*Antara* 3 November 1954; *Merdeka* 16 May 1957).

Further nationalization was postponed, probably due to a shortage of funds available for such purchases in 1956 and 1957. The total cost of acquiring the remaining privately owned electricity and gas firms was estimated at Rp. 300 million, at a time when the government budget deficit was increasing from Rp. 2.3 billion to Rp. 5.3 billion (*Antara* 15 August 1957; Bank Indonesia 1958:82). However, pressure from the labour unions was mounting. In 1956, during a special congress in Solo, the Serikat Buruh Listrik dan Gas Indonesia (SBLGI, Union of Indonesian Electricity and Gas Workers) had demanded the immediate nationalization of those utilities still in Dutch hands. In early 1957 the labour union produced a formal petition, and the Department of Public Works drew up plans for new rounds of nationalization.[22] Eventually, intentions were realized and in December 1957 all Dutch-owned electricity and gas companies were placed under direct military command.

All Jakartans were familiar with the local bus company Bataafsche Vervoers Maatschappij (BVM, Batavian Transport Company), which was privately owned but received subsidies from the state to keep fares low. In early 1953 the state decided to discontinue its financial support. The Dutch owners responded by announcing their intention to liquidate the company, as it was now

20 ANRI, Jakarta: Kabinet Presiden 1526, 6-3-1952, 1550, 20-10-1953.

21 Bank Mandiri, Jakarta: Jaarverslag NHM Factorij 1953, I:43, 1955, I:34; *Dunia Ekonomi* 30-1-1954.

22 ANRI, Jakarta: Kabinet Presiden 1658, 27-2-1956; *Merdeka* 6-2-1957, 11-3-1957.

operating at a loss. The two major bones of contention were the combination of low fares without state subsidy and the widespread evasion of payment on overcrowded trams and buses, which made public transport unprofitable and ruled out investment in new equipment. In March 1953 BVM's exploitation was taken over by the state, with two representatives of the Jakarta municipal government as directors. They declared that nationalization was imminent. The government's purchase of shares proceeded slowly, with as much as 90 per cent of equity still in private hands by the end of the year. Emergency legislation in 1954 opened the door to a rapid acquisition of equity, and in less time than it takes to relate the news, BVM was transformed into the fully state-owned Perusahaan Pengangkutan Djakarta (Jakarta Transport Company) (*Antara* 27 March 1953; *Times of Indonesia* 14 January 1954). Nationalization had been speeded up by the Dutch owners' decision to pull out. The Indonesian government fully realized the necessity to maintain tram and bus transport facilities in the national capital.

The private railways in Java and Sumatra formed another obvious target for nationalization. The matter was studied in detail by a committee chaired by Treasurer-General Soetikno Slamet, at the time serving as the government representative at the Java Bank, later Minister of Finance and Governor of Bank Indonesia. Soetikno's committee reported to the government in February 1953. The conclusion was hardly encouraging: if the government wished to take over the railways prior to the expiration of concessions, it would have to pay 25 times net gains calculated over an average of five good years. A few years later, the Secretary-General in the Department of Communications, Abdul Danuningrat, complaining that the Dutch owners asked too much for the railways, said that 'it would be better to nationalize paying zero rupiah' (*lebih baik nasionalisasi dengan pembajaran 0 rupiah*), which anticipated the later take-overs. In one remarkable case, that of the Kediri Stoomtram (Steam Tram) in East Java in 1957, discussions about nationalization stopped all of a sudden when it became known that the railway was operating at a loss (*Antara* 18 February 1953, 23 April 1956, 13 June 1957).

Disagreement characterized the discussions relating to the valuation of assets, always a sensitive issue when compensation is to be paid after a transfer of ownership. Opinions differed strongly in the case of the Deli Spoorweg Maatschappij (Deli Railway Company), in charge of more than 500 km of railways in Sumatra and employing 3,500 people, with all the supervisors and managers being Dutch. The government repeatedly assured trade unions and nationalists that nationalization was pending, it was only awaiting the 'right moment' (*saat jang tepat*). The price was to be based on an estimate of the company's actual value and the government was surely not going to pay for 'scorched-earth losses' (*kerugian bumi hangus*). As it turned out, a vast capital injection, some Rp. 600 million over five years, was needed to modernize the railway's worn-out rails and equipment (*Antara* 25 September 1956, 15 October 1957; *Waspada* 27 September and 15 October 1956).

Compared to electricity and public transport, port facilities were of less immediate concern to the public at large, but they were obviously of paramount importance in an economy highly dependent on shipping. Several stevedoring firms and warehouses were owned and operated by Dutch private capital, again a feature inherited from the colonial economy. The decisive step towards shifting control from foreign to Indonesian hands was a decree, PP 61/1954, barring non-Indonesian citizens from establishing new port facilities. Foreign-owned firms were supposed to transfer business to domestic counterparts. However, this proved difficult to accomplish, primarily due to a 'lack of means' on the part of the latter. Dutch shipping companies were not unwilling to divest their warehouses and stevedoring activities, especially since operations were increasingly plagued by labour union militancy and massive pilfering, provided they were paid adequate compensation. The rub was that a gradual transfer was unworkable and was depicted as a 'major obstruction' (*zeer remmend*) to shipping operations. Some Dutch-owned warehouses quietly changed hands and came into the possession of ethnic Chinese.[23]

Tanjung Perak in Surabaya was Indonesia's busiest port, and discussions about how to implement 'PP 61/1954' soon centred on the situation there. In early 1955 the two main Dutch-owned warehouses, Stroohoeden Veem and Soerabaja Veem, were supplemented by five national firms, a number rising to fourteen in the following year. One widely debated idea was to give the national firms priority access to state-owned storage facilities in the harbour, a practice already tested in Semarang and now spreading throughout Indonesia. The idea met with several objections, for instance that it would infringe upon the historical rights of the two Dutch-owned warehouses to have permanent access to storage space, and also that exclusive use by national firms would leave the state-owned facilities under-utilized. Eventually, in October 1956, agreement was reached on a division of labour, with national warehouses handling local and inter-island shipping, and their Dutch competitors handling all international shipping (*Antara* 18 February and 23 September 1955, 27 October and 1 November 1956).

Despite government protection, the new warehouses were unable to take over much of the foreign-controlled business in the port, either in Surabaya, in Semarang, or in Belawan near Medan. Then the government changed its strategy. In 1956 the purchase of Stroohoeden Veem by a state-supported consortium was negotiated. This consortium, under the leadership of

23 Bank Mandiri, Jakarta: Jaarverslag NHM Factorij 1956, I:33; *Antara* 14-3-1956; Anspach 1969:184.

H. Djamaludin Malik, paid Rp. 14 million for the firm. The former Dutch managers were retained as advisors. Rumour had it that Stroohoeden Veem Indonesia, as it was now called, was still being run as a Dutch enterprise, with the Indonesian managers condescendingly being referred to as 'directors only in name' (*orang-orang jang menamakan diri direktur*) (*Antara* 16 November 1956, 25 January 1957).

Time and again dissatisfaction was voiced about the lack of national control of warehouses and stevedoring. Yet another measure introduced by the government, the imposition of uniform storage tariffs for all warehouses, was said to disadvantage smaller national firms, reducing their gains to a 'gift of generosity on the part of foreign shipping' (*'hadiah' atau 'presen' dari kemurahan hati pihak perkapalan-perkapalan asing*). Observers even advised against the government extending credit to Indonesians to allow them to purchase foreign facilities, as the foreign owners were likely to inflate the asking prices (*Antara* 10 September 1957; Merdeka 15 February 1957). The question of who was to be in charge of essential facilities in Indonesian ports was far from resolved when the wave of take-overs of Dutch firms began in December 1957.

Two common features marked the efforts made by the Indonesian government to gain full control over operations in those parts of the economy that can be classified as falling within the public domain. One was the apparent lack of progress in achieving *Indonesianisasi* of personnel in higher positions. Hardly ever do we come across evidence of Indonesian staff members moving up the ladder, as it were, in enterprises providing public utilities and transport facilities. The other common feature was state ownership. Transfers from private Dutch ownership to private Indonesian ownership were rarely, if ever, considered. Inevitably, nationalization without *Indonesianisasi* enlarged the role of the state in the Indonesian economy.

The tendency for the state to become increasingly involved was also apparent in industries outside the public sector. Sometimes, as in mining, the Indonesian state inherited a direct commitment from its colonial predecessor.[24] The Ombilin coal mines in Sawah Lunto, West Sumatra, had been managed by Indonesian staff from late 1945, when the Japanese army units withdrew. However, during the late 1940s both labour force and output declined dramatically. By 1950 the mine employed only 1,200 workers and produced fewer than 25,000 tons, compared to almost 600,000 tons shortly before the Pacific War (*Indisch Verslag* 1941). Dutch advisors to the government are said to have recommended closing the mine altogether, but operations gradually recovered and by 1957 the mine was producing 90,000 tons with a total labour

24 Commitments of the Indonesian state in oil exploitation and tin-mining are discussed below (Chapter VII), as they were intimately linked to cooperation with foreign private enterprises.

force of 2,200 (*Antara* 2 May 1953; Zaiyardam Zubir 2004). When in 1956 KPM closed its own coal mine, Parapattan in Berau, East Kalimantan, the local authorities showed an interest in continuing to operate the mine. The Berau regional government paid Rp. 3.5 million for the mine, which was engulfed in difficulties on reopening, one example being that the private individual entrusted with making the mine operational had his cheques refused at the local branch of Bank Kalimantan (*Antara* 4 October 1956, 8 April 1958).

Fresh state involvement covered a wide range of economic activities. Some scattered examples will suffice to illustrate this. In 1952 the local government in Yogyakarta purchased the cigar factory Negresco, a transaction that had been pending for some time, as well as a small-scale metal goods factory (*Antara* 3 September 1952; Sutter 1959:800). The regional government of Central Java purchased the majority equity in the sugar factory Gondangwinangun in Klaten, and the sugar factory Pakis, formerly part of the Oei Tiong Ham concern, reopened in Kedu in Central Java under government ownership. The asphalt factory Buton on the island of the same name was purchased from its Dutch proprietors, as was a tea plantation, Kabawetan, in Bengkulu in southwestern Sumatra (*Antara* 18 June 1956, 27 April, 21 and 22 August 1957). The variety of state involvement in economic life seemed endless.

As a rule, voluntary nationalization unaccompanied by *Indonesianisasi* of the personnel did not proceed smoothly. For a final illustration we return to the central bank, in its imposing new head office on Jalan Thamrin, downtown Jakarta. In July and August 1954 a conflict developed between the top management of Bank Indonesia under Governor Sjafruddin and the local branch of the union Sarekat Buruh Bank Indonesia (SBBI, Union of Indonesian Bank Employees). At issue was compensation for the loss of bonuses incurred when the Java Bank was transformed into Bank Indonesia. A lengthy protest was organized by SBBI, which summoned the Governor and the other members of the directorate to appear for negotiations at a set time. Sjafruddin, seconded by Director Indra Kasoema, called this move by the union a 'destructive action' and declined to be summoned in such a presumptuous manner. In exasperation they added that it was 'very interesting to note that the SBBI spokesmen at BI [Bank Indonesia] had never put forward such demands when the Java Bank was exclusively managed by foreigners' (*sangat menarik perhatian bahwa SBBI Komisariat BI tidak pernah mengadjukan tuntutan apapun semasa DJB melulu dipimpin oleh bangsa asing*).[25] Unquestionably, voluntary nationalization brought a host of changes but did not solve all problems.

25 Bank Indonesia, Jakarta: DJB 3353, no. 17.

CHAPTER VI

Economic nationalism

'A cornered mouse jumps in strange directions' (*kutjing kedjepit memang lontjatnya aneh*). That is how in April 1954 people in Jakarta reportedly perceived attempts by Minister of Economic Affairs Iskaq to counter accusations of corruption made in Parliament. But, as a Chinese newspaper maliciously remarked, such assessments must surely come from 'mean people' (*orang djail*), lacking in national spirit (*a-nasional*) and also lacking special licences (*a-lisensi-istimewa*) (*Keng Po* 21 April 1954). The scandal was all about the controversial Benteng policy intended to wrest control of the nation's economy from foreign elements. The very tone in the press, as soon as news of the controversy about the Benteng policy broke, indicates that the concept of *nasional*, whether applied to importers, enterprises or even goods, carried strong legal and emotional connotations. Meeting in March 1956 in Surabaya, the national importers' organization, Kongres Importir Nasional Seluruh Indonesia (KINSI, All-Indonesian Association of National Importers), maintained that a declaration of love for the nation should be made by anyone aspiring to obtain recognition as a national trader (*harus mengandung pernjataan tjinta terhadap negara*) (*Antara* 21 March 1956).

This chapter discusses the juxtaposition of reason and emotion in policies of positive discrimination in the name of economic nationalism during the 1950s. It begins with a brief note on the many priorities in economic policy competing for the attention of the Indonesian government immediately after the transfer of sovereignty. This provides the broader context in which the measures to bolster economic nationalism were applied, although it is impossible to offer an exhaustive description of economic development and economic policies in Indonesia at the time. Subsequently, the Benteng policy itself is examined and assessed. We then turn to auxiliary policy measures regulating trade and credit which accompanied the Benteng policy. Finally, the chapter pays special attention to the ethnic Chinese, in recognition of the axiom that positive discrimination in favour of one group inevitably implies negative discrimination of others.

Conflicting priorities

In the early 1950s the Indonesian economy benefited from a rapidly rising demand in world markets for its two chief export commodities, oil and rubber. Growth was export-driven and macroeconomic performance compared favourably with most other Third World countries, not to mention with Indonesia's own dismal record in the early and mid-1960s. An average rate of real GDP growth (after correction for inflation) of 6 per cent per year enabled per capita income to rise significantly despite a very rapid population growth (Van der Eng 1992:369; Dick et al. 2002:178, 192; see also the section 'Post-colonial trends' in Chapter II). Nevertheless, the new power holders had reason to be less than satisfied. The Korean War boom was short-lived and large parts of the export sector were not doing well at all. More fundamentally, the economic expansion was driven by exports of unprocessed raw materials, just as it had been during the late-colonial period, precisely at a juncture at which industrialization held greater promise for sustained long-term growth. Vital growth sectors were still largely controlled by foreign capital, usually Dutch private firms. In this context, the Indonesian government went to considerable lengths to promote industrialization and secure national control of key parts of the services sector in the 1950s (Chapters IV and V).

Top priority was increasingly given to the development of indigenous entrepreneurship. The 1950s saw a proliferation of new businesses, many of which were indigenous, with some maintaining a prominent position for decades to come (Chapter IV). This is where the Benteng policy of positive discrimination fits in, although there is room to wonder whether the truly successful indigenous entrepreneurs of the 1950s would not have been better off without protection. A case in point is Soedarpo Sastrosatomo, who later vehemently denied that he had enjoyed the privilege of being designated a national importer under the Benteng policy (Thee Kian Wie 2003:153-4).

The Benteng policy also fitted into the more general budgetary and trading policies of the Indonesian government. As might have been expected in a nation that had only just gained independence, expectations were very high concerning what the state could and should spend. The 1950 budget operated at a large deficit, corresponding to 40 per cent of government revenue. In 1951, by contrast, the government enjoyed a lavish share of rising export revenues so that a surplus of 12 per cent was generated. After that, however, government expenditure continued to rise or was adjusted only slightly downwards, whereas the high level of revenues in 1951 could not be sustained. Deficit financing became a characteristic feature of Indonesian economic policy (DJB 1953:27; Paauw 1960:433). The government's excessive dependence on trade taxes rather than on income taxes was a fundamental problem (Dick et al. 2002:175-6). One reason for this preference was practical, the other political. Trade levies were obviously easier to collect than income taxes. But, more importantly, trade taxes were paid largely by non-*pribumi* subjects, in particular foreign nationals and ethnic Chinese. Imposing income tax on the huge *pribumi* peasant population would have met with fierce opposition from almost all members of Parliament.

Taxing foreign trade for the purpose of financing government expenditure necessitates a great deal of regulation. Rationing foreign exchange for purposes of trading had been introduced by the returning Dutch colonial administration in 1946. Although the system was taken over by the Indonesian authorities after the transfer of sovereignty, it was applied to different ends. Starting in March 1950 foreign exchange certificates were issued whereby the rate of exchange varied according to the type of transaction. This inaugurated the highly complex system of multiple exchange rates in use in Indonesia throughout the Sukarno period. An alteration of the system in March 1951 replaced export inducements by new import certificates sold directly by the government at a price twice the level of the official rate of exchange. Even so, these certificates were not valid for all types of imports.[1] The multiplicity of foreign exchange rates shifted from exports to imports and grew ever more bizarre in its complexity.

The main aims of the Indonesian trade policy were to generate a surplus in the balance of trade and fund the government budget. To this was added the third aim of enhancing the share of indigenous Indonesian businessmen, 'newcomers' in the jargon of the day, especially in the import trade. Targeting this sector was not accidental. Import trade did not require much initial capital investment or access to specialized know-how or technology. Above all, it was known to be highly lucrative. In early 1950 the well-informed directors of the Java Bank dryly remarked that the Indonesians too wished to 'reap the fruits of the money tree' (*van de rijke boom plukken*).[2]

In January 1950 Indonesia counted about 100 'newcomers', who between them were responsible for a mere 10 per cent of total imports. By contrast, the eight largest Dutch trading firms handled 60 per cent of imports of consumer goods, which constituted about half of all imports.[3] This group of eight included the famous 'Big Five', namely Borsumij, Internatio, Jacobson van den Berg, Lindeteves, and Geo. Wehry. The very fact that eight Dutch companies pocketed three times as much profit from imports as all indigenous Indonesian importers taken together was clearly viewed as an anomaly

1 Bank Mandiri, Jakarta: Jaarverslag NHM Factorij 1952, I:31-2; DJB 1951:39-43.

2 Bank Indonesia, Jakarta: DJB 1584, 4-2-1950. A similar statement was made publicly at a slightly later stage (DJB 1952:24-5).

3 Amstutz 1958:47; Glassburner 1971:78-9. The cited percentage applies to the eight largest Dutch importers in 1952, but it is unlikely to have been lower in 1950.

President Sukarno and Prime Minister Ali Sastroamidjojo in 1955 at the time the Benteng policy was implemented (KITLV 42118)

inherited from Dutch colonialism.

Pursuing several disparate aims simultaneously in one area of economic policy was no easy task, although far from uncommon elsewhere. Far-reaching intervention in foreign trading as a means of generating state revenue raised costs, discouraged investment in production capacity, and acted as a powerful stimulus to smuggling (Dick et al. 2002:176). However, even more regulation of trading was required to implement the Benteng policy, the prime manifestation of economic nationalism in Indonesia during the first half of the 1950s.

The policy that backfired

In April 1950, Djuanda, Minister of Prosperity (*Kemakmuran*) in the Hatta cabinet, launched the Benteng policy, promising that indigenous Indonesian importers would receive government protection in order to be able to compete with foreign importers. Newcomers would be given access to credit from the government and a priority allocation of what in imports were known as Benteng goods. In order to qualify newcomers had to possess an office large enough to house several full-time employees, and at least 70 per cent of the firm's capital had to be furnished by indigenous (*bangsa asli*) Indonesians. This last requirement evoked an immediate protest from Siauw Giok Tjhan, member of Parliament for PSI, claiming that it violated the Manifesto Politik of 1 November 1945, which took a firm stand against racial discrimination. In his response, Djuanda referred to article 11 of the Finec Agreement, stipulating the right of the Indonesian government to take measures in the interests of the 'protection of economically weak groups' (*Ronde Tafel Conferentie* 1949:27; Amstutz 1958:47-8). It is ironic that the agreement with the Dutch provided ammunition when the government was accused of not upholding its own principles.

The registration of newcomers on the basis of the published criteria was soon set in motion. By December 1950 the number had increased to 250, and to 740 by April 1952, although newcomers still accounted for no more than 20 per cent of all importers (*Indonesian Review* 1951:36; Sutter 1959:1021). Initial attention focused on a list of Benteng goods. At first the list was limited, affecting only 10 per cent of total imports. In November 1952 Sumitro Djojohadikusumo, Minister of Finance in the Wilopo cabinet, criticized his predecessors for not having achieved enough and announced that another 25 per cent of import goods outside the Benteng list were to be reserved for accredited newcomers. Two months later, in January 1953, import goods falling outside the Benteng list were reduced to less than half of all import products. Still there were demands for even more goods to be put on the list

(*Times of Indonesia* 29 January 1953; Meek 1956:169; Anspach 1969:170-1).

A second round of registration of newcomers was announced on 30 May 1953, days before the fall of the Wilopo cabinet. Requirements pertaining to the size of the office and sufficient capital reserves were reiterated, but this time a full 100 per cent of the capital had to be provided by 'Indonesians'. The definition was unclear; in practice half of the capital could be indigenous and the other half non-indigenous. By September 1953, after three months of re-registration, 1,500 newcomers had been accredited (*Antara* 7 September 1953; Amstutz 1958:50).

There was little real disagreement among the major political parties about the Benteng policy, with only minor differences of opinion arising between factions or individuals. Nevertheless, the controversy surrounding this policy grew more intense after Iskaq had been appointed Minister of Economic Affairs in early June 1953 in the (first) Ali Sastroamidjojo cabinet. Iskaq became notorious as what might be called the 'bagman of PNI', the person assigned to collect and redistribute dirty money. He was a fervent economic nationalist. In September 1953 he issued a regulation, 'P [*Peraturan*] 41', reserving fifteen major categories of imports exclusively for Benteng traders, raising their share in the total from 40 to 60 per cent. There was an outcry of indignation, especially from ethnic Chinese. Central bank President Sjafruddin insisted that Iskaq withdraw the regulation, as the proper procedure had not been followed. 'The interests of the people must not be sacrificed to the interests of the importers', Sjafruddin exclaimed. Iskaq complied and quietly replaced the director of the Kantor Pusat Urusan Impor (KPUI, Central Office for Regulating Imports). KPUI bore the primary responsibility for implementing the Benteng policy and already employed more than 500 civil servants.[4]

Only a few months later, in November 1953, Iskaq was again involved in controversy regarding Benteng goods. KH (Kiai Haji) Tjikwan from Masjumi asked questions in Parliament about the latest regulation issued by KPUI, 'P 51', reserving imports of cambric for members of the association of Indonesian batik cooperatives, the GKBI. Siauw Giok Tjhan added fuel to the parliamentary debate by drawing attention to the exclusive character of the GKBI, which effectively closed the door to Indonesian citizens of 'foreign descent' (*keturunan asing*), namely ethnic Chinese. He called upon the government to end this type of discrimination and compel the GKBI to admit Indonesian citizens of whatever ethnic origin.[5] Siauw's request was reasonable. In Cirebon,

4 Bank Mandiri, Jakarta: Jaarverslag NHM Factorij 1953, I:39-40; *Antara* 15-9-1953, 22-4-1954; *Harian Rakjat* 15-9-1953.

5 ANRI, Jakarta: Risalah Rapat DPR 222, rapat 75.

to give but one example, local Javanese batik producers obtained priority access to imported fabrics and clearly benefited at the expense of their ethnic Chinese rivals (Abdul Wahid 2004).

The system of allocating foreign exchange for purchases from abroad, as revised in March 1951, offered ready-made opportunities for discrimination, not to mention corruption. Foreign exchange certificates effectively became import licences, a substantial part of which could be reserved for national importers in a way analogous to applying the list of Benteng goods. In 1952 43 per cent of all foreign exchange was allocated to indigenous Indonesian importers, which was more than the proportions obtained by either European firms (31 per cent) or ethnic Chinese traders (26 per cent) (Amstutz 1958:78). But this was still not enough to satisfy Iskaq, who aimed at 80 to 90 per cent. Public announcements to that effect and a simultaneous lowering of requirements on down payments in rupiahs prompted a rush to register as a national importer, beginning in September 1953. By February 1954 Indonesia had about 3,000 national importers, half of all importers, but many were readily recognizable as strawmen for ethnic Chinese or for the 'Big Five' (*Antara* 18 February 1954; compare Bisuk Siahaan 1996:168). A new concept introduced into the public discourse was that of the 'briefcase importer' (*importir aktentas*), the national importer ready to produce his licence at all times pretending that he was conducting his own business, when in fact he was a front man financed by others.

Cooperation between strawmen and their patrons lurking in the background was founded on mutual benefit. The national importer had prioritized access to scarce foreign exchange, but limited funds to run a trading business. The larger trading firm, controlled by ethnic Chinese or foreign capital, encountered a bottleneck in its attempts to access sufficient amounts of foreign exchange. Both stood to gain from cooperation. The government and the public, however, expected national importers to act out of nationalist sentiment and not simply out of the desire for personal profit. Whatever it was intended to achieve, the Benteng policy soon developed into a blatant rent-seeking operation.

The necessity of cooperation in import trading was appreciated at a very early stage by the directors of NHM in Jakarta. In 1951 the directors commented on the allocation of Benteng goods to newcomers, adding that in most cases these importers had to be 'financially supported by the larger European, Chinese or Indian trading houses which also took care of distribution'. The extension of the list in 1952 was greeted at NHM by the conviction that national importers would not be able to import the goods allocated to them without financial support from third parties. A flourishing trade in import licences towards the end of 1952 elicited stern warnings from the public prosecutor, who even threatened to take action against foreign importers 'eager to buy' (*kooplustige buitenlandse importeurs*). The NHM directors do not seem to have been impressed.[6]

A popular term in the public discourse of the early 1950s was 'Ali Baba', referring to a pseudo-joint venture between indigenous Indonesians and ethnic Chinese.[7] No similar term was coined for cooperation schemes between national importers and major European trading firms. In 1953, when Iskaq's policies reduced direct access to foreign exchange even further, NHM had already made 'provisions to secure our share in the businesses of Indonesian importers' (*een regeling getroffen waardoor wij ons van een aandeel in de zaken van de Indonesische importeurs hebben kunnen verzekeren*).[8] Whatever secret adjustments were needed, cooperation with scores of national importers did substantially enlarge the total network of local clients for major trading houses such as NHM.

A new registration round of national importers followed in March 1954, this time stipulating that firms had to be fully owned by Indonesian citizens in order to qualify. The number of national importers, who between them obtained 85 per cent of all import licences, increased to 4,000 (*Antara* 13 March, 28 April 1954). An unofficial but very lively auction system evolved whereby import licences sold at 200-250 per cent of their nominal value and indigenous intermediaries pocketed Rp. 2,000-5,000 each month (*Antara* 24 June 1954; Anspach 1969:174). Such practices demonstrate that rent-seeking lay at the core of how the Benteng policy was implemented. Deputy Prime Minister Wongsonegoro of the Persatuan Indonesia Raya (PIR, Union of Great Indonesia) was convinced that as many as 80 per cent of all licences allocated to national importers were in fact sold on to non-indigenous traders (*Aneta* 26 April 1954). The Benteng policy was quickly becoming a national scandal.

Corruption abounded at KPUI, the agency entrusted with executing the Benteng policy. Gifts were left on the doorstep, 'for people inside' (*untuk orang dalam*) (*Berita Ekonomi* 10 September 1954). In April 1954 the indefatigable Tjikwan submitted a motion of no confidence in Parliament against Iskaq on charges of corruption and, as seen earlier, Iskaq failed to convince the public of his innocence. By June 1954 he had again replaced the director of KPUI and in July he admitted publicly that KPUI was 'vulnerable' (*kwetsbaar*) (*Antara* 28 July 1954).

Uneasiness increased among national importers, with 900 attending a

6 Bank Mandiri, Jakarta: Jaarverslag NHM Factorij 1950-51, I:68, 1952, I:39.

7 'Ali' refers to the indigenous Indonesian partner, whereas 'Baba' derives from *babah* or *wa wa sze*, a term with derogative connotations used by Chinese born in China when addressing Chinese born in Indonesia.

8 Bank Mandiri, Jakarta: Jaarverslag NHM Factorij 1953, I:86, 1954, I:93.

meeting in October 1954 in Jakarta; the atmosphere was very tense and all but a handful left before it ended (*Antara* 8 October 1954). Iskaq became embroiled in an embarrassing conflict with Hasjim Ning, arguably the most prominent indigenous businessman of his day. Hasjim claimed that import licences were given only to people with good connections with the PNI leadership. Iskaq responded by trying, in vain, to topple Hasjim from his position as President-Director of his flagship company ISC (Navis 1986:134-5).

The final showdown for Iskaq and the most aggressive phase of the Benteng policy came in November 1954. There were rumours about that KPUI demanded kickbacks from people wanting to register as national importers, subsequently channelling the money into the funds of the ruling party PNI. The two Muslim parties in the coalition, NU and PSII, allegedly enjoyed preferential treatment too, as did some well-placed individuals, along with no less than Deputy Prime Minister Wongsonegoro. It was all denied by Achmad Ponsen, the third director of KPUI in fourteen months, but Iskaq was forced to resign and Wongsonegoro also stepped down.[9] A few weeks later Vice-President Hatta spoke at the All-Sumatra Economic Conference, held in Medan at the renowned Hotel De Boer (now Dharma Deli). He equated the common set up of a national importer fronting operations and foreign capital and management behind the scenes to 'a disease which must be eradicated' (*penjakit jang mesti dibasmi*) and cited Achmad Ponsen's internal estimate that no more than one national importer in ten was bonafide (*Antara* 26 November 1954; Amstutz 1958:66, 144).

Roosseno, who succeeded Iskaq as Minister of Economic Affairs, took swift action. Upon the insistence of the government body regulating foreign exchange, LAAPLN, new instructions required applicants for licences to present more detailed evidence of their financial strength (*financieele draagkracht*). Roosseno ordered a rescreening of the 4,300 persons already accredited as national importers, primarily in order to reduce their numbers. The total amount of foreign exchange available was Rp. 2,750 million, working out to only Rp. 640,000 each, which, as Roosseno admitted, inevitably meant that some foreign firms must be employing as many as ten 'licence scavengers' (*tukang tjatut lisensi*). The ultimate aim, Roosseno assured his fellow politicians, remained unchanged: to have national importers take over the function currently fulfilled by the 'Big Five' (*Antara* 6 and 24 December 1954, 12 and 27 February 1955; Amstutz 1958:38-72). It proved difficult to turn the tide. Roosseno's well-intended efforts did little to restore the Benteng policy's tarnished reputation.

9 *Antara* 9-11-1954. Six years later, in 1960, Iskaq Tjokrohadisurjo was convicted of corruption.

Primary responsibility for implementing the Benteng policy shifted from the Department of Economic Affairs to Finance when the Harahap cabinet assumed office in August 1955. Sumitro Djojohadikusumo, still representing the small PSI, reappeared as Minister of Finance and immediately ordered a reorganization of the entire system. KPUI was closed and replaced by a new agency responsible for foreign exchange management, the Biro Devisen Perdagangan (BDP, Bureau for Foreign Exchange in Trading), with a total staff of only 35 people, of whom nineteen were transferred from the former KPUI. New application procedures were devised, including safeguarding the anonymity of applicants by using codes instead of names, as well as the active involvement of three staff members in the processing of each application. A simplified 'natural screening' based on importers' variable financial strength was launched, with minimum deposits for accreditation set at Rp. 500,000 for national importers and Rp. 5 million for 'foreign' importers. The latter were now permitted to use licences allocated to the former if they paid a 5 per cent commission, which effectively legalized the practice of employing indigenous strawmen (*Antara* 1, 10 and 20 September 1955; Amstutz 1958:69-71). It was a bold attempt to turn a vice into a virtue.

A new rescreening of all importers got underway and, by 1 November 1955, had counted 3,545 importers, 55 per cent of whom were designated national importers. However, most of the non-national importers were loath to pay the deposit of Rp. 5 million. By January 1956 only 44 firms, almost all European ones, had done so. Most lent the Rp. 500,000 to indigenous businessmen and paid the 5 per cent commission when the foreign exchange certificates were issued. Sumitro responded by relaxing the Rp. 5 million deposit for 'foreign' importers while making it more difficult to become a national importer. No longer was it sufficient to be an Indonesian citizen born in Indonesia; now the applicant's father also had to be Indonesia-born. It was to little avail. By mid-February 1956 fewer than 100 importers had paid their deposit, whereas BDP had so far registered almost 3,500 national importers. Sumitro aptly observed that the 'natural screening' was not proceeding 'very well' (*tidak lantjar*) (*Antara* 2 November 1955, 9 and 10 January, 7 February 1956; Neuman 1956:701).

The failure of Sumitro's 'natural screening' became all too apparent in late 1956, as 175 importers in Jakarta, almost all indigenous Indonesians, were blacklisted for failing to comply with BDP's requirement to report their debt obligations. Some were eventually taken off the list but almost half were denied access to foreign exchange. Due to the openings offered to foreign firms prepared to pay more, the entire import trading sector had now been reduced to a 'free for all' (*Antara* 21 December 1956, 21 January 1957). By this time, however, attention was already drifting away from the Benteng policy.

All observers were disappointed with the achievements of the policy.

Moh. Hatta, who by then had resigned as Vice-President, lamented: 'Under the guise of national economic development, Indonesian traders have obtained privileges which have cost the country tens if not hundreds of millions of rupiahs while the suffering of the whole society increases' (Faauw 1960:76). Sumitro too had few illusions. Commenting on the Benteng policy in retrospect, he stated that 'if you gave assistance to ten people, seven might turn out to be parasites, but you might still get three entrepreneurs' (Sumitro Djojohadikusumo 1986:35). Actual achievements fell short of even that estimate.

The Benteng policy has gone down in history as a complete failure; negative outcomes clearly predominate as we draw up the balance-sheet. The original aim of transferring control over economic assets to indigenous Indonesians cannot possibly have been achieved when nine out of ten national importers in fact served as strawmen of precisely those targeted for a reduction in their economic power. Dutch trading firms do not appear to have been seriously disadvantaged. In late 1955, when the policy had already been in force for more than half a decade, national sugar traders in East Java still complained about fierce competition from the 'Big Five', which they depicted as 'cats' competing against 'mice' (*Antara* 25 November 1955). Only a few months later, Dutch sources claimed exactly the opposite: that the distribution of sugar in East Java had almost entirely passed into the hands of Indonesians![10]

In late 1956 it was still openly stated in Parliament that the power of foreign capital was the foremost obstacle (*penghalang terutama*) to the development of a truly national economy. A few months later complaints were heard in the regional parliament of East Java that even the central government opted for foreign trading firms instead of national ones, in direct violation of its own directives.[11] One final piece of circumstantial evidence can be given. According to an estimate cited in Parliament in April 1956, 70 per cent of all import trading was still handled by foreign banks, whereas the capacity of national importers constituted only 6 per cent of the total capacity of foreign importers.[12] The evidence is overwhelming. Benteng simply did not achieve its main objectives.

Perhaps even more seriously, the balance-sheet also shows that the Benteng policy had outright negative consequences, corruption being one of them. The policy was singularly effective in fostering corrupt practices in dealings with officials entrusted with its execution. By 1954 there was talk of 'moral decay' (*kemerosotan moral*) and salary increases for civil servants were considered the

10 Bank Mandiri, Jakarta: Jaarverslag NHM Factorij 1956, I:67.
11 ANRI, Jakarta: Risalah Rapat DPR 222, 18-12-1956.
12 ANRI, Jakarta: Risalah Rapat DPR 127, 15-4-1956.

sole remedy for this situation (*Berita Ekonomi* 10 September 1954). It would perhaps be a bridge too far to say that the Benteng policy was the main cause of later widespread corruption in Indonesian society, but it incontrovertibly reinforced corrupt practices which were encouraged by the bizarre system of trade taxes and multiple exchange rates (Dick 2004:187-9).

Moreover, the Benteng policy was closely linked to the resurgence of anti-Chinese sentiment, which will be discussed in the final section of this chapter. Yet another negative side-effect was the erosion of confidence in private capital as the foundation of economic development in Indonesia. By discrediting private indigenous entrepreneurship, the Benteng policy paved the way for a far greater direct involvement in economic life by the state (Thee Kian Wie 1996:317). Apprehension about the operations of the free market and private capitalism often lurked beneath the surface of writings by leading nationalists. Vice-President Hatta became the very personification of the cooperative movement, and both Sjafruddin and Sumitro probably saw themselves as social democrats (Hatta 1957; Thee Kian Wie 2003:52-5, 85). Soejono Hadinoto did not hesitate about the direction Indonesia should take in its transformation from a colonial to a national economy when he wrote: 'Our aim is the development of democratic socialism' (*tudjuan kita adalah pembangunan demokratis sosialisme*) (Soejono Hadinoto 1949:66). The distance between social democracy and Sukarno's 'Guided Economy' (*Ekonomi Terpimpin*), introduced in the wake of his 'Guided Democracy' in 1959, was considerable, but the Benteng policy did make the transition easier.

Did the Benteng policy bring Indonesia closer to economic decolonization? Not really. This scheme of positive discrimination could have served as one possible avenue towards that aim but, as the balance-sheet shows, it failed to do so. The real problem was that the whole policy was a political fix from the outset, not a serious measure of national economic policy. It was doomed to fail and to backfire.

Auxiliary policies

Agoes Moesin Dasaad was no great friend of the Dutch. Employing a metaphor common in the 1950s, he likened Dutch businessmen to 'cats confronting mice' (*kutjing menghadapi tikus*), smiling at them but in fact ready to eat them. He preferred to do business with Germans, whom he described as 'tough and rude but professional' (*keras dan kasar tetap zakelijk*) (*Antara* 24 March 1956). Not long after he had publicly voiced his opinions, Dasaad departed for Europe to pave the way for a state visit to West Germany by Sukarno. As a national importer, he reaped some benefits from the positive discrimination under the Benteng policy, although the generally favourable prospects for well-connected indigenous businessmen were probably at least as important in securing his commercial success.

The Benteng policy did not stand alone. It brought with it various measures in trading and credit regulation which have received far less attention in the literature. This section discusses a few auxiliary policy measures which may contribute to a fuller understanding of economic nationalism as it took shape in Indonesia during the 1950s.

A good point of departure for any discussion of economic nationalism is a break-down of national income by ethnic origin. How much is contributed by indigenous subjects as opposed to aliens (or those considered as such)? Around 1950 about 25 per cent of Indonesia's Gross National Product (GNP) was contributed by foreign, primarily Dutch, enterprises and firms owned by ethnic Chinese. The non-indigenous share of GNP consisted of all estate agriculture, most modern manufacturing, half of mining and transport, and virtually all services in the private sector. The indigenous Indonesian share of GNP, 75 per cent of the total, comprised all peasant agriculture, fisheries, and traditional manufacturing, as well as government-owned mining, transport facilities (in each case about 50 per cent of the sector total), and public services (Neumark 1954:354, 371; Anspach 1969:113-4). Ten years later, following the nationalization of Dutch enterprises, the combined share of foreign and ethnic Chinese capital was smaller, but this outcome cannot be attributed to the Benteng policy.

Evidence of outright discrimination is rare in the records of private Dutch firms. In early 1953 the Wilopo cabinet went so far as to deny accusations made by the Netherlands government that Indonesia discriminated against Dutchmen (*Antara* 27 March 1953). In September 1954, however, import licences were denied to the Philips radio assembly factory in Surabaya on account of its failure to appoint Indonesian distributors. The factory closed down within half a year (*Aneta* 29 September 1954, 12 February 1955).

Selective credit policies formed a logical supplement to the identification of Benteng goods and national importers when allocating foreign exchange. Outstanding credit designated for use in import trading rose from Rp. 94 million in December 1950 to Rp. 383 million in December 1952, corresponding to a jump from 18 to 30 per cent of all credit extended to the private sector by commercial banks other than BNI.[13] BNI targeted national importers to an even higher degree. Functions and assets were taken over from the former Dutch colonial organization for imports, which went into liquidation in March 1950. The total outstanding debt increased very rapidly, reaching Rp. 1 billion at the end of 1951, including Rp. 64 million to members of the Gabungan

13 Bank Indonesia, Jakarta: DJB 184, 19-9-1952.

Pembelian Importir Indonesia (Gapindo, Association of Indonesian Import Purchasers). Gapindo members had a reputation for failing to repay their debts. Apparently, this aspersion applied to BNI clients in general, causing frequent disappointment.[14] The ever-active Siauw Giok Tjhan voiced complaints in Parliament alleging that BNI discriminated against ethnic Chinese importers. By the end of 1953, when many short-run debts had in fact been repaid, total outstanding debts at BNI amounted to Rp. 500 million, of which 45 per cent (more than Rp. 220 million) had been allocated to national importers (Amstutz 1958:162). In early 1957 President-Director Abdul Karim, who had succeeded Margono in 1953, asserted that domestic banks were still handling only 15 per cent of all imports (*Antara* 28 March 1957).

For most of its implementation period, the Benteng policy targeted import trading. Much less attention was paid to exports. Dutch predominance, as symbolized by the notorious 'Big Five', was far more visible in import trading, and the import business was also considered easier for indigenous newcomers to enter. Indigenous smallholders, in particular in Sumatra and Kalimantan, were already proving highly successful in exporting their products and scarcely in need of special protection. Government intervention in export trading served an entirely different aim of economic policy, that of financing state expenditures.

Export and import taxes increasingly furnished funds for government spending. In 1956-1957 trade taxes of various kinds contributed half of all government revenue, which is high by any standard (Paauw 1960:181). Increasing reliance on such sources of revenue implied that far-reaching regulation was now also extended to exports. In October 1955 a new agency was set up for implementing export regulations, Kantor Pusat Urusan Ekspor (KPUE, Central Office for Regulating Exports), the counterpart of the former KPUI, which had been replaced by BDP in the preceding month. In September 1956 the NU Minister of Economic Affairs Burhanuddin in the second Ali Sastroamidjojo cabinet introduced a new type of certificate, Bukti Pendorong Ekspor, expressly designed to stimulate exports. The link between exporting more and obtaining easier access to foreign exchange for imports was re-established. This appeared advantageous to foreign traders, but Burhanuddin was keen to reassert the government's original aim of accomplishing a transition to a national economy through greater participation in the distribution sector by indigenous Indonesians (*Antara* 28 August and 5 September 1956).

The next step followed in June 1957. The latest type of official document

14 Robison 1986:45; Bank Mandiri, Jakarta: Jaarverslag NHM Factorij 1950-51, I:39. The NHM directors added, condescendingly, that BNI played no role of any significance in the Indonesian economy.

in trading was the Bukti Ekspor (BE, Export Certificate), representing a value equal to the nominal value of expected foreign exchange earnings. It could be traded at a higher rate than the nominal value and the government was entitled to 20 per cent of the proceeds from the sale of such certificates. Importers in need of foreign exchange first had to obtain a permit by depositing 20 per cent of the expected merchandise value, after which they had to purchase a BE certificate to be submitted in order to effectuate the transaction. At this stage a surcharge also had to be paid directly to the government, depending on the type of goods imported, up to a maximum of 175 per cent of the nominal value of the BE certificate.[15] The system was almost unbelievably complex, but it did provide the government with plenty of revenue.

Complaints abounded on all sides. The two major organizations of Indonesian importers, KINSI and Persatuan Importir Indonesia (PII, Union of Indonesian Importers), demanded that all imports be handled by indigenous importers, with the government fixing the rate of BE certificates so as to prevent speculation. One representative of Indonesian exporters in North Sumatra argued that the new regulation was primarily benefiting foreign firms with a great deal of capital and those few domestic producers capable of exporting on a similar scale, a viewpoint later reiterated by PKI in Parliament.[16] KPM then announced increases of 50 per cent in its freight tariffs, on the grounds that it incurred higher costs due to the new regulation (*Antara* 15 July 1957). Smuggling soared, eventually reaching an estimated 30 per cent of total exports (Rosendale 1978:151). The long-term viability of the trading system was sacrificed for short-term cash gains for the government.

This brief overview reveals that the ill-fated Benteng policy was part and parcel of a whole package of measures inspired by economic nationalism and that it was designed to promote indigenous entrepreneurship at the expense of foreign firms and ethnic Chinese. Indigenous Indonesian entrepreneurship did in fact flourish in the 1950s. However, as in the case of the Benteng policy itself, this outcome materialized despite, rather than because of, the government's positive discrimination measures.

Squeezing the Chinese

When Roosseno, Minister of Economic Affairs in the Djuanda cabinet, officially abandoned the Benteng policy in December 1957, he ostensibly did so in order to eradicate discrimination on racial grounds (Widigdo Sukarman

15 Bank Agro, Medan: AVROS, 24-6-1957.

16 ANRI, Jakarta: Risalah Rapat DPR 370, 19-12-1957; *Antara* 25-6-1957, 30-6-1957.

2005:56). Inadvertently, he thereby touched upon the single most sensitive aspect of the policy, namely the question of whether positive discrimination in favour of indigenous Indonesians by definition implied discrimination against ethnic Chinese. Or, in terms of the theoretical concepts applied here, was *Indonesianisasi*, as made manifest in the Benteng policy, the equivalent of *pribumisasi*? This section examines the position of the ethnic Chinese as potential and actual victims of the policy of positive discrimination during the 1950s.[17]

Siauw Giok Tjhan always kept a watchful eye on the authorities and raised the matter of racial discrimination on many occasions. In December 1953 he filed a formal complaint in Parliament about discrimination against ethnic Chinese by the Ministry of Economic Affairs, especially in the section for the manufacturing industry and the accreditation of national importers. The government assured him that citizenship alone, not ethnic origin, was the criterion for being designated a national importer (*Antara* 7 December 1953; *Keng Po* 7 December 1953). This answer is revealing because it shows how keen even a nationalist cabinet such as the first one headed by Ali Sastroamidjojo was to honour the ideals of racial equality laid down in the Manifesto Politik of 1945 – at least in principle. The answer is also revealing because it ignored all the complexities associated with applying such a seemingly straightforward criterion as citizenship.

The origin of the confusion surrounding the citizenship of ethnic Chinese was twofold. The first was a legacy from colonial rule which only distinguished between a 'Dutch citizen' and a 'Dutch subject' (*onderdaan*). When Indonesian independence was acknowledged by the Dutch, the former of these two terms applied only to persons eligible for emigration to the Netherlands; the latter term disappeared altogether. Former Dutch subjects of indigenous origin became citizens of the Republic of Indonesia. However, this did not apply automatically to ethnic Chinese, as Indonesian law ruled out dual nationality, which brings us to the second source of confusion.[18]

The Chinese empire, later the Kuomintang government and the People's Republic, applied the principle of descent by blood (*jus sanguinis*) in granting

[17] It must be emphasized that the current account cannot possibly offer an exhaustive discussion of the fate of ethnic Chinese during the Sukarno era.

[18] The situation was different for Indonesians of Arab descent, who by definition were not indigenous either. They were immediately eligible for Indonesian citizenship, as they possessed no other citizenship. In addition, their assimilation into indigenous society was eased by sharing the same religion and the use of personal names inspired by Islam. In 1948, when the Republican government in Yogyakarta introduced the term 'new citizens' (*warga negara baru*) for non-indigenous nationals, it had already met with vehement protests from organizations of Indonesians of Arab descent, claiming that full citizenship had been obtained automatically at the proclamation of independence in 1945 (ANRI, Jakarta: Kementerian Penerangan 207, 28-8-1948).

citizenship, a practice which was not abandoned until 1982. Consequently, Chinese citizenship was held both by those who had immigrated to Indonesia from China (*totok*) and by those who had been born in Indonesia, often offspring of families living there for generations (*peranakan*). Chinese ancestry was what counted, which implied an unequivocal identification with Chinese society, including the use of Chinese personal names.[19] Hence, the Chinese concept of citizenship differed fundamentally from the one based on place of birth (*jus soli*), as applied in Western society and adopted by Indonesia at independence. The two come into conflict when a nation decides not to allow dual citizenship.

In 1950 Indonesia was home to about 2.1 million ethnic Chinese, of whom approximately 75 per cent were *peranakan* and 25 per cent *totok* (Anspach 1969:113). *Peranakan* Chinese were allowed a grace period of two years to formally choose Chinese citizenship. If they failed to do so, they would, by default, become Indonesian nationals. About 80 per cent of the *peranakan* Chinese, 1.2 million out of 1.5 million, chose the default option, presumably because they identified more strongly with Sukarno's Indonesia than with the People's Republic of China (Thompson and Adloff 1955:51). They were understandably enraged when in 1953 new procedures were introduced for obtaining Indonesian citizenship, requiring that an 'active choice' be made (Willmott 1960:40-3). As a result, the citizenship status of a large group of *peranakan* Chinese remained ambiguous throughout the years during which the Benteng policy was implemented. This ambiguity offered ample opportunity for discrimination without having to resort to ethnic or racial criteria.

In August 1950 Indonesia had been one of the first countries to establish diplomatic relations with the People's Republic of China, and Sukarno was increasingly keen to get rid of obstacles to further cooperation such as the dual nationality problem. Negotiations on the matter commenced in November 1954 and produced a formal agreement between Chou En-lai, Prime Minister of the People's Republic, and Minister of Foreign Affairs Sunarjo in the wake of the Afro-Asian Conference at Bandung in April 1955. Under this agreement, *peranakan* Chinese were again offered the opportunity to choose their nationality, within two years of ratification, while the People's Republic relinquished its citizenship claims on those wishing to become Indonesian nationals. The treaty on dual nationality was ratified by the People's Republic in December 1957. However, not until January 1960, almost five full years after the Bandung conference, was the treaty ratified by the Indonesian gov-

19 Skinner 1963:97. The distinction between *totok* and *peranakan* Chinese is less defined than it appears on the surface. An immigrant from China could become *peranakan* by virtue of rapid assimilation, whereas a Chinese born in Indonesia could remain *totok* due to a strong identification with Chinese culture such as the ability to speak Mandarin or any other Chinese dialect.

ernment. About one million people were then, at long last, in a position to make a definite choice about their nationality. An estimated 65 per cent chose Indonesian citizenship.[20] This ended the ambiguity in citizenship status.

In the public discourse of the 1950s there was more disagreement about the interpretation of the term 'foreign' (*bangsa asing*) as opposed to 'indigenous' (*bangsa asli*) than there was about the implementation of the Benteng policy as such. In 1951 Sjafruddin Prawiranegara, newly appointed president of the central bank, complained that terms like 'domestic capital' (*nationaal kapitaal*) and 'domestic economy' (*nationale economie*) were not defined carefully enough in the government's ambitious economic plans. He asserted that the sole criterion for distinguishing between 'domestic' and 'foreign' lay in the propensity to remit profits abroad. It was in that domain, and no other, that Indonesia needed clear and unambiguous regulations (DJB 1951:40-2). Sjafruddin's firm stand against any designation of Indonesian Chinese as 'foreign' represented the opinion commonly held by economic nationalists of the moderate type.

Sumitro Djojohadikusumo strongly favoured positive discrimination as an instrument to boost indigenous entrepreneurship. He was prepared to accept some level of corruption in the process, but shared Sjafruddin's and Hatta's refusal to distinguish between different types of Indonesian citizens. When ordering the reform of the Benteng policy in late 1955, he removed the distinction between 'indigenous citizens' (*warga negara asli*) and 'non-indigenous citizens' (*warga negara tidak asli*) which had become institutionalized in procedures for the allocation of foreign exchange certificates. National importers, whether *asli* or *tidak asli*, were henceforth entitled to the same protection (*Antara* 1 and 28 December 1955). Clearly, moderate nationalist politicians sometimes felt uneasy about the racial bias in the implementation of the Benteng policy and the lack of cooperation which some ethnic Chinese encountered even after they had become Indonesian citizens (Anspach 1969:168-79).

More militant economic nationalists such as Iskaq were inclined to add the finer distinction *asli/tidak asli* to the formal distinction based on citizenship alone. This was done despite assurances to the contrary given by Prime Minister Ali Sastroamidjojo in response to complaints in Parliament, notably by Siauw in December 1953. In August 1954 a meeting took place between Iskaq and representatives of a Chinese organization, the Federasi Tionghoa Siang Hwee Seluruh Indonesia (Chinese Federation Siang Hwee of All Indonesia). Targets for involvement in future investment activities were

20 Willmott 1960:118-39; Mackie and Coppel 1976:11. The figure of 65 per cent is derived from Indonesian government sources. Leaders of the Chinese community in Indonesia claimed that 70-90 per cent opted for Indonesian nationality.

formulated, reserving 75 per cent for indigenous Indonesians, 15 per cent for non-indigenous Indonesians, labelled 'new citizens' (*warga negara baru*), and a final 15 per cent (*sic*) for investors of foreign nationality. The men from the Siang Hwee Federation expressed the hope that their capital would be considered 'domestic', serving a 'national' function (*Antara* 28 August 1954).

The gradations became a shade more complex when economic statistics on domestic enterprises began to differentiate on the basis of ethnic origin of the capital. A case in point is the distribution of investment capital in the weaving industry of Bandung, as published by the military authorities in the 'Second Autonomous Region' (*Daerah Swatantra II*) of Bandung, presumably in the early 1950s. Total invested capital amounted to Rp. 145 million, of which 62 per cent was in foreign-owned enterprises, including firms whose owners had chosen Chinese nationality. The remaining 38 per cent was distributed across three different categories of domestic firms. One, responsible for 17 per cent of the grand total, operated with 'alien' capital that had been supplied primarily by ethnic Chinese who had chosen not to become Indonesian citizens. A second category, of equal size, worked with 'citizen' (*warga negara*) capital, a euphemism for ethnic Chinese. The third category (only 4 per cent) relied on indigenous Indonesian capital (Pramoedya Ananta Toer 1960:185, attachment).

Circumstances visibly deteriorated for the ethnic Chinese in 1954, under the (first) Ali Sastroamidjojo cabinet. Two government regulations made use of the ambiguity of the citizenship status of *peranakan* Chinese to advance indigenous control of economic assets. The first, *Peraturan Pemerintah* (PP, Government Regulation) 42/1954, stipulated that Indonesian citizens must supply the capital of and take responsibility for management of all rice-mills in Java, 90 per cent (138 out of 154) of which were then owned by ethnic Chinese (Sutter 1959:802-3). The deadline for the transfer was set at March 1955 but was later extended by two years. In reality, ownership often remained unchanged but the mills were rented to indigenous Indonesians, which suggested compliance with the government regulation although little of substance had changed (Suryadinata 1992:132; *Antara* 23 July 1956). The second regulation, PP 61/1954, ordered a similar transfer for warehouses in major ports to indigenous Indonesians, affecting both Dutch and ethnic Chinese owners. The deadline was set at 1956 but later extended to mid-1959 (*Antara* 1 March 1956; Anspach 1969:184).

Anti-Chinese undertones increasingly coloured public discourse, and even on occasion official statements by government bureaucrats. In early 1955 the chairman of the government's supervisory agency, Djabatan Perdagangan Pusat (Central Trading Office) , insinuated that 'certain groups' (*golongan tertentu*) were using the deterioration of the economy to damage the government (*Antara* 9 February 1955). Worse was yet to come. In 1956 outright anti-

Chinese sentiments were voiced by the group around Assaat, a prominent politician and former businessman who had served briefly as Minister of Domestic Affairs in the Natsir cabinet.[21] In a motion at a meeting of KINSI in Surabaya in March 1956, Assaat asserted that 'national enterprises' had to be fully controlled by people who qualified as *asli* even when jointly owned by *asli* and ethnic Chinese (*warga negara*). He demanded special protection for indigenous business against competition from 'foreign business in general, Chinese business in particular' (*pihak asing umumnja, golongan Tionghoa chususnja*). The motion, described by many as revolutionary and 'firm' (*tegas*), was accepted (*Antara* 24 March 1956). Reactions varied. Support committees were set up by indigenous businessmen at various locations to defend the distinction between *asli* and *bukan asli* (non-indigenous) within the wider category of Indonesian citizens.[22] By contrast, moderate organizations and PKI argued that government protection should be based on class, not race.

In mid-1956 Assaat's group, popularly known as 'the Assaat movement', was flourishing.[23] Assaat's explicit goal was the transfer of all economic assets into indigenous hands. Charges of racial discrimination were soon raised in Parliament but were denied by Assaat (*Indonesian Observer* 30 July 1956). It was a broadly-based group of businessmen who formed a lobby, shrewdly combining the government's professed aim of promoting 'national enterprise' with a definition of 'national' which discriminated unequivocally against ethnic Chinese (Mackie and Coppel 1976:14). In the words of one eloquent historian of Indonesia, the late Herbert Feith, the Assaat movement 'expressed with shattering directness feelings which Indonesians had long had, but hesitated to express in public' (Feith 1962:481).

Matters culminated at the KENSI meeting on 5-9 August 1956 in Surabaya. In his opening speech, Djuanda, then Minister of Planning, spoke at length about the necessity to ensure that 'the people were given protection against certain groups' (*rakjat diberi perlindungan terhadap golongan tertentu*), which could be construed as an official endorsement of the aims of the Assaat group. As a member of the congress presidium, Assaat personally defined 'national' as a business in which management and equity were fully controlled by indigenous Indonesian citizens, adding that firms with ethnic Chinese shareholders would have to give a guarantee that decision making rested

21 Between 27-12-1949 and 17-8-1950 Assaat served as President of the Republik Indonesia (RI, Republic of Indonesia), a constituent state in the federation named the Republik Indonesia Serikat (RIS, United Republic of Indonesia), with Sukarno as its head of state. Assaat's position became redundant when the unitary Indonesian state was formed (Bambang Purwanto 2004:3).

22 Bank Mandiri, Jakarta: Jaarverslag NHM Factorij 1956, I:32.

23 The full name of the group was Gerakan Kemerdekaan Ekonomi Bangsa Indonesia (Movement for Economic Independence of the Indonesian People).

with indigenous partners. The KENSI delegates accepted Assaat's hardline approach and formulated 26 separate resolutions containing specific measures to ensure indigenous control of economic assets. A task force on *badan perdjuangan* (literally 'the body for the struggle') was created to carry out these KENSI decisions. It was a triumph for the Assaat movement, but critics pointed out that the KENSI meeting in Surabaya was not fully representative of the community of Indonesian businessmen. Two national organizations had not participated: Perusahaan Pengusaha Dagang Ketjil (Small Trading Businessmen) with 45,000 members and Gabungan Perserikatan Perusahaan Rokok Nasional (GAPPERON, Associated Union of National Cigarette Manufacturers). However, the latter organization counted only 600 members. Peasants were not represented at all (*Antara* 6, 8, 9, 13 August, and 22 December 1956).

The KENSI resolutions forced all political parties to take sides. PNI kept insisting that discrimination on ethnic grounds violated the nation's ideals. Masjumi and PSI maintained that Chinese capital and management were badly needed in Indonesia, whereas PKI attached higher priority to the distinction between national and 'imperialist' capitalists, which makes one wonder in which category the ethnic Chinese would be placed (Anspach 1969:186-7). Having failed to gain endorsement from the leading political parties, the Assaat movement evaporated almost as quickly as it had emerged. It was fatally compromised in 1958, when Assaat joined the PRRI rebellion.

Anti-Chinese sentiments resurfaced in 1959, when the Republic was on the verge of ratifying the 1955 agreement with the People's Republic. By now there was no longer any talk of the Benteng policy as an instrument with which to promote indigenous entrepreneurship. On 14 May 1959 NU Minister of Trade Rachmat Muljomiseno announced a government regulation in the making which would ban foreign nationals from trading in rural areas, including those ethnic Chinese who by 4 May 1959 had still not acquired Indonesian citizenship. The idea was not new. As of May 1955 a steady stream of resolutions from regional parliaments requested the Jakarta government to ban 'foreigners' from trading, small-scale industry, and unskilled labour in rural areas. In December 1956 a similar recommendation was made by the Masjumi national congress. It is worth noting that statistical surveys of commercial enterprises at this time invariably distinguished between shops by mentioning the ethnic origin of the owner (*Warta Niaga dan Perusahaan* 20 November 1959). The intended measure would affect thousands of small enterprises. According to one estimate, in 1959 Indonesia had 168,000 'alien' firms, 125,000 of which were involved solely in trading. We may safely assume that an overwhelming majority, 95 per cent or more, consisted of ethnic Chinese who did not hold Indonesian citizenship (*Antara* 23 October 1959).

Reactions were predictable. The Chinese retail traders' organization was appalled, and during the next few weeks a steady flow of letters from individual businessmen reached the desk of President Sukarno. The Kiem Siong in Kutoarjo near Purworejo in Central Java, to mention just one example, stated that he and his family were going to 'suffer greatly' (*sangat menderita*) if the announced changes were implemented.[24] Indonesian business organizations, by contrast, spoke of 'a long overdue step to help Indonesian nationals out of their economic backwardness' (*Warta Niaga dan Perusahaan* 10 August 1959). The much-feared government regulation, labelled PP 10/1959, was issued on 18 November 1959 and became effective on 1 January 1960. Rural areas, defined as being outside cities and district (*kabupaten*) capitals, witnessed the extraordinary spectacle of army units forcibly removing ethnic Chinese traders. A severe economic disruption and an exodus of ethnic Chinese Indonesians took place during the following year (Mackie 1976:83-97). In 1962 there were about 2.5 million ethnic Chinese living in Indonesia, 60 per cent of whom were *peranakan*, including a sizeable group of 250,000 people who were either the children of Chinese citizens or had themselves rejected Indonesian citizenship (Mozingo 1961).

As a vehicle to achieve economic decolonization, the Benteng policy was not directed first and foremost against ethnic Chinese, except in the minds of those militant enough to view local Chinese as allies of the one-time colonial power. In this respect, the policy differed fundamentally from the New Economic Policy (NEP) in Malaysia a couple of decades later. NEP was occasioned by ethnic riots in Kuala Lumpur in May 1969 and the policy was pursued throughout the 1970s and 1980s, with the professed intention of advancing indigenous (*bumiputera*) Malaysian control of the economy at the expense of Chinese Malaysians in the first place and foreigners, especially British ones, in the second. In the event, the indigenous or *bumiputera* share in total corporate equity rose tenfold between 1970 and 1990, from 2 to 20 per cent, whereas the foreign share fell from 63 to 25 per cent, implying an increase in the proportion held by Malaysians of Chinese descent (Rajah Rasiah 1997:128). Incontrovertibly, the Benteng policy provided the context for discrimination against ethnic Chinese because it happened to coincide with the period of ambiguity regarding their citizenship status.

Economic nationalism coloured much of the public discourse and had a strong impact on the choice of priorities in economic policy in Indonesia during the 1950s. The Benteng policy, with related policy measures and its association with anti-Chinese sentiment, was the most conspicuous expression of a kind of economic nationalism which, as we have seen, delivered very little of what was intended. Throughout the period of its implementation hundreds

[24] ANRI, Jakarta: Kabinet Presiden 1695, 31-5-1959.

of foreign enterprises, in particular Dutch businesses, continued operating in key sectors of the Indonesian economy.

After focusing on events outside these foreign firms, whether in private Indonesian companies, in government-controlled segments of the services sector, or in economic policy, the time is ripe to look at what was happening at the foreign firms that remained active in Indonesia.

CHAPTER VII

Indonesianisasi

Reminiscences of three men, selected from among many, highlight how the situation was changing in the Dutch-owned enterprises staying on in Indonesia during the 1950s. The three men were all born in 1924 and worked for Dutch-owned companies. They witnessed their superiors trying desperately to continue doing business as usual. L.P. Jager and Pieter Verhage were planters in North Sumatra, employed by the Dutch trading concern HVA and stationed at the palm oil estate Dolok Sinumbah and the fibre estate Laras, respectively. They saw senior Indonesian staff members increasingly taking over responsibilities in day-to-day management and were both refused re-entry permits due to their involvement in military actions against the Republic in the late 1940s. The third man was A. Rosemer, born in Malang (East Java) and from 1948 an employee of the oil giant BPM. He had Indonesian citizenship and was promoted to the rank of personnel manager, first in Cepu near Surabaya, later in Balikpapan (East Kalimantan). He personified the process of *Indonesianisasi* taking place in Dutch companies at the time. As a locally recruited employee, he was paid less than his expatriate subordinate.[1]

The commitment of Dutch enterprises to *Indonesianisasi* was laid down in the Finec Agreement. Under article 12 (d), Dutch employers were obliged to make efforts (*hebben mede te werken aan*) in 'including qualified Indonesians in management and staff (also boards of directors) of the companies as soon as possible' (*zo spoedig mogelijk opnemen van daartoe geschikte Indonesiërs in de leiding (ook directies) en staven der bedrijven*). The aim was that after 'a reasonable time' (*zekere redelijke termijn*), the majority of the supervisory staff of the firms would consist of Indonesian citizens (*het overwegende deel van het leidend stafpersoneel der bedrijven te doen bestaan uit Indonesische staatsburgers*) (*Ronde Tafel Conferentie* 1949:24-9, 1950). To representatives of Dutch business interests this may have appeared a cheap concession in view of the far-reaching guarantees given by the Indonesian government to Dutch firms, making it possible for

1 Steijlen 2002:218-9, 305-6, 576-8. Original interviews in: KITLV, Leiden: Oral History Project Collection, 1271, 1372, 1713.

them to continue operating in Indonesia. The agreement did not include any timetable for *Indonesianisasi* nor did it specify at what level more Indonesians should be put to work. It was widely recognized that the acute shortage of Indonesians with formal management skills stood in the way of too speedy an implementation. In September 1950 Prime Minister Natsir publicly urged foreign firms to create opportunities for training Indonesian managers and supervisors (Donnithorne 1954:27).

This chapter discusses the process of *Indonesianisasi* in the narrow sense of the term, the promotion of Indonesians to management and supervisory positions in firms with foreign, in particular Dutch, ownership. This process is examined in the wider context of how foreign enterprises, particularly Dutch firms, operated in early independent Indonesia. First, an overview is given of the changing conditions in the operational environment after the transfer of sovereignty. This is followed by the adjustment strategies adopted by private foreign-owned companies. The record in the implementation of *Indonesianisasi* is reviewed through case studies representing two broad categories of business, differentiated by the leverage they were able to apply in their dealings with the Indonesian authorities. The first category consists of oligopolies, leading companies dominating their branch of industry. Such firms had a high profile and could to a great extent set their own priorities. The second category consists of companies operating in highly competitive sectors, in which the individual company had less bargaining power but was also less conspicuous than an oligopoly. The final section adds a comparative perspective by paying attention to achievements at non-Dutch foreign firms.

Changing conditions

On occasion Dutch managers found it difficult to know what attitude to adopt under the rapidly changing political constellations in newly independent Indonesia. There were embarrassing incidents. At the Handelsbank, the former Nederlandsch-Indische Handelsbank, the management refused to hoist the Indonesian flag alongside the Dutch flag even after sovereignty had been transferred. The bank's director, G.A. Dunlop, had openly supported military intervention in the late 1940s and remained convinced that it would take a long time for Indonesians to acquire sufficient skills to run their own economy (Baudet and Fennema et al. 1983:172). The tone was very different in statements issued by brokers Van der Werff and Hubrecht at the Amsterdam Stock Exchange. In the mid-1950s these brokers assured Indonesians that Dutch companies were not asking for any special favours, merely the right to transfer profits in order to satisfy shareholders at home (*Antara* 29 August 1955). Such contradictory Dutch attitudes were symptomatic of a bilateral economic relationship which came under increasing strain.

The time was long gone when the Netherlands formed the main market for Indonesian exports or was the foremost supplier of imports to Indonesia. Although still ranking first among Indonesia's trading partners in Europe, in the early and mid-1950s the Netherlands received no more than one-fifth of Indonesia's exports, while supplying only one-eighth of Indonesia's imports (Appendix 2, Table 6). Statistics on Dutch private investment in Indonesia during the 1950s are scarce and offer little more than an extrapolation from more robust pre-war data which had put the accumulated total at 2.25 billion guilders ($ 900 million), to which must be added post-war costs of reconstruction of at least 450 million guilders ($ 200 million) (Creutzberg 1977:21; Lindblad 1998:14). Estimates of the total value of Dutch corporate assets in Indonesia in 1950 range from 3.15 billion to 3.5 billion guilders ($ 1.26-1.4 billion) (Meijer 1994:648; Fennema and Rhijnsburger 1981:85). In early 1954 the Indonesian government submitted a memorandum to Parliament citing a lower total, 2.5 billion guilders, which almost coincided with the figure from the late-colonial period (*Times of Indonesia* 21 February 1954; Baudet and Fasseur 1977:334).

Colonial Indonesia was a rich source of income for private Dutch capital, both through direct ownership of the production means and through participation in Indonesia's foreign trade, whether with the Netherlands or with third countries. The later Nobel Prize Laureate Jan Tinbergen and his associate at the Centraal Bureau voor Statistiek (CBS, Central Bureau of Statistics) in The Hague, J.B.D. Derksen, estimated that colonial Indonesia directly contributed 8 per cent of Dutch GDP in the late 1930s, rising to 14 per cent if including secondary multiplier effects accruing from the spending of primary income (Derksen and Tinbergen 1945). This figure is high by any international comparison. It came in handy as an argument for both Dutch policy makers mobilizing public support for military intervention and for Indonesian nationalists keen to discredit Dutch strategies in the eyes of the international community (Sumitro Djojohadikusumo 1946; Maddison 1989:24; Van den Doel 2000 271).

Indonesia's contribution to Dutch national income declined sharply during the Indonesian Revolution; it was estimated to be only 2-3 per cent at the time of the transfer of sovereignty. This percentage began to rise as soon as reconstruction was completed. It neared 4.5 per cent in 1950-1952, but fell to 3 per cent in the mid-1950s, and by 1956 and 1957 amounted to only 2 per cent. Two-fifths of this income flow stemmed from trading activities, while transfers of profits accounted for about one-eighth (Baudet and Wijers 1976; Meijer 1994:649).

In 1952 there were still approximately 120,000 Europeans living in Indonesia, 107,000 of whom were Dutch citizens, mostly of mixed Indo-European origin. The Indonesian civil service employed 7,000 Dutchmen and the exodus of Dutch supervisory and technical staff in the Indonesian merchant fleet had

Employees at the BPM oil refinery in Plaju, South Sumatra, in 1948 (KITLV 41495)

barely begun.[2] A sizeable group of Dutchmen occupied key positions in private firms and the Dutch language was widely used. Nevertheless, Dutch had been abandoned as a language of instruction in primary schools in 1950, in secondary education in 1951, and at universities in 1952, when the Dutch professors were required to start teaching in English. A foundation for preserving Dutch language education in Indonesia, Stichting voor Nederlands Onderwijs in Indonesië, was established. It claimed that there were 92 schools in Indonesia using Dutch. Under an ordinance passed in the early 1950, notary acts had only to begin and end in Indonesian, while the body of the legal text could still be in Dutch.[3] A continued strong Dutch presence in Indonesia's economy and society thus formed the context in which the Sukarno administration decided to assert control over the nation's economy. Confrontations with foreign firms developed in two arenas in particular, those of property rights and labour relations.

At the Round Table Conference Hatta had promised that all Dutch properties seized were to be returned to their lawful owners. This took effect as of January 1950 but, according to Dutch observers, progress was 'disappointing'. Difficulties frequently arose as many estates had in fact been occupied by locals.[4] It was an operation of considerable size. East Java alone had 247 Dutch-owned estates which had to be restored to their owners, including 128 in the Besuki region as well as 81 around Malang, 16 in Kediri, and another 16 in the vicinity of Surabaya.[5] Long-winded disputes often stood in the way of the resumption of production at full capacity, and conflicts over property rights could drag on for years.

One highly publicized case concerned the BPM oil installations in Pangkalan Brandan, North Sumatra, the oldest installations of their kind in Indonesia, having been built by the newly founded Royal Dutch in the 1890s. Upon the withdrawal of the Japanese army in 1945, the labourers had taken command of the installations. The Republican government declined to return the property on the grounds that BPM had forfeited its rights when it had ordered the installations to be destroyed in the face of the approaching Japanese army in 1942. Operations had been resumed and were now handled by the Indonesian military, albeit at a level far below full capacity. Following the RTC Agreements, BPM demanded the installations back. The Natsir and Sukiman cabinets were both reluctant to take a final decision. In July 1952 the

2 ANRI, Jakarta: Sekretariat Negara 781, 23-6-1951; Thompson and Adloff 1955:141-2; Meijer 1994:655.

3 Bank Indonesia, Jakarta: DJB 131, 18-8-1951, 3351. See also Groeneboer 1998:291.

4 Bank Mandiri, Jakarta: Jaarverslag NHM Factorij 1950-51, II:7.

5 Personal communication from Tri Chandra Apriyanto, MA, at the University of Jember, East Java.

Panitia Pertambangan Negara (Committee on State Mining Affairs) advised Sumanang, Minister of Economic Affairs in the Wilopo cabinet, to return the installations to BPM. There was an outcry of indignation in Parliament and the advice was not acted upon (*Berita Indonesia* 21 July 1952).

The matter became a real dilemma for the next cabinet. Nationalization might work as a precedent and scare off foreign investors, but the return to the Dutch of an installation already being operated by Indonesians would be seen as a political defeat.[6] In late 1954 an agreement was reached between BPM and Masjumi, dominant partner in the Harahap coalition. The oil fields and refinery were to be returned, but the current supervisor Djohan was to be retained as superintendent (*Harian Rakjat* 22 January 1955). In the event, nothing much happened. In May 1956 the second Ali Sastroamidjojo cabinet decided not to restore the BPM concession but to prolong its status as an army-controlled enterprise called Tambang Minjak Sumatera Utara (North Sumatra Oil). In charge of operations was Colonel (later General) Ibnu Sutowo, who decades later was to acquire fame and notoriety as President-Director of the state oil company Pertamina (*Waspada* 9 May 1956). In October 1957 the Pangkalan Brandan unit became the core production facility for Pertamina's forerunner Permina (Bartlett 1972; Purnawan Basundoro 2004:184).

One of the most extraordinary conflicts over return of property concerned the sugar estates Tjolo Madu and Tasik Madu that had previously belonged to the Mangkunegaran court in Solo. In September 1949 a Foundation for the Properties of the Mangkunegara Realm (Fonds van Eigendommen van het Mangkoenegorosche Rijk) was authorized by the returning Dutch government to claim two sugar estates that had been seized by the Republican government when the Mangkunegaran court sided with the Dutch during the Indonesian Revolution. The Indonesian government refused to return the property, local peasants boycotted the estates, and eventually, in 1952, a Presidential Decree nullified the claim altogether. The foundation requested Rp. 3.2 million in compensation, which was never paid (Wasino 2005:56).

Land occupation by local peasants became another problematic issue confronting Dutch-owned estates even after the restoration of property. During the Japanese occupation and the Indonesian Revolution, considerable tracts of land had been put to use by local inhabitants for housing and for growing their own food crops. Now, in the early 1950s, the local dwellers were reluctant to move.[7] Again, the issue turned into a dilemma for the government, even bringing down the Wilopo cabinet after a violent confrontation between locals

6 Bank Mandiri, Jakarta: Jaarverslag NHM Factorij 1953, I:43.

7 Whether or not such use of the land should be considered an unlawful act, especially when the land in question was not under cultivation, is a separate and very interesting question.

and police at Tanjung Morawa, North Sumatra (Stoler 1985:15). The government lent a sympathetic ear to the claims of locals that the land was theirs, but at the same time it was obliged to uphold the legal rights held by the foreign firms. Once more the government was extremely slow in formulating and pursuing an unambiguous policy in favour of the foreign owners of estates.

It was by no means a marginal matter. According to one estimate, of the 130,000 hectares of tobacco land restored to foreign owners in North Sumatra, 20,000 hectares or 15 per cent of the total had already become a 'a conglomeration of villages' (*perkampungan*) (*Antara* 13 April 1953). The total area of estate lands in North Sumatra in permanent use by local inhabitants neared 80,000 hectares in mid-1954 and rose to more than 120,000 hectares by the end of 1957 (GAPPERSU 1960:table xiii). This 50 per cent increase, even after the government had adopted an increasingly uncompromising attitude, reveals both how ineffective government policies were and how strong the conviction was on the part of the occupiers that they were entitled to the land. Such convictions were fuelled by massive popular support for the peasants. PKI in particular offered active support to land occupations by local peasants.

In November 1954 the latent conflict between locals and landowners came to a head in Kalisat in the northern part of Jember, East Java. Just as had happened in the Tanjung Morawa incident, locals were accused of illegally occupying and cultivating land on a Dutch-owned estate, Kotta Blater. Mass protests followed and some 340 peasants were arrested by the police upon the estate owner's request. The demonstrators were held in custody for only a couple of days, but a local court declared the protests unwarranted and illegal. During subsequent conflicts the local peasants of Jember received full support from PKI and from the peasants' union Barisan Tani Indonesia (BTI, Indonesian Peasant Front) (*Trompet Masjarakat* 30 November 1954, 24 December 1955).

The government kept threatening local land occupiers with severe punishment, including fines and prison sentences of up to six months, but to little avail. Firm policies in Jakarta were undermined by vehement opposition from various quarters, including the PNI chapter in North Sumatra, the region most affected (*Waspada* 2 October 1956). Meanwhile, negotiations with estate owners continued and in September 1957 an agreement was reached. The estates agreed to release land not considered essential to profitable operations in return for a consistent enforcement of existing regulations (Pelzer 1982:165-6).

The second arena of confrontation with foreign firms concerned labour relations. Trade union activity intensified and the unions grew increasingly militant after the transfer of sovereignty. The trade union Sarikat Buruh Perkebunan Indonesia (Sarbupri, Union of Indonesian Estate Workers) regularly called strike actions, particularly at foreign-owned companies. Several long strikes in 1950 involved almost half a million workers; production losses attributable to labour unrest in that year alone were estimated at 216 million guilders ($ 90 million). One director at the central bank suggested, strictly in private, that the Dutch owners should for the time being hand over the operation of their estates to the government, but his associates labelled such an opinion 'mortally dangerous' (*levensgevaarlijk*).[8]

Strike activity ebbed and flowed with peaks at the national level in 1950, 1951, 1953, and from 1955 (Appendix 4). North Sumatra, a stronghold of Dutch corporate power, showed a different pattern, with a steady increase in labour unrest up until December 1956, when martial law was imposed after the abortive rebellion led by Colonel Simbolon.[9] Most labour disputes as well as the largest number of workers involved were in manufacturing, accounting for 40 per cent or more of the total, whereas about one-third of the disputes occurred in agriculture. Manufacturing was the sector with the highest proportion of skilled labour and the highest degree of trade unionism. This is where labour disputes that aimed to improve material conditions for its members were fought. The sudden eruption of strike activity reflected the urgency for economic decolonization once political independence had been internationally acknowledged.

Strikes in the region of Central Java during one single year illustrate the intensity of labour activism shortly after the transfer of sovereignty. In 1951 Central Java registered seventeen labour conflicts. The largest one took place in January in the port of Semarang, where 6,000 workers went on strike for ten days demanding higher wages. Three strikes involved more than 3,000 workers each. Two of them occurred in Solo in March and were interrelated. Workers at the cigarette factory Perperi walked out in solidarity with striking labourers in two adjacent factories, Menara and Lestari. In October 1951 strikes hit a number of estates in the region with workers demanding wage rises in accordance with an agreement reached between Sarbupri and the Dutch employers' organization, Algemeen Landbouw Syndicaat (ALS, General Agricultural Syndicate). Among labour conflicts of smaller dimensions, eight out of thirteen were in manufacturing, while three were in firms with ethnic Chinese owners, the Tiong Hwan soap factory, the cigarette factory Poo Hien, and the copra oil refinery of the Kwee Seng concern. Only one

8 Bank Indonesia, Jakarta: DJB 3352, no. 30-1.

9 The extraordinary discrepancies in the number of strikes and working days lost in North Sumatra, exceeding corresponding figures for the entire country, testify to the lack of reliability of these statistics. The Department of Labour, from which Bank Indonesia obtained national data, counted fewer strikes and fewer working days lost than the employers in North Sumatra did. The latter were likely to have applied a more liberal definition of what constituted a strike. Figures which are obvious underestimates have been placed in brackets in the table.

conflict was directed at a recognizably Dutch owner, the trading firm Crone, which decided to close down its pineapple-fibre factory Mentotulakan in Wonogiri near Yogyakarta, only to be met with demands from laid-off workers for additional pay.[10]

The main board of mediation, Panitia Penjelesaian Perselisihan Perburuhan – Pusat (P4P, Central Committee for Resolving Labour Conflicts), grew increasingly powerful. In February 1953 alone P4P made decisions in conflicts about dismissals at the American oil company Stanvac, about working hours at the huge Goodyear estate Wingfoot, and about relocation costs of workers whose contracts had expired at HVA estates. In July a large-scale general strike was announced at KPM, due to Indonesian employees being angry about receiving smaller bonuses than their Dutch colleagues (*Antara* 14 February 1953; *Times of Indonesia* 7 July 1953). In mid-September of the same year, more than 300,000 estate labourers went on strike for three days to force employers to accept a Sarbupri demand for a wage rise of no less than 200 per cent. P4P attempted a compromise, which was not accepted by Sarbupri. The (first) Ali Sastroamidjojo cabinet then pleaded with the employers' organizations to accept an increase in wage rates of at least 20 per cent. The employers resigned themselves to the inevitable with no expectation that an increase in labour productivity would be sufficient to compensate them for the larger wage bill.[11] Scarcely had this conflict been settled when a large-scale strike erupted at KPM, where workers demanded a higher bonus for 1952. P4P ordered KPM to pay (*Harian Rakjat* 24 September 1953). Only a couple of months later, in January 1954, some 5,000 KPM workers went on strike for more than two weeks over rates of pay (*Antara* 1 February 1954).

In the early 1950s employers complained incessantly about the theft of products and equipment by workers, although this was a matter rarely mentioned in the formal negotiations with labour unions. One such occasion was in January 1954, when P4P was called in to resolve a conflict about wages on the rubber estates in Sumatra. In its arbitration, P4P requested the employers to accept a 25 per cent increase in wage rates but AVROS, representing the employers, retorted that production costs were excessively high due to the prevalence of theft on the estates. Sarbupri countered the argument by asserting that the AVROS statistics on theft were wrong (*Antara* 31 January 1954). When both sides in a conflict have a vested interest in portraying different realities, it becomes difficult for the historian to find out where the truth lies.

10 Data on strikes in the province of Central Java were collected in 2003 from local sources by Rumekso Setyadi, under supervision of Bambang Purwanto at the Pusat Studi Sosial dan Asia Tenggara of Gadjah Mada University in Yogyakarta.

11 Bank Indonesia, Jakarta: DJB 184, 30-9-1953.

Dutch corporate adjustment

In the early 1950s few involved in the Dutch companies would have denied that there was an urgent need to redefine business strategies. The Finec Agreement seemed to offer a basis for carrying on business as before, but such hopes were quickly dashed by changes in the operating environment. Conflicts about property rights and a successive deterioration in labour relations were compounded by the complex regulations on foreign exchange and restrictions on employing foreign staff. An assessment of capital committed, costs of maintenance, and risks of new investment had to be made. Several options were available, such as extracting as much profit as possible but investing elsewhere, retaining earnings which could not be remitted, undertaking limited new investment, or selling to private owners or to the Indonesian government. The option of setting up a joint venture with Indonesian partners was rarely chosen.[12] In reality, it boiled down to two choices. One was whether to look at the future from a short-term or a long-term perspective, the other was whether to adapt to changing circumstances in Indonesia or to look for new opportunities elsewhere.

The time horizon in a business strategy is most clearly revealed by dividend policies and fresh investment commitments. Transfers of profits to the Netherlands (excluding oil) totalled about 320 million guilders (Rp. 960 million) over the period 1950-1952. Assuming for the sake of argument that capital injections since 1945 had merely restored the pre-war value of corporate assets, this transfer of slightly more than 100 million guilders annually would correspond to a dividend payment of about 5 per cent, which was very similar to the results in the late-colonial period.[13] Individual firms invariably made the headlines whenever high dividend rates were reported. In 1952, for instance, the trading firm Hagemeijer paid out dividends of 9 per cent, while the Moluksche Handelsvennootschap (Moluccan Trading Company) and the estate company Deli-Atjeh offered their shareholders 8 per cent (*Harian Rakjat* 3 September 1953).

In the early 1950s the Indonesian government introduced a bewildering array of regulations on the remittances of profits. Profits of foreign firms were heavily taxed and authorizations for overseas transfers were usually slow in coming. In 1955 Minister of Finance Ong Eng Die ordered 40 per cent of the profits of foreign corporations to be blocked, awaiting permission to transfer funds overseas. On the whole, Dutch trading firms estimated that half of all profits generated in Indonesia actually ended up in the Netherlands, albeit

12 I am indebted to Howard Dick for this analysis.
13 Bank Indonesia, Jakarta: DJB 3235, 27-3-1952, 3352 no. 47A.

after considerable delays (*Merdeka* 12 February 1957; Jonker and Sluyterman 2000:267). As a result, substantial portions of profits were retained in Indonesia and ploughed back into the businesses where they were generated. In 1952, for instance, NHM sought official permission to extend a loan of Rp. 19 million for constructing the new palm oil factory of the Serdang Cultuur-Maatschappij (Serdang Cultivation Company) in North Sumatra, claiming that non-transferred profits were available for repayment of the loan.[14]

Direct transfers to the Netherlands by private Dutch companies included profits, dividend, and interest payments, as well as contributions to pension funds and employee savings funds. The aggregate approached Rp. 1.1 billion in 1953 but declined to Rp. 840 million in 1954. For 1955 Dutch calculations gave a sum total of Rp. 810 million (270 million guilders), whereas the Indonesian authorities quoted a higher figure, Rp. 970 million. Differences between the estimates of profit transfers became larger still in 1956 and 1957, as Dutch calculations showed a decline to Rp. 500 million while the Indonesian press reported twice that amount (*Antara* 6 March and 4 May 1956, 9 December 1957; Meijer 1994:649). Wherever the truth may lie, transfers of profits and related funds were impressive, considering the restrictions imposed by the Indonesian authorities.

Substantial profit remittances reflected a preference among Dutch corporations for a short-term horizon in planning operations in Indonesia compared to the situation in the late-colonial era (Lindblad 1996a:223-4). Direct transfers to the Netherlands by private Dutch firms over the period 1950-1957 added up to almost 2.4 billion guilders. This amount exceeded incoming flows of fresh investment. Estimates of such flows in the literature for the years 1950-1957 range from 710 million to 1.5 billion guilders. The former figure includes a sizeable proportion of the expenditure required for reconstruction, and the latter is likely to be too high (Creutzberg 1977:21; Van der Zwaag 1991:288; Meijer 1994:497). High priority was given to immediate gains derived from the boom in the Indonesian export economy, rather than investing in future profit-generating capacity.

Most Dutch firms in Indonesia followed a strategy of accommodation despite the continued deterioration of working conditions. Although emotional ties were undeniable, the Dutch company owners and managers remained rational decision makers. Three reasons have been advanced in the Dutch language literature to explain why Dutch companies so stubbornly insisted on accommodation. The first was the lack of viable alternatives outside Indonesia. The second was the undeniably great potential of the Indonesian economy. The third, and possibly decisive, reason was the widely held conviction that

14 ANRI, Jakarta: Kementerian Keuangan 418, 30-4-1953.

Dutch management was indispensable to Indonesia and likely to remain so for a long time to come (Sluyterman 2003:218).

However, the preference for accommodation did not preclude attempts to find new fields of operations outside Indonesia. In the late 1940s trading houses such as Borsumij and Hagemeijer were already setting up branch offices in Singapore, and Internatio explored the Chinese market. Lindeteves established a subsidiary in Africa, the Nieuwe Afrikaanse Handelsvennootschap (New African Trading Company). Internatio, Borsumij, and Hagemeijer all tried out ventures in East Africa or the Belgian Congo, Jacobson van den Berg went to Mozambique, Geo. Wehry to Ghana. HVA tried, in vain, to copy the success of the Java sugar industry on the dry soils of Ethiopia. Others experimented with operations in Latin America. Most incurred heavy losses. The experience gained in a tropical country like Indonesia did not readily lend itself to emulation elsewhere (*Antara* 8 April 1954; Baudet and Fennema et al. 1983:153-6, 163-4; Goedkoop 1990; Jonker and Sluyterman 2000:273-81; Sluyterman 2003:220-1).

In October 1956, less than fifteen months before the take-over of Dutch enterprises, the directors of the trading concern Internatio admitted that the situation in Indonesia was becoming almost untenable and that it was 'increasingly difficult for Dutch firms to stay afloat' (*het wordt voor de Nederlandse ondernemer steeds moeilijker zich te handhaven*). Nevertheless, the directors assured trustees, 'we certainly fulfil functions here which are still useful, important and hopefully also profitable' (*wij vervullen er bepaaldelijk nog nuttige, belangrijke, en naar wij hopen ook lucratieve functies*) (Jonker and Sluyterman 2000:269; Sluyterman 2003:218-9; Van de Kerkhof 2005a:199). Their firm belief in a lasting commitment to operations in Indonesia compelled company directors and managers to favour accommodation.

Nevertheless, alongside accommodation, whether or not accompanied by trial investment projects elsewhere, there was always the exit strategy. Some Dutch firms quietly gave up altogether and sold off their property. In 1952 one estate in five in Java was Chinese-owned, usually acquired from departing Dutch owners (Anspach 1969:182). By 1956 180 estates in North Sumatra were occupied by new owners. In early August 1956 the strongly nationalist Madjelis Usaha Veteran Indonesia (Muvi, Advisory Council for Indonesian Veterans' Affairs) suspected that most of these estates had not been acquired by indigenous Indonesians and requested the government to look into the matter. As it happened, the national congress of economists, KENSI, met in Surabaya the same week. One delegate at the meeting proposed that the government should nullify all estate transactions which had not ended up in the possession of 'national businessmen' (*ternjata tidak didjatuh ke tangan pengusaha2 nasional*). The Minister of Communications, Suchjar Tedjasukmana, present in Surabaya, responded enthusiastically. He judged it a 'very good idea' (*Antara* 9 August 1956; *Waspada* 11 August 1956). A couple of months later, in late 1956, another thirty foreign-owned plantations were put up for sale and in 1957 the country's largest single estate, the Pamanukan and Ciasem Lands in West Java, covering 47,000 hectares, was offered on the market for Rp. 90 million (*Antara* 19 November 1956, 12 October 1957).

Meanwhile, the political diplomacy with the one-time colonial power had deteriorated, primarily as a result of the unresolved dispute about the future of the western part of New Guinea (later Irian Jaya, now Papua). There was an increasing appreciation among Dutch businessmen in Indonesia that their interests were not necessarily best served by the Dutch official policy towards Indonesia. Contacts were discreetly made between a group of leading Dutch businessmen around Unilever's top executive, Paul Rijkens, and President Sukarno to reach a secret understanding outside of the negotiations with the Dutch government (Meijer 1994:553-4). Concrete results failed to materialize, but the initiative as such is illustrative of the basic strategy of accommodation chosen by Dutch firms in Indonesia.

Where a strategy of accommodation was perceived to be born of commitment or the conviction of being indispensable, one would expect to find efforts in the direction of *Indonesianisasi* in the sense of promoting Indonesians to higher positions. However, Dutch managers allegedly had to stay on due to the lack of qualified Indonesians to take over. One would also expect the preparation of Indonesian staff for higher positions to be adopted as an integral part of accommodation, but often this did not happen. In the final analysis, it was down to the individual accommodating Dutch firm to decide whether or not to include *Indonesianisasi* among its chief priorities.

The record of oligopolists

In August 1950 President Sukarno received a three-man delegation from the oil company BPM. They were H. Bloemgarten, Director of Royal Dutch, K. Scholtens, Acting Director for BPM in Indonesia, and the high-ranking Javanese staff member K.R.T. Notonegoro. It was a pleasant conversation and Sukarno expressed the hope that BPM would undertake serious efforts to encourage *Indonesianisasi*. Five and a half years later, in February 1956, a BPM delegation was again received at the presidential place. Now it was concluded that *Indonesianisasi* at BPM 'could be expected to continue to develop apace' (*dapat diharapkan akan berkembang selandjutnya dengan baik*). In July 1956 Notonegoro gave a presentation to the assembled press at the Djakarta Club in the capital's downtown business district. He elaborated on BPM's achievements. The company's management and supervisory staff consisted of 2,200 personnel, or 10 per cent of the total labour force. The staff was divided into three categories of employees: (1) foreign staff, (2) local Indonesian staff, and (3) 'local foreign' staff, as ethnic Chinese were euphemistically labelled. Since 1949 the share of category (1) had fallen from 60 to 39 per cent and that of category (3) from 35 to 11 per cent. The big gains were made by the indigenous Indonesian group, whose share climbed from 5 to 50 per cent. A complete replacement of expatriates by Indonesian nationals was expected to take place within the next ten years (*Antara* 19 September, 31 October 1956; *Dunia Minjak* 1956-57:no. 7).

This section focuses on how *Indonesianisasi* was implemented in some selected Dutch oligopolists enjoying a dominant position in their industry. Such companies usually maintained a high profile in Indonesian society, with a good public image and considerable leverage in dealings with the authorities. Besides the highly significant oil sector, examples have been selected from finance and tin-mining.

It was no coincidence that BPM sought maximum publicity for its achievements in *Indonesianisasi* in 1956. Its 'Let Alone' agreement had just expired and negotiations for renewal were in progress. The Indonesian government was prepared to extend the oil company's privileges on condition that BPM enhance its 'national' character by appointing an Indonesian executive director and by moving the head office from The Hague to Jakarta. Plans for new investment worth Rp. 300 million ($ 25 million) were announced.[15] The special understanding with the Indonesian government, as laid down in the 'Let Alone' agreement, permitted BPM to adopt a more long-term perspective than most other Dutch firms. It effectively endorsed investment in *Indonesianisasi* of the company staff.

Education and training lay at the core of BPM's efforts. A secondary school for technical staff in the oil sector, Pendidikan Ahli Minjak (PAM, School for Oil Professionals), in Prabumulih, South Sumatra, was opened in 1950, offering a five-year curriculum. In 1955 it was followed by a similar institution in nearby Plaju. The cumulative number of graduates from the two PAMs rose from 77 in 1956 to 147 in 1958 and 231 in 1960, of whom 90 per cent found employment with BPM. In addition, six-month training courses were offered yearly in Bandung from 1953. The groups were small, usually twelve participants, and were invariably ethnically balanced, including both indigenous and ethnic Chinese as well as Indo-Europeans. BPM also awarded scholarships for university study in Jakarta, Yogyakarta, and Bandung, on occasion even in the Netherlands (*Dunia Minjak* 1953-54, 1956-57; *Antara* 18 October 1957, 28 September 1958, 17 February 1960). Although outlays on education were modest compared with the company's huge turnover, it is clear that

15 Bank Mandiri, Jakarta: Jaarverslag NHM Factorij 1954, I:76; *Antara* 25-10-1956, 18-11-1956.

BPM went a great deal further to implement *Indonesianisasi* than most other Dutch companies.

BPM cooperated directly with the Indonesian government in the joint venture Nederlandsch-Indische Aardolie-Maatschappij (NIAM, Netherlands Indies Petroleum Company) which operated oil fields in Jambi, southern Sumatra, and on the island of Bunyu off the northeast coast of Kalimantan. At the transfer of sovereignty, the 50 per cent of equity held by the Netherlands Indies government automatically passed into the hands of the Indonesian government. Yet to all intents and purposes, NIAM was run as an integral part of BPM. The ethnic composition of the top management was gradually altered in a way similar to what was happening at the nation's central bank. Moh. Sediono, Secretary-General in the Department of Economic Affairs, represented the Indonesian government, and the Board of Trustees consisted of three Indonesians, including chairman Muchjidin Affandi, and two Dutchmen (*Antara* 30 October 1957). There was a solid Indonesian majority in top policy making, but responsibility for day-to-day management rested with the Dutch executives in BPM.

In August 1956 BPM requested an extension of the NIAM concession in Jambi that was due to expire in 1960. The government responded by demanding that NIAM become fully independent of BPM. Discussions in Parliament gravitated towards nationalization, but doubts were voiced as to whether there were enough Indonesian technical staff to continue operations without BPM. Eventually, in 1958, NIAM was renamed Perusahaan Minjak Indonesia (Permindo, Indonesian Oil Enterprise), but the directors feared that production would fall dramatically if the BPM staff was 'prematurely withdrawn' (*djika 'ontijdig' dikeluarkan*).[16] The Indonesian technical staff were 'still too young and not yet ready to lead operations' (*masih terlalu mudah belum siap memimpin usaha2*). At the time NIAM/Permindo was exceptional among Dutch firms in Indonesia in the sense that *Indonesianisasi* and nationalization occurred simultaneously.

Foreign banking in Indonesia was characterized by an oligopoly resembling that in the oil industry. A traditionally strong Dutch predominance coexisted with competition from a handful of foreign players. The three private Dutch banks – NHM, Handelsbank, and Escompto – were all larger than the four non-Dutch foreign banks – the Chartered Bank, HSBC, the Bank of China, and the Overseas Chinese Bank. The Dutch lead was especially pronounced in the handling of international transactions.

NHM was the largest of the three and had the longest standing, with a history going back to 1824. It was known for its close cooperation with the

16 ANRI, Jakarta: Muh. Yamin 346; *Antara* 30-8-1956, 17-9-1956; Bartlett 1972:120.

Dutch colonial government in the past, including direct participation in the running of the Cultivation System in the nineteenth century, as well as for its pragmatism in adjusting to changing conditions in the post-colonial situation. The Handelsbank, ranking second, was among the staunchest supporters of the restoration of Dutch colonial rule, a standpoint which was modified in the course of the 1950s as the directors realized the necessity of accommodation (Baudet and Fennema et al. 1983:171-2). The smallest of the three, Escompto, did occasionally attract public attention. In 1956, for instance, it announced its intention to pay out 25 per cent dividends to shareholders in the Netherlands, which was immediately construed as capital flight in response to the unilateral Indonesian repeal of the Finec Agreement. Escompto's plan was 'to remove its capital from Indonesia quickly' (*dengan tjepat melarikan modalnja dari Indonesia*). It seems that *Indonesianisasi* of the staff at the Dutch-owned banks got underway only after the Indonesian government took over operations in 1958 (*Antara* 8 June 1956; *Suluh Indonesia* 7 February 1958).

The NHM directors in the palatial bank building opposite the Kota railway station in Jakarta usually expressed a cautious optimism about continued operations in Indonesia. Dutch banking skills were believed to be indispensable. The directors professed a willingness to maintain and develop good personal contacts with the Indonesian authorities. An agreement about the transfer of profits to the Netherlands was reached at an early stage and from 1950 NHM initiated expansion, both in Indonesia and elsewhere. The bank was critical of the official Dutch policy towards New Guinea, and Indonesia's repeal of the Finec Agreement came as no surprise (Baudet and Fennema et al. 1983:170-1).

NHM reaped substantial profits from its banking business in Indonesia. Accumulated profits over the four-year period 1951-1954 amounted to Rp. 77 million, of which Rp. 56 million (72 per cent) was transferred to the Netherlands, apparently without much difficulty. Profitability remained high in 1955 and 1956, but bureaucratic obstacles delayed remittances. The expansion of activities required the recruitment of new staff. During 1951-1954 NHM appointed 77 new members to its banking staff, but only fourteen of these were Indonesians, with at least one being ethnic Chinese. The pattern was repeated in 1956, when thirteen of the fifteen newly recruited staff members were Dutchmen. The slow pace of *Indonesianisasi* can be attributed to the shortage of formal banking skills among Indonesian applicants, which in turn may also have made it easier to obtain the necessary entry permits for Dutch recruits. All nineteen NHM branch offices in Indonesia were headed by Dutchmen. Decisive changes did not take place until a late stage. The share of Indonesian nationals in the management rose from 16 per cent (23 out of 142 people) in 1956 to 44 per cent (47 out of 106) in 1958. By that time, however, the conclusion of NHM's operations in Indonesia was in sight.[17]

Our final case study from the realm of oligopolists is drawn from tin-mining. Here the configuration was akin to the arrangement at NIAM. The two main producers were the state-owned Bangka Tin Mines and the Gemeenschappelijke Mijnbouwmaatschappijen 'Billiton' (GMB, Consolidated Mining Companies of Billiton) located off the eastern coast of southern Sumatra on the islands of Bangka and Belitung, respectively. GMB was a joint venture between a private Dutch corporation, Billiton, and the Indonesian government, which had inherited 62.5 per cent of equity from the Dutch colonial government. By virtue of contracts concluded in 1948, Billiton was entrusted with the management of the mines of both GMB and Bangka.

Management at Billiton initiated changes in operating conditions at an early stage. The training of technical personnel was set up at Belitung, and by 1950 the labour force consisted of 69 per cent indigenous Indonesians compared to 58 per cent in 1947. This increase was achieved largely at the expense of ethnic Chinese, and scarcely affected the higher echelons of the management hierarchy. Yet it was hailed by Billiton as a sensible measure that would have been taken even in the absence of official pressure. A different kind of change in personnel was taking place at Bangka. Civil servants were increasingly replaced by Billiton staff in an attempt by Billiton to appear indispensable when its management contract came up for renewal in 1953 (Sutter 1959:846; Van de Kerkhof 2005c:128-9).

Indonesian opposition to prolonged exclusively Dutch control over the management of the country's main tin mines was increasing. In August 1951 Teuku Hasan, chairman of the Parliamentary Committee for Trade and Industry, urged that a thorough investigation of problems and prospects in the mining industry be undertaken to form the basis for decision making about Billiton's management contracts after their expiry in 1953. Government officials privately assured the Billiton directors that the Dutch firm could count on continued responsibility for management of the mines, provided the Indonesian character of the firm was given more emphasis. Tedious and difficult negotiations followed. In September 1952 PNI turned against plans for continued Dutch management. At the very last moment, on 28 February 1953, a compromise was reached: Billiton withdrew from the management of the Bangka mines but obtained a five-year extension of the contract for GMB (Sutter 1959:847; Van de Kerkhof 2005c:132-5).

The rather passive role played by the Indonesian partner in the joint venture raised the hackles of PNI economic nationalists, in particular Minister

17 Bank Mandiri, Jakarta: Jaarverslag NHM Factorij 1950-51, 1952, 1953, 1954, 1956, letter about PP 22/1958, 8-7-1958.

of Economic Affairs Iskaq Tjokrohadisurjo. In November 1953 he had two Dutchmen on the Board of Trustees of GMB replaced by Indonesians, thereby securing an Indonesian majority of three to two members on the board. In February 1954 he secretly instructed the Indonesian board members to take steps to strengthen government control at the expense of Billiton. To Billiton's dismay, the Indonesian chairman, Muchjidin Affandi, proved very active taking an interest in many management matters. Meanwhile, Iskaq continued to press for changes which would bring out the Indonesian character of the tin-mining corporation more strongly. In October 1954 Iskaq and Billiton came to an understanding. After the expiry of the management contract in 1958, Billiton was to provide technical assistance and execute day-to-day management in return for a full *Indonesianisasi* of GMB personnel within six years (*Antara* 19 November 1954; Sutter 1959:848-50; Van de Kerkhof 2005c:137-8).

Billiton went to considerable lengths in order to retain its control over the management of the tin mines. It was a policy of accommodation which would eventually require a more significant *Indonesianisasi* of the staff. Indonesian insistence on efforts in this direction during the negotiations in 1954 combined with the reported shortage of skilled staff after the departure of the Billiton supervisors in 1958 suggest that GMB's record was not particularly impressive. This is consistent with operating for short-term gain. Tin-mining was known to be highly profitable and dividend payments were lavish, for instance 20 per cent in 1954 and 15 per cent in 1955. Such payments could not fail to attract attention in the press, as did the charge levelled in May 1955 that 90 per cent of all new investment by Billiton was made outside Indonesia (*Antara* 16 May 1955 and 11 April 1956; Van de Kerkhof 2005c:143).

The record of major Dutch oligopolists in Indonesia in implementing *Indonesianisasi* varied: massive training at BPM, accommodation but little change in the balance of personnel at NHM, and high-level intervention at Billiton. All three had a strong bargaining position vis-à-vis the Indonesian government due to their leverage and the specialized skills needed to run operations. Each had a high profile and was expected to set an example for Dutch enterprise in general. Some responded to that challenge, others did not. Certainly the situation was markedly different for the many smaller Dutch enterprises in sectors such as trading and estate agriculture. These firms operated in a highly competitive environment and generally had less direct contact with the authorities. It is to their record that we now turn.

Achievements under pressure

The Finec Agreement was followed up by a gentlemen's agreement with Dutch business leaders that indigenous Indonesian employees would eventually make up 70 per cent of the total workforce. Nowhere was it clearly stated when this target had to be met or whether it also applied to higher management positions (Meijer 1994:352). Implementation was on a strictly voluntary basis and the Indonesian authorities had few means of enforcement. Achievements in *Indonesianisasi* among Dutch agricultural estates and trading firms reflected the juxtaposition of inducements from within the firm with continuous external pressure from the authorities taking a different tack to the one among the oligopolies. The strongest pressure of all was exerted within the Indonesian civil service itself, where numerous Dutchmen stayed on, even after the transfer of sovereignty.

Dutch employers often paid only lip service to the goal of *Indonesianisasi*; in practice they were reluctant to promote Indonesian employees to higher-ranking management positions. The Indonesian government soon began looking for means to exert more pressure. One effective tool was the issuing of entry and work permits to expatriates from the Netherlands. In 1950 and 1951 Dutch nationals could still enter Indonesia freely and take a position with a Dutch company. In mid-1952, however, the government introduced strict immigration controls. Employers had to demonstrate that the vacancy could not be filled locally before the permission to recruit overseas would be granted. As a result the number of work permits issued to Dutchmen was drastically reduced. In 1953 the authorities issued 1,000 permits, which was clearly insufficient to replace departing Dutch employees and fill new vacancies (Meijer 1994:353). *Indonesianisasi* was becoming increasingly less voluntary.

Bottlenecks caused by strict immigration controls were aggravated by a declining willingness among qualified Dutch personnel to work in Indonesia. Long-term prospects in Indonesia were uncertain, whereas the domestic economy in the Netherlands had already embarked on a post-war path of sustained catch-up growth (Griffiths 1996:174-5). The trading firms Internatio and Hagemeijer tried to stem the exodus of qualified Dutch staff by offering a generous bonus, 25-33 per cent of salary, but to no avail (Jonker and Sluyterman 2000:267-8; Van de Kerkhof 2005b:193-4).

Indonesianisasi did gain ground but remained confined largely to the lower and middle echelons, as Dutch employers were reluctant to let control pass into Indonesian hands. They now encountered a different obstacle. It was increasingly difficult to find sufficiently qualified Indonesian applicants to fill vacancies in lower and middle management. Indonesians with formal education displayed a clear preference to work for the government rather than for a private Dutch firm (*Antara* 27 April 1957). Thus the Dutch employers found themselves dealing with one bottleneck after another.

The Dutch traders with the highest profile in Indonesia were the 'Big Five', specialized in import trading and the local distribution of consumer goods. Stiffening competition in trading coincided with pressure to speed up

Indonesianisasi within these companies. Replacing Dutch staff by Indonesians became a hallmark of accommodation. At Borsumij the Dutch staff was reduced by half, from 320 people in 1953 to 160 in 1957; the Indonesian staff was increased concomitantly (Jonker and Sluyterman 2000:268).

In the mid-1950s the situation at Internatio was typical of the industry at large. Unquestionably, doing business in Indonesia remained highly profitable. In 1955 profits pocketed in Indonesia more than compensated for losses incurred elsewhere. The rub was that transferring profits to the Netherlands was becoming increasingly problematic. Transfers fell sharply between 1952 and 1954, and an increasing proportion of profits was retained in Indonesia. Internatio used these funds to set up a vast distribution network embracing seventy agencies, most of them headed by an Indonesian employee (Van der Zwaag 1991:290; Jonker and Sluyterman 2000:269; Van de Kerkhof 2005b:197).

In 1954 Internatio created a separate category of personnel labelled 'Indonesian staff' (*staf Indonesië*), composed of locally recruited employees qualified to function at a level comparable to that of expatriate staff. The size of *staf Indonesië* increased from 86 in January 1956 to 97 in January 1957. Meanwhile, the number of expatriates declined from 186 to 163, resulting in the ratio of *staf Indonesië* to total expatriate staff rising from 46 to 60 per cent. However, 52 per cent of the *staf Indonesië* category consisted of ethnic Chinese. The rapid change in the ethnic composition of higher management was an impressive achievement according to Internatio's definition of *Indonesianisasi*, but not according to the definition preferred by the Indonesian government, whose officials tended to equate it with *pribumisasi*. Furthermore, in 1957 all top management positions at Internatio were still held by Dutchmen. Only two branch offices, in Bandung and in Cirebon, had Indonesian managers (Van de Kerkhof 2000b:194-7).

The 'Big Five' expected to be able to retain their leading position in Indonesian trading in the long run. The Benteng policy posed a weak threat that could easily be averted, and *Indonesianisasi* was inevitable anyway. Profits from the booming Indonesian economy contrasted starkly with the dismal results of halfhearted attempts at ventures outside Indonesia. A few examples will suffice to illustrate this. Lindeteves did not seem in the least discouraged by the Indonesian abrogation of the RTC Agreements in 1956, and Borsumij and Internatio tried to stay on in Indonesia even after their premises had been seized in December 1957 (Baudet and Fennema et al. 1983:162-3; Van de Kerkhof 2005a:202-3). Managers at the 'Big Five' were firmly convinced that Dutch know-how in trading was indispensable in Indonesia, possibly not realizing that trading skills were less scarce than the highly specialized skills required in the oil industry and in finance. Perceptions among managers unashamedly reflected a sense of superiority. Some Dutchmen may also have been lulled into complacency by the pleasant atmosphere characterizing informal contacts with senior Indonesian civil servants, who were fluent in Dutch and steeped in Dutch culture and custom.

Despite optimism and convivial talk, the 'Big Five' were viewed with great suspicion. They symbolized the colonial past and were known not to eschew unscrupulous business methods. In 1954 it was reported that the 'Big Five' shrewdly made use of the complex system of distributing foreign exchange through commissioned agents in order to circumvent the restrictions on access to currency needed in overseas transactions. Most of the foreign exchange allocated to Indonesian traders was in fact said to flow into foreign pockets, 'including those of [ethnic] Chinese' (*Berita Ekonomi* 1 August 1954).

In January 1957 a scandal erupted. The 'Big Five' were rumoured to have concluded a secret agreement among themselves to 'squeeze' (*gentjet*) domestic distributors through price manipulations. The idea was to raise prices steeply when goods were acquired by domestic distributors, then to flood the market with the very same products at vastly reduced prices, thereby forcing the domestic firms to seek assistance from the cash-rich foreign firms (*Antara* 5, 8 and 17 January 1957). Whatever the truth of the charge, it did little to improve the already tarnished image of the 'Big Five'.

Prospects for effective *Indonesianisasi* at the several hundred Dutch-owned agricultural estates in Java and Sumatra presented quite a different picture. The extreme pyramidal structure of the labour force focused attention on the top and intermediate levels of management and supervision, where expatriate predominance was likely to remain unchallenged. In 1953 Raden Imam Supeno, head of agricultural inspection in Central Java, listed a number of problems encountered in estate management, including an acute shortage of qualified and experienced supervisory personnel. Over and above this, he criticized owners for overzealous thriftiness (*krapgeldpolitiek*), and remarked that some supervisors could not accept that circumstances had changed since Indonesian independence (*Dunia Ekonomi* 19 December 1953). The general impression is that, at the time of the inspection tour in early 1953, *Indonesianisasi* had scarcely begun.

The estate company LMOD in East Java was quick to include an Indonesian on its senior staff as early as 1950, but the main function of former TNI officer Soedirman was to act as a go-between with the Indonesian authorities. In 1954 the company submitted a long list of Indonesian managers, which however failed to impress the authorities as it consisted primarily of foremen (*mandur*) and petty clerks. The local authorities promised leniency in immigration cases and successfully insisted on the recruitment of five Indonesians holding degrees from an agricultural college. This was the beginning of a more active policy of *Indonesianisasi*. By the time of the take-over of the LMOD estate in December 1957 it employed 171 workers, of whom 134 (78 per cent) were Indonesians.

Out of 35 management positions 26 were still occupied by Dutchmen (*Antara* 3 February 1958). LMOD's selective version of *Indonesianisasi* was probably typical of Dutch estate companies (Van der Zwaag 1991:290).

The Indonesian authorities exerted increasing pressure on Dutch planters to make serious efforts to bring about the *Indonesianisasi* of their senior staff. Nevertheless, they also realized that the scarcity of Indonesians with the necessary qualifications formed a real problem. In November 1950 two crash courses were launched with the purpose of creating a pool of suitable candidates, one in Bogor for upland plantations (coffee and tea) and the other in Pasuruan (East Java) for sugar factories.[18] Results were slow to materialize and failed to satisfy Indonesian representatives of the industry. The associations of sugar producers and traders, Persatuan Ahli Gula Indonesia (PAGI, Union of Indonesian Sugar Professionals) and Persatuan Pedagang Gula Indonesia (PPGI, Union of Indonesian Sugar Traders), kept urging the implementation of *Indonesianisasi* measures, to be carried out 'immediately' (*dengan segera*), as well as the establishment of more training facilities (*Antara* 7 April, 11 August, 29 December 1956).

Economic nationalists in Indonesia felt progress in *Indonesianisasi* was never fast enough, but to Dutch employers it was always too fast. The acceleration of the process during the years 1954-1957 met with criticism from very different quarters. In May 1957 the organization of rubber planters in Sumatra, AVROS, claimed that *Indonesianisasi* jeopardized the transfer of experience to a younger generation on the estates.[19] A couple of months previously, even former Vice-President Hatta had voiced a similar opinion, asserting that those appointed to management positions through *Indonesianisasi* 'mostly lacked the commensurate knowledge of economics' (*kebanjakan dengan tiada berpengetahuan ekonomi jang berpadanan*) (*Pikiran Rakjat* 7 February 1957). *Indonesianisasi* remained controversial.

The civil service was the sector of the economy where *Indonesianisasi* could most easily be implemented. Although the RTC Agreements had guaranteed the contracts and salaries of Dutchmen in the Indonesian civil service for several years, even after the transfer of sovereignty, working conditions were far from satisfactory. Dutch civil servants were bypassed by Indonesian superiors, who often received a lower salary, a situation not exactly conducive to good office relations. Dutch was replaced by Bahasa Indonesia as the official language of communication, adding to the frustrations of those Dutch civil servants without proficiency in Indonesian. Tensions involving Dutch expatriates in the Indonesian civil service became a recurrent theme of arbitration in

18 Bank Mandiri, Jakarta: Jaarverslag NHM Factorij 1950-51, II:7-8.

19 Bank Agro, Medan: AVROS, 24-5-1957.

deliberations between the High Commissioner of the Netherlands in Jakarta and the Indonesian authorities.[20]

As the entire government bureaucracy expanded rapidly the share of Dutchmen fell. On 1 January 1952, two full years after the transfer of sovereignty, the central government employed about 440,000 civil servants, of whom 7,110 (1.6 per cent) were identified as 'foreigners' (*bangsa asing*), most of them Dutch. One year later, on 1 January 1953, the overall number had risen to 533,000, but there were now no more than 3,170 foreigners in the civil service (0.6 per cent).[21]

Although a disproportionate number of Dutchmen were found in the echelons receiving the highest remuneration, this did not necessarily equate to influence in decision making. Perceptions about the presence of Dutchmen in the service of the Indonesian government were also changing. Indonesians asserted that they had unwillingly put up with a great number of Dutch civil servants and actually needed far fewer of them than expected. The Dutch side retorted by claiming that these arrangements had been explicitly requested by the Indonesian delegates at the Round Table Conference in 1949 (Meijer 1994:172). Dutch civil servants were likely to stay the longest in places where highly specialized skills were needed, notably in the Department of Economic Affairs, Bank Indonesia, and the foreign exchange agency, LAAPLN.

A comparative perspective

In a speech made in Palembang, in March 1952, Sumitro Djojohadikusumo stressed how essential the presence of foreign companies was to economic development in Indonesia. To get rid of foreign investors without having a viable alternative was tantamount to 'digging our own grave' (*menggali lobang kubur kita sendiri*), he claimed (*Berita Indonesia* 13 March 1952). A welcoming attitude, at least in principle, towards foreign direct investment characterized virtually all cabinets up until 1957, including the Wilopo cabinet which Sumitro was on the verge of joining as Minister of Finance at the time of his appearance in Palembang. This positive attitude applied in particular to foreign capital originating from countries other than the Netherlands. Although decolonization was not at stake in these cases, the government still insisted on *Indonesianisasi* of the personnel. The two processes, however, did not always go hand in hand, which is demonstrated by examples from leading non-Dutch foreign firms.[22]

20 ANRI, Jakarta: Muh. Yamin 72; Meijer 1994:171.

21 ANRI, Jakarta: Kabinet Presiden 63, 1479.

22 The Anglo-Dutch joint ventures BPM and Unilever both escaped nationalization after

Despite the good intentions of policy makers such as Sumitro, in the 1950s Indonesia was not an attractive place for foreign direct investment. Inflows of private long-term capital were small, the equivalent of 1.5 per cent of the trade surplus in 1953, or even negative, as in 1954. The sole exception to the rule was investment by the two American oil companies, Stanvac and Caltex. Their new investment commitments averaged Rp. 330 million in 1955 and 1956, although this barely offset outflows of capital from other foreign firms. Total American investment in Indonesia is estimated to have increased from $ 130 million in 1949 to $ 401 million in 1959. After the nationalization of Dutch firms in 1959 American companies, in particular those operating in oil and rubber, emerged as the predominant category of foreign direct investment in Indonesia (Bank Indonesia 1955:91, 1957:123; Gould 1961:79; Lindblad 1998:105-6).

Stanvac was identical to Standard Oil's renamed subsidiary 'Koloniale' in Indonesia and holder of a large concession near Palembang in South Sumatra. Although more than 80 per cent of its managers were Dutchmen, Stanvac was keen to promote its identity as an American enterprise. In 1948, when its 'Let Alone' agreement had just been concluded, the company had immediately sent three Indonesian employees to the United States for training. The Dutch Ambassador in Washington commented that it was 'the first time ever'.[23] Stanvac's 'Let Alone' agreement expired on 1 January 1952 and was replaced by a temporary arrangement granting Stanvac full access to revenues from sales of petroleum products on the world market. Negotiations began, to establish conditions under which continued operations in Indonesia would be safeguarded.

Two issues predominated the talks between Stanvac and the Indonesian government. One concerned ambitious plans for investment totalling some $ 70-80 million, including a vast enlargement of productive capacity at the refinery in Sungai Gerong in Palembang. The other issue was the *Indonesianisasi* of the personnel. A process of appointing Indonesian employees to technical and administrative positions had been initiated some years previously and new plans were geared towards the 'training of employees to take the highest positions possible' (*Antara* 6 September 1954; Anspach 1969:135). In the course of the negotiations, in July 1953, Minister of Finance Sumitro spoke of 'the great importance that I attach to the aspects of "human investment" by your company'. Sumitro wished to see an outline of Stanvac's programme for the

December 1957 because they were considered not to be Dutch companies. Both firms had excellent relations with the Indonesian authorities. BPM is discussed together with Dutch oligopolists, as 60 per cent of equity was owned by the 'Koninklijke' (Royal Dutch) and 40 per cent by Shell Transport and Trading. In contrast, Unilever was half owned by the British Lever Brothers, and is therefore discussed along with the non-Dutch foreign enterprises operating in Indonesia.

23 ANRI, Jakarta: Algemene Secretarie 912, 4-6-1948.

training of Indonesian nationals and a list of intended promotions to positions of 'responsibility and importance' before agreeing to fiscal incentives in support of continued operations and investment.[24] It is difficult to imagine a more direct link between commitment to *Indonesianisasi* and privileges granted to a foreign investor.

Stanvac was granted its new agreement, running for four years as of 1954; new investment was undertaken, and efforts to implement *Indonesianisasi* redoubled. By 1956 the total staff consisted of 763 people, of whom 40 per cent were American, 35 per cent Dutch, and 25 per cent Indonesian. Numerous Dutch employees had been replaced by Americans, a process possibly speeded up by difficulties in obtaining re-entry permits for Dutchmen. The impressive increase in the number of Indonesian nationals employed, including ethnic Chinese, from zero in 1948 to 182 in 1956, coincided with an enlargement of the total staff, from 547 to 763 (Bank Indonesia 1955:109; *Antara* 3 December 1956, 30 July 1957). This suggests that *Indonesianisasi* was achieved by a process resembling the creation of a separate category of employees, *staf Indonesië,* as happened at Internatio, discussed above.

Stanvac's management disguised their failure to replace Dutch managers with Indonesians 'with an avalanche of talk for the time being about training Indonesian employees' (*dengan diselimuti perkataan2 untuk sementara mendidik tenaga bangsa Indonesia*). Increasing numbers of Indonesians were sent to the United States for training, 22 in 1955-1956 and 42 in 1957-1958. Stanvac's investment in human resource development was considerable in comparison with most Dutch firms, with the possible exception of BPM. Yet such efforts apparently did little to change the system of rigid social segregation in the company compounds in Palembang, were Stanvac had two sports clubs, Pendopo Sosial Sport Club (PESOS) for Indonesian employees and Pendopo Rekreatie Club (PRC) for foreign staff. PESOS members complained that only PRC members were allowed to use the main swimming pool (*Antara* 30 March 1955, 31 January 1958).

The other large American oil company in Indonesia, Caltex Pacific, developed from the Nederlandsche Pacific Petroleum Maatschappij (Dutch Pacific Petroleum Company) and underwent rapid expansion in the early 1950s with the opening of the lucrative oil fields near Pekan Baru in Riau, Central Sumatra. The newly built refinery at Dumai on the Straits of Malacca soon became the largest in Indonesia, easily surpassing Sungai Gerong and Plaju at Palembang and Balikpapan in East Kalimantan. In 1957 Caltex accounted for 46 per cent of Indonesia's output of crude oil, compared to 34 per cent for Royal Dutch/Shell (BPM and NIAM combined), and 20 per cent for Stanvac.

24 ANRI, Jakarta: Kementerian Keuangan 351, 15-7-1953.

Caltex's 'Let Alone' agreement ran until 1 January 1954, so a renewal needed to be negotiated. Again, a general licence to pay for imports and retain export revenues was issued from LAAPLN in return for lofty investment plans and promises of more *Indonesianisasi* (Bank Indonesia 1955:109, 1959:251).

Caltex boasted an impressive record when it came to investment. During the development of the new oil fields in the early 1950s the firm was reported to have spent as much in one single year, $ 50 million in 1952-1953, as Stanvac had done during the six years since the conclusion of the Pacific War, 1945-1951. New plans in the mid-1950s included port facilities in Dumai worth $ 100 million and a paved road through the mountains over a distance of 170 km from the oil fields. The total labour force in Central Sumatra already approached 3,500, including circa 280 supervisors and managers. When Caltex started out in 1951 the number of Indonesian managers had been 'very small', but by 1955 this had climbed to 9 per cent (24 Indonesians out of 280). Between 1955 and 1958 the total managerial staff at Caltex nearly doubled, whereas the share of Indonesian nationals rose to one quarter, 140 out of almost 545 (*Antara* 3 September 1954, 23 October, 8 November 1956; Suwardi 2005). Again, *Indonesianisasi* was achieved primarily through a rapid expansion of the total staff, but here, in contrast to Stanvac, there were fewer Dutchmen needing to be replaced.

Unilever enjoyed a good reputation with the Indonesian authorities. The stigma of a colonial past did not cling to it, possibly because it had emerged in the embryonic manufacturing sector of Indonesia only towards the end of effective Dutch colonial rule, and perhaps also because the management downplayed the company's partially Dutch character, emphasizing that it was 50 per cent a British firm. The Indonesian government expected Unilever to bypass the 'Big Five' and rely on 'national traders' in the distribution of its merchandise. Over the years Indonesian traders were indeed responsible for an impressive proportion of distribution. Sales of soap will serve as an illustration. The share of Indonesian traders in the sales of the Sunlight soap, for instance, was 33 per cent in West Java, 40 per cent in Manado, and 90 per cent in Central Sumatra. At least half of the soap sales passed through Indonesian traders in Semarang, Medan, and Makassar. Nevertheless, Unilever refused to stop using the Dutch 'Big Five' as intermediaries, which was greeted with openly expressed dismay by Deputy Minister of Economic Affairs F.F. Umbas (*Antara* 27 August 1956, 12 March 1957; Fieldhouse 1978:300-2).

Unilever's favourable public image was boosted by a policy of *Indonesianisasi* initiated and vigorously pursued since 1950. Within six years forty managers out of a total of 160, or 25 per cent, were Indonesian nationals. The gradual promotion of Indonesian employees was underpinned by an active training programme involving sending several people each year to the company's headquarters in Europe. The management stated explicitly that 'we do not want Indonesian managers in name only, without any authority' (*kita tidak mengingini adanja anggota staf bangsa Indonesia jang namanja sadja anggota staf tetapi tidak mempunjai kekuasaan*). By the end of the 1950s the personnel newsletter was fully run by Indonesian employees, and an indigenous member of the top management team had already replaced the former Dutch director of marketing.[25]

Scattered examples in industrial production may be added from other non-Dutch foreign firms. The Belgian-owned cigarette manufacturer Faroka in Malang, whose plant dated from the early 1930s, started sending Indonesian employees to Europe to study production techniques soon after resuming operations in the late 1940s. Tyre producer Goodyear had 40 per cent of its foreign technical personnel replaced by Indonesians in the course of the 1950s (Gerungan 1952; Anspach 1969:135).

Although the evidence remains fragmentary, it does suggest that non-Dutch foreign firms did more to achieve *Indonesianisasi* than Dutch companies did. Some of this difference may be attributable to the greater role of oil companies among non-Dutch firms. Quite clearly, BPM, Stanvac, and Caltex have a better record than companies in other lines of production. Another reason for the difference relates to the legacy of colonialism. There was more mutual distrust and suspicion between Indonesians and Dutch firms than there was between Indonesians and foreign investors from other countries.

It is difficult to assess whether the Dutch companies did enough, since no standards or yardsticks were agreed upon. It remains a matter of subjective, almost intuitive, judgement. The prevalence of internal considerations of personnel management and the kinds of achievements seen in trading firms and agricultural estates suggest that *Indonesianisasi* was implemented highly selectively, in a way that reflected company priorities. The conclusion appears inescapable that the Dutch companies continuing to operate in independent Indonesia could have accomplished a great deal more than they did to replace foreign managers by Indonesians.

In the course of the 1950s the relationship between Indonesia and the Netherlands continuously deteriorated. Tensions lurked beneath the surface and were slowly building towards an eruption. The future had a more violent confrontation in store for the Dutch firms than demands for *Indonesianisasi* of personnel.

25 *Antara* 29-1--1957; *Suara Unilever* 1959. Active participation by Indonesians at all levels of management has remained a characteristic of human resource policy at Unilever. In the late 1990s an Indonesian woman served as executive director of PT Unilever Indonesia.

CHAPTER VIII

Take-over and nationalization

On a Dutch-owned coffee estate in Java administrator Haai gets up one morning and is completely taken aback when he goes outside. He sees 'all the walls and doors of his house smeared with a dirty fluid resembling tar. "Property of RI [Republik Indonesia]", the writing said, and "Dutch go home"' (*semua tembok dan pintu rumahnja ditjoret2 dengan tjairan kotor mirip ter. Milik RI begitulah bunji tulisannja, dan Belanda enjahlah*) (Jacob 1986:142). This fictional character, whose name by no coincidence translates as 'Shark', had in no way anticipated the expropriation of Dutch business by Indonesians. His story reflects the real-life experience of many Dutchmen in Indonesia in December 1957.

The events of December 1957 sparked off the final phase of economic decolonization, as remaining Dutch corporate assets were seized and subsequently nationalized. It was a dramatic and often painful transition that has left many questions unanswered. Were the Dutch caught unprepared because of a firm belief that they were an indispensable cog in the workings of the Indonesian economy? In other words, because so little had been achieved in terms of *Indonesianisasi* of Dutch enterprises? Did Indonesians revert to such draconian measures because progress had been so limited in gaining effective control over the country's economic resources? Was it inevitable, bound to happen sooner or later, as has been argued in the literature (Glassburner 1971:94)? This chapter recounts the dramatic events of take-over and hostile nationalization and seeks to improve our understanding of the processes at work.

The account is chronological, commencing with the prelude to the take-overs, continuing to the critical period in 1958, when the enterprises remained under Dutch ownership but were managed by Indonesians. Then follow the waves of nationalization, or formalization of the transfer of command that had already been effected. A separate account offers a glimpse of what happened during the aftermath of nationalization in the early 1960s; the final settlement with the Dutch concludes the chapter.

The road to take-over

Ide Anak Agung Gde Agung, the Balinese Minister of Foreign Affairs in the Harahap cabinet, was convinced that Dutch insistence not to include western New Guinea (West Irian) in the transfer of sovereignty represented a 'total misjudgement of the Indonesian psychology [that] was to cost the Netherlands very dearly' (Ide Anak Agung Gde Agung 1973:70). How high the cost would be in terms of expropriated economic assets was surely not foreseen in 1949. Profound disagreement about the fate of West Irian inexorably soured Dutch-Indonesian relations in the course of the 1950s, although a group of Dutch businessmen in Indonesia under Unilever's Rijkens went to considerable lengths to reach a separate understanding with President Sukarno. This section traces the origins of the take-over of Dutch firms in 1957 back to unresolved conflicts between the former colony and its one-time master.

Indonesian concessions at the RTC in 1949 were inspired by pragmatism, with the aim of obtaining an immediate transfer of sovereignty. This was not always fully appreciated by Dutch negotiators or later politicians. After the original federalist construction had been disbanded in favour of a unitary Indonesian state on 17 August 1950, nobody doubted that other provisions in the RTC Agreements would eventually come up for revision as well. In August 1954 a joint protocol at ministerial level envisaged the dissolution of the union between the Netherlands and Indonesia, with the Finec Agreement remaining intact. However, this protocol was never ratified. Instead, the Indonesian government began efforts to put 'Irian' on the agenda of the General Assembly of the United Nations. International pressure on the Netherlands had worked to Indonesia's advantage before, in 1949, and it was now tempting to tread a similar path. Although support from several Asian and African member states proved insufficient to obtain the required two-thirds majority in the General Assembly, the dispute about West Irian attracted international attention, which in turn led to formal negotiations between the Netherlands and Indonesia on neutral ground.

Talks began in December 1955 in Geneva. They were adjourned for Christmas, resumed in early January 1956, broken off, and resumed again for a few days in February. The failure of the conference was acknowledged by both sides, but opinions differed as to why no agreement could be reached. The Dutch Minister of Foreign Affairs, Joseph Luns, insisted that the Indonesian delegates had secret instructions to ensure that the conference would fail, but this was flatly denied by Anak Agung, leader of the Indonesian delegation. Whatever the truth may be, the immediate consequence was the unilateral abrogation of the union with the Netherlands by Indonesia on 13 February 1956. As the main reason, President Sukarno cited the Dutch refusal to give up West Irian (Ide Anak Agung Gde Agung 1973:161; Gase 1984:45-9;

De Geus 1984:77-8; Penders 2002:254-5).

A draft law to formalize the termination of the union was accepted by Parliament in late April, effective retroactively as of 15 February 1956. It nullified all agreements made at the Round Table Conference, including the Finec Agreement. The remaining debt to the Netherlands was cancelled, and remittances of profits and depreciation as well as pension allowances by Dutch companies were prohibited for the time being. Even payment of rent to railway companies for the use of rolling stock on lines operated by the government was discontinued (*Antara* 21 April 1956).[1]

The cancellation of debt obligations can hardly be construed as a major blow to the Dutch. Of the three billion guilder total debt payable directly to the Netherlands 90 per cent, or all but 311 million guilders, had already been paid (*Waspada* 3 May 1956; Anspach 1969:189). A great deal of speculation ensued about the consequences of the repeal of the Finec Agreement. Dutch firms adopted a wait-and-see attitude and undertook no investment other than what could be financed with profits which could not be transferred to the Netherlands anyway. Suchjar Tedjasoekmana, chairman of Dewan Ekonomi Indonesia Pusat (DEIP, Central Council for the Indonesian Economy), feared 'serious consequences for continuity in the nation's economy'. A few months later Suchjar's successor as chairman of DEIP, Kosasih Purwanegara, expected substantial cash gains for Indonesia. He was joined in his optimism by Dasaad, who had already predicted 'enormous gain' (*Antara* 18 February, 2 and 24 March, 29 June, 6 August 1956).

Emotions ran high during the months following the abrogation of the RTC Agreements. The new cabinet, a broad coalition of the three largest political parties led by Ali Sastroamidjojo, was often criticized for being too timid towards Dutch enterprises. The cabinet's preference for a thirty-year time frame to allow a transfer of ownership from foreigners to Indonesians in the estate sector was too conservative, even for members of the moderate Masjumi party. No longer a minister, Sumitro even accused the cabinet of indirectly supporting the flight of Dutch capital by dismissing the head of the foreign exchange fund LAAPLN when he opposed pressure exerted by his superiors at Bank Indonesia to allow transfers by Dutch firms by means of foreign exchange manipulations. Perbana urged that foreign banks be curtailed in their operations. The national congress of economists, KENSI, held in Surabaya in August 1956, demanded tougher measures, including the treatment of all investment dating from before 1 January 1950 as 'domestic' and keeping a close eye on the Dutch banks (*Antara* 9 March, 13 August 1956; *Keng Po* 28 May 1956).

1 ANRI, Jakarta: Risalah Rapat DPR 132, 21-4-1956.

Main office of the shipping concern KPM in Jakarta, where the takeover of Dutch-owned corporate assets began in December 1957 (KITLV 4225)

Attitudes towards Dutch enterprises hardened after Hatta's resignation as Vice-President on 1 December 1956 and the introduction of martial law in early 1957. One small incident in East Java is illustrative. A Dutch supervisor at the sugar factory Wonodjati in Jember, referred to as *tuan Bosch* ('mister Bosch'), was said to have used abusive language towards two workers, who alerted the local branch of the nationwide labour union Sarbupri, which in turn sent a letter to Jakarta. Sarbupri did not simply demand that disciplinary measures be taken by the Dutch owners, Vereenigde Majanglanden (United Majang Lands), but also requested the government to take 'unequivocal steps against foreigners who deliberately adopt such behaviour in order to minimize nationalist sentiments' (*langkah jang tegas terhadap warga negara asing jang dengan sengadja mengadakan tindakan-tindakan jang dapat meminimalkan rasa sentimen nasional*).[2] Politics had now entered day-to-day communication at the workplace.

In August 1957 a group of Asian and African nations once again moved to put the conflict over West Irian on the agenda of the United Nations General Assembly. From that moment on, this matter figured almost daily in the Indonesian media. At the celebration of the national holiday 'Day of the Youth Oath' (*Hari Sumpah Pemuda*) on 28 October 1957, a mass rally was organized in Jakarta at which Sukarno in a fiery address officially launched the Campaign to Liberate West Irian (*Perdjuangan Pembebasan Irian Barat*). A four-day boycott of Dutch firms throughout Indonesia followed. A few weeks later Sukarno spoke at rallies in Maluku and Nusatenggara, explicitly mentioning the possibility that the government would have to cut trade relations with the Netherlands and seize Dutch possessions (*harus diputuskan hubungan perdagangan dengan Belanda dan dipotong milik-milik Belanda*) should the move at the United Nations fail (*Antara* 14 November 1957; *Merdeka* 15 November 1957). The climax was drawing nearer.

Meanwhile events were developing on other fronts. Negotiations with the Japanese government on reparations payments were at long last producing tangible results. A proposal reported just before the mass rally in Jakarta cited a total sum of $ 800 million, half of it war reparations, and half long-term technical assistance. Only the details remained to be worked out. On 28 November 1957 an agreement was reached between Sukarno and Prime Minister Nobosuke Kishi about the $ 800 million aid package from Japan, but it was only officially announced by the Japanese Minister of Foreign Affairs, Aiduro Fujiyama, on 7 December 1957 (*Antara* 22 October, 7 December 1957; Nishihara 1976:51-4; Van Poelgeest 1999:189-91).

The timing of these happenings gives rise to intriguing questions. Were

2 ANRI, Jakarta: Kabinet Presiden 1505, 22-1-1957.

the Japanese keen to reach an agreement precisely because open conflict with the Dutch was becoming inevitable, which would create a vacuum in the Indonesian economy into which Japanese firms could step? Did Sukarno need to secure Japanese financial and technological assistance before unleashing forces which had been smouldering over the past months? Incidentally, this presupposes that the government at least sensed what was about to happen. Knowledge that the reparations agreement was about to be concluded with Japan must have buoyed up Sukarno's courage to strike against the Dutch.

These were tumultuous days, not least for Sukarno personally. On Saturday 30 November it became known that the resolution in the General Assembly had failed to drum up the required two-thirds majority (it was still Friday in New York). On the same day an attempt was made to assassinate Sukarno in Cikini in downtown Jakarta, leaving two people dead and at least thirty wounded, while the President escaped unscathed. On Sunday 1 December the extra-parliamentary cabinet headed by Djuanda agreed on the first set of reprisals. A nationwide 'General Strike Day' (*hari mogok total*) was announced on the radio by Minister of Information Soedibjo, chairman of the coordinating committee of the 'liberation campaign', seconded by Minister of Labour Samjono, ordering employers to pay wages to workers who had been on strike that day. KLM landing rights in Jakarta were withdrawn and Dutch newspapers and films were prohibited (*Merdeka* 2 December 1957).[3] More far-reaching measures were just around the corner.

On Tuesday 3 December 1957 a delegation led by union activist Mamesah entered the office of President-Director De Gous of the KPM shipping company at Jalan Gambir in central Jakarta. In the presence of two other directors, Ter Braake and Brandt, Mamesah read out a 'proclamation of appropriation of authority' (*proklamasi pengambilan oper kekuasaan*). The KPM directors refused to sign. A 'heated discussion' (*perdebatan jang penuh semangat*) followed and the three Dutchmen were invited to leave their offices, which they did 'with pale faces and shaking hands' (*dengan muka putjat dan tangan gemetar*). De Gous grabbed a folder of important documents, which one of the activists unsuccessfully tried to snatch from him. A few minutes later all the employees gathered in front of the KPM building. Mamesah read out the proclamation again. The KPM flag was lowered and replaced by the Indonesian national flag and the plain red union flag. Following these dramatic events staff returned to work (*Antara* 3 December 1957; *Pedoman* 4 December 1957).

The take-over of KPM affected facilities on shore as well as about forty ships, one-third of the fleet. Most of the other ships had moved into interna-

3 Bank Agro, Medan: AVROS, 27-12-1957.

tional waters in the Java Sea and elsewhere. Captains had previously been given instructions to set course for Singapore or the nearest foreign port should a signal be given, which indeed happened on 3 December. KPM had taken the additional precaution of insuring its fleet against seizure (Dick 1987a:23-4). KPM's take-over set the pattern for a series of similar take-overs throughout the country over the next few days. In all cases, it should be noted, they were effected without bloodshed or violence. Management at the three Dutch banks passed into the hands of a trade union committee, Serikat Buruh Bank Seluruh Indonesia (SBBSI, All-Indonesian Union of Bank Employees). Representatives of the trade union soon hung banners with white letters outside each branch office reading *Milik RI* ('Property of RI'), an example to be followed by many. At Borsumij and Geo. Wehry the Dutch staff locked the cash register and kept the key, but their offer to run the firm jointly was politely turned down by union representatives (*Merdeka* 2 December 1957; *Antara* 4 and 7 December 1957).

There was a great deal of confusion during that eventful first week of December 1957. Strikes broke out at trading companies such as Borsumij, Geo. Wehry, Hagemeijer, Jacobson van den Berg, and Internatio, and also at BPM, which along with Unilever escaped take-over as it was not a fully Dutch-owned company. Elsewhere Dutch goods were boycotted, and in some cases Dutch people were refused service in shops and hotels, for instance in Surabaya and Malang. In Jakarta there was a run on the Dutch banks, as depositors wanted to obtain their money before it was too late (*Antara* 6 December 1957; *Merdeka* 7 December 1957). On Thursday 5 December 1957 the cabinet met in an extraordinary session and assumed responsibility for further take-overs. Henceforth all expropriated companies were to be operated under the direct responsibility of the government. A 'committee of authority' (*panitia penguasa*) was installed at KPM (*Antara* 5 and 6 December 1957; *Merdeka* 6 and 7 December 1957; Mackie 1961:340-3). All Dutch nationals were told that they had to leave Indonesia within the next few months unless informed otherwise by the government, a measure affecting about 50,000 individuals, many of mixed European and Indonesian descent. Between December 1957 and August 1958 a total of 33,600 Dutch people left the country (Palmer 1962:108).

The military soon began to play an important role. Martial law still prevailed throughout the country, and the military became increasingly preoccupied with the recurrent unrest in the Outer Islands. On 6 December trade unions handed over various Dutch-owned manufacturing enterprises in Bandung, including publishing company De Kleyne, to the local military authorities. Four days later the cooperation with the armed forces was institutionalized as the BKSBM, Badan Kerdjasama Buruh dan Militer (BKSBM, Body for Cooperation between Labour and Military), was set up in Bandung and entrusted with the management of all Dutch-owned firms in West Java. When take-overs of estates began in North Sumatra on 7 December the regional military command was involved from the outset. On 9 December the reins of power at the three Dutch banks passed from the SBBSI to the military command, the Komando Strategis Angkatan Darat (KSAD, Strategic Command of the Army), the following day saw the 15th Infantry regiment of Surakarta entering a sugar factory in Klaten, Central Java, and on 11 December 34 Dutch-owned companies were placed under military command in South Sulawesi alone (*Pikiran Rakjat* 7 and 11 December 1957; *Merdeka* 9, 10 and 17 December 1957; *Antara* 11 December 1957; Heru Suytino 1996).

General guidelines were issued by General A.H. Nasution, Army Chief of Staff, on 13 December 1957. From then on, all Dutch corporate properties seized were subject to military authority. The Diponegoro division took command on estates and at sugar factories in Central Java, and the Siliwangi division ran both the OGEM power plant and the Philips factory in Bandung. The 23 cinemas of the Dutch-owned Sirnagalih company, located throughout Java, and the highly reputed Grand Hotel Preanger in downtown Bandung, came under control of military personnel (*Suluh Indonesia* 2, 3 and 6 January 1958; Bambang Purwanto 2005). By quickly placing the companies seized under direct military command, the government prevented control of vital economic assets by trade unions and PKI (Feith 1962:584). There was a profound antagonism between the military establishment and the national central organization of Indonesian workers SOBSI, known for its close links to PKI. In an incident in mid-December 1957 a group of SOBSI leaders was even arrested by the army and kept in custody for a while (Maraden Panggabean 1993:266).

The dimensions of the take-over in December 1957 were impressive, even aside from the many thousands of Dutch people affected. About 500 Dutch estates were seized, and operations were entrusted to the Pusat Perkebunan Negara-Baru (PPN-Baru, New Centre for State Estates), which had been hastily extablished. Its director, the engineer Saksono, was transferred from the existing PPN organization, dating from the 1940s. Highest priority was given to safeguarding the continuity of operations on the estates (*Merdeka* 11 December 1957).

In total more than 700 Dutch-owned enterprises were expropriated. One of the first to protest was KPM, demanding 120 million guilders in compensation for ships seized. Prime Minister Djuanda retorted by claiming that for some time already KPM had been busy liquidating operations in Indonesian waters (*formule likwidasi sudah lama ada*) (*Antara* 12 and 17 December 1957). Predictably, there was enormous disagreement about the actual value of the Dutch enterprises seized. According to official estimates, the book value was $ 1.2 billion, or perhaps even $ 1.5 billion, but unofficial figures were far lower, around $ 200 million. During the KENSI congress of August 1956 it had been publicly asserted that many Dutch firms had zero book value, having 'written off' (*susut*) their assets and repatriated their capital long ago. In January 1958 the international press reported as follows: 'Borsumij and other Dutch traders are using a variety of techniques to get what they can out of their Indonesian holdings' (*Antara* 24 August 1956; *Business Week* 11 January 1958; Cholil 1971:2).

There were several incidents in the tense days following the take-overs, as Dutch travellers busily scrambled for the few remaining cabins on board ocean liners leaving for Europe or at least tried to get to Singapore to board a KLM flight to Amsterdam. In Makassar excited youths on open trucks forced Dutch cars to assemble in front of Hotel Negara, and some even tried to enter private homes. The Dutch people involved reported these intrusions to the police. The military dispatched a tank, reprimanded the youths, and order was restored to the streets of Makassar. In central Jakarta a flag incident occurred at the premises of the trading company Jacobson van den Berg. A Dutch employee lowered the Indonesian flag which had just been hoisted by the union. The commanding officer, a lieutenant, dismissed the employee on the spot. In Medan a conflict developed between employers and trade unions when the former refused to pay wages to workers who had failed to show up for work because they had returned late to the estates after attending a mass rally in the central square of Medan.[4]

In hindsight two interesting questions arise when viewing the take-overs in December 1957. Were they inevitable? And what was the role of the government?

It was clearly a matter of political prestige. The take-over of Dutch firms was prompted by the failure to place 'Irian' on the agenda of the General Assembly of the United Nations; everybody knew that it would be virtually impossible to achieve the required two-thirds majority. In that sense, the take-overs were indeed inevitable.

The government's backing of the take-overs was officially explained as a direct consequence of the 'stubborn attitude of the Dutch' (*bersikap kepala batu*) in the dispute about West Irian. It did not take long before a direct link was made with *Indonesianisasi*, or rather the lack of it. Minister of Labour Samjono complained that efforts to achieve this had 'not delivered the results for which the government had hoped' (*tidak mempunjai hasil jang kita harapkan*) (*Suluh Indonesia* 12 December 1957; *Antara* 18 December 1957). There would surely have been a less acute sense of urgency to take drastic action had achievements in implementing *Indonesianisasi*, whether perceived or real, been less disappointing.

4 Bank Agro, Medan: AVROS, 27-12-1957; *Antara* 13-12-1957; *Suluh Indonesia* 21-12-1957.

A careful analysis of the event by a young Indonesian historian has produced yet another interesting and highly plausible explanation. In late 1957 the political and economic situation in Indonesia was highly volatile and growing increasingly tense. Dutch firms easily fell into the role of scapegoat for everything that was going wrong, especially in the economy. Both Communist and nationalist groups knew that they could count on widespread popular support if they were to take action against the Dutch. The sense of drama and urgency reached a climax with the failed vote in the General Assembly and the attempt to assassinate Sukarno. From this point of view, the take-overs were inevitable due to the dialectics of the drama itself (Bondan Kanumoyoso 2001:106-7).

There are two strands of thought in the literature about the role of Sukarno and the cabinet. According to one view, the take-overs were by no means premeditated and the cabinet was just as much taken by surprise as were the Dutchmen affected. This theory is supported by the fact that no blueprint existed about how to proceed once the take-overs had been accomplished. The government stumbled from one improvisation to the next, as the highly critical Sjafruddin Prawiranegara immediately pointed out (Kahin and Kahin 1995:111; Bondan Kanumoyoso 2001:78-9). This view concurs with official statements made by Prime Minister Djuanda that the government had been bypassed by the trade unions (*Suluh Indonesia* 30 December 1957). Considering its own expressed threats, the government had little choice but to step in and legitimize the take-overs retroactively.

The alternative theory claims that the government orchestrated the take-overs. A scenario had been devised in which angry masses would attack various properties, thereby paving the way to government intervention in the name of security. This view has gained a stubborn popularity due to a statement attributed to Sukarno that the take-overs had been his idea (Fischer 1959:300; Gardner 1997:142). Although this theory does not tally well with the actual course of events, the possibility of some wishful thinking on the part of Sukarno cannot be ruled out. The president may have had information that something was about to happen, without knowing the details, and sensed that it would be to his own advantage to let history take its course.

Running somebody else's business

The cement factory in Padang discussed earlier in relation to the Indonesian Revolution had been operated by its Dutch owners for almost a decade when the wave of take-overs reached West Sumatra. The company's name had been altered so as to no longer reflect the colonial past. At 150,000 tons, total output was approaching pre-war levels. A new manager, J.E. van der Laan, had replaced the veteran W.J. van Konijnenburg. Just as elsewhere, the local SOBSI branch took charge in December 1957, but the army lost no time in putting the factory under the command of Colonel Soeprajogi. During the PRRI rebellion two months later cement factory workers fled to the forests, either to join PRRI units or to escape them. Continued military command at the factory was not deemed advisable once the armed forces were ordered to suppress the rebellion. Padang Cement was therefore placed under a new executive administration of state firms in manufacturing and mining, Badan Penjelenggara Perusahaan-Perusahaan Industri dan Tambang (BAPPIT, Body for Management of Manufacturing and Mining Enterprises), which was set up in April 1958 in Jakarta (*Antara* 14 April 1958).

At a brief ceremony on 5 July 1958 the Padang cement factory was officially surrendered to the Indonesian government, pending formal nationalization. Van der Laan spoke, in Indonesian, and is reported to have said that he understood that this course of events was inevitable. By this time all Dutch technical staff had left with the exception of one person, F. Boom, who played a vital role in keeping production going by single-handedly training a group of young workers who hitherto had only hands-on experience. Boom worked closely with a Javanese engineer, Setjatmo, who was sent from the Gresik cement factory in Surabaya to serve as associate manager, although barely thirty years old. In 1958 total output fell to only 80,000 tons but recovered in 1959, reaching 121,000 tons, which corresponded to two-thirds of full capacity (Asmulyadi 1994:34-5, 42; Mestika Zed, Hasril Chaniago and Khairul Jasmi 2001:150-7). The example of the Padang cement factory illustrates the general situation of seized firms during 1958. Formally the firms were still Dutch-owned, but the Dutch administrators and supervisors had left, or were about to leave. The management vacuum was filled by Indonesians, often senior employees of long standing with the company, while the military or newly created civilian agencies filled supervisory positions.

The general context in 1958 was one of confrontation and suspicion. On 23 January 1958 a telegram signed by the owners of 94 Dutch estates was sent to President Sukarno and Prime Minister Djuanda protesting sharply against the take-overs. The estate owners claimed that the immediate gain to the Indonesian state lay between one and two billion dollar. By that time the take-overs had included some fifty sugar factories across Java. One of them, Gondangliporo near Yogyakarta, was not allowed to resume production at all, due to the 'poor attitude' (*sikap tidak baik*) of the owner, Smutzer of Amsterdam. Several Dutch-owned warehouses in major ports were rented out, but Indonesian rivals swiftly drew the conclusion that the tenants served as 'puppet representatives' (*golek djonggol*). In the port of Surabaya, Tanjung Perak, fifty out of eighty warehouses were considered to be run by straw-men. Public discourse was enriched by a new term, 'briefcase warehouse' (*veem aktentas*), analogous to Benteng's 'briefcase importer' (*importir aktentas*) (*Antara* 23 January, 4 February, 30 May, 15 September 1958).

Indonesianisasi was now fully implemented at all levels. Henceforth foreign exports should be handled by domestic firms, not Dutch ones. Import trading licences and sole agencies were transferred from Dutch holders to Indonesians. When KPM's Dutch supervisors were preparing to return to the Netherlands, leaving behind some 8,800 Indonesian employees, it was wryly noted that this was 'the opportunity to achieve 100 per cent *Indonesianisasi*' (*Antara* 13 January 1958; *Harian Rakjat* 29 January 1958). The process was accelerated to an unprecedented degree. One year after the take-overs it was estimated that 75 per cent of banking and 60 per cent of foreign trade were in Indonesian hands (Anspach 1969:193).

A new institutional framework was needed in large parts of the economy to handle the suddenly transferred management functions. PPN-Baru became an exceptionally powerful umbrella organization for several hundred agricultural estates. One of its guidelines, laid down at an internal conference in Bandung in early March 1958, was to avoid exporting to the Netherlands. As a direct consequence, the year's harvest from the tobacco fields of LMOD in Besuki, East Java, was shipped to Bremen and Antwerp, not to Amsterdam and Rotterdam as had been done previously.[5] Nevertheless, sources preferring to remain anonymous claimed that Dutch importers made liberal use of British, German, and Belgian intermediaries, who asked only a modest commission (*Antara* 5 March, 14 May, 5 November 1958). Acting in conjunction with the government-controlled trading firm CTC, with roots in the Indonesian Revolution, PPN-Baru handled almost the entire agricultural output destined for foreign markets. In its turn, CTC ventured into shipping and enlisted one-time advisors to the Permesta rebellion to gain control of the copra trade from Manado (*Antara* 29 April, 24 August and 20 September 1958).

A separate body, Panitia Pengawasan Perusahaan2 Belanda (P3B, Committee for Supervision of Dutch Enterprises), acted as a temporary authority before the seized enterprises were allocated to a specialized department or agency. In February 1958 P3B received a request from seventeen Dutch-owned companies in the services sector, including one of the 'Big Five' (Lindeteves) plus a law firm, a piano shop, and a motor car service station. The firms' interim managers asked for permission to transfer the business to 'national' businessmen, allegedly because the workers demanded it. But this

5 Prior to December 1957 ocean shipping to Europe was dominated by Scheepvaart-Maatschappij 'Nederland', Rotterdamsche Lloyd, and NSM (Nederlandsche Scheepvaart Maatschappij, Dutch Shipping Company) 'Oceaan'. In early 1958 NSM 'Oceaan' switched its vessels back to the British flag, and two German lines, Hapag (Hamburg-America) and Nord-Deutsche Lloyd, filled the gap. I owe this information to Howard Dick.

did not fit with official policy for regulating management matters in anticipation of a legal and more general settlement of the ownership issue.

A host of specialized government agencies emerged for various branches of industry. All Dutch-owned pharmacies, for instance, were formally under the jurisdiction of the Department of Health, but the supervision of management rested with an agency created specifically for this purpose, Badan Pusat Penguasa Perusahaan2 Pharmasi Belanda (BAPPHAR, Central Body for Administration of Dutch Pharmaceutical Companies) (*Antara* 8 February, 6 September 1958). The specialized agency responsible for the supervision of manufacturing and mining enterprises, BAPPIT, where Padang Cement ended up, kept expanding. BAPPIT had its head office in Jakarta and branch offices in Bandung, Semarang, Surabaya, and Medan. Eventually, this agency supervised 179 individual companies (Bisuk Siahaan 1996:332).

The 'Big Five' posed a separate problem. By mid-1958 all had been brought under tight government supervision. One of them, Borsumij, expressed a willingness to continue operations in Indonesia with only a minimal Dutch staff, a dozen people at most, compared to the several hundred Dutchmen employed prior to the take-over. This company had also been exceptionally quick to appoint an Indonesian manager following take-overs by local union leaders (*Antara* 4 January, 23 April, 20 June 1958). In the shadow of the overall reorganization of the 'Big Five', substantial parts of Borsumij's assets were acquired by the ethnic Chinese conglomerate Mantrust.

The military involved itself with a will on receiving the green light to keep a supervisory eye on operations in the expropriated Dutch enterprises. In Jakarta more than 300 residential houses left behind by departing Dutch people were seized by the local commander and distributed among military and civilian personnel (Bambang Purwanto 2005). In North Sumatra a seemingly endless succession of ordinances was issued by the region's 'War Authority' (Penguasa Perang). There were prohibitions against removing Dutch property or using Dutch-owned land without permission from the military; financial transactions with Dutch banks were regulated in detail, and movements of foreign staff were monitored by a separate agency, Badan Koordinasi Pengawasan Orang Asing (Coordinating Body for Supervision of Foreign Nationals).[6] The main tasks of the military officers on the seized estates were to restore the internal administration, normalize and improve production, and implement *Indonesianisasi*. The officers fulfilled these tasks by functioning as intermediaries between the seized company and external institutions, both private firms and state agencies, as well as the company

6 Bank Agro, Medan: AVROS, 28-1-1958; SPA, 26-3-1958, 19-5-1958, 27-5-1958, 17-6-1958.

head office and other estates with the same owner.[7] It goes without saying that such far-reaching prerogatives substantially enhanced the military's influence on economic life in Indonesia.

Some military units went a step beyond performing the supervisory functions entrusted to them. The Diponegoro division in Semarang under then Colonel Soeharto set up a shipping company, Pangeran Lines, in cooperation with Bob Hasan (The Kian Seng), a personal friend of the future president. It is still not clear whether Pangeran Lines owned or actually operated any ships. It later merged with a one-ship firm, Kidang Mas, to form Wasesa Lines. The foundation YPTE under Soeharto's direct command invested in trading, fisheries, and a sugar factory (Elson 2001:63). Such activities were a precursor to what was later to become widespread practice.

The big bottleneck was, of course, the dearth of management skills among Indonesian managers, a direct consequence of the limited degree to which *Indonesianisasi* had been accomplished in Dutch firms at an earlier stage. The problems were not new. Shortly before the take-overs, in early September 1957, the Indonesian government had purchased the 'Sringin' estate in Bojayang near Semarang from the Dutch trading firm Internatio for about Rp. 1 million. The new owners instantly encountered great difficulties in continuing operations due to the extreme shortage of skilled staff. In all of Central Java the total number of supervisory staff on seized estates actually declined, from 890 in December 1957 to 630 in December 1958, with Dutch staff being reduced from 216 to only two. The positions and tasks of departing Dutchmen were taken over by Indonesian staff already there, but the latter were not replaced in the lower ranks of the hierarchy (*Merdeka* 6 September 1957; *Antara* 14 December 1958). This pattern was replicated elsewhere. On the estates of the Deli Company in North Sumatra the total supervisory and technical staff shrank from 138 to 72 people in the course of 1958.[8]

An acute shortage of managers, engineers, and accountants was reported on many occasions and there is no lack of anecdotal evidence confirming that remaining directors had a hard time continuing routine management under the changed circumstances (*Suluh Indonesia* 4 June 1958; Pipit Rochijat 1985:37). Beginning in June 1958 BAPPIT organized an industrial management course at NHM's magnificent 300-room office complex in downtown Jakarta. PPN-Baru was co-sponsor, and seven lecturers from the University of Indonesia and the Institut Pertanian Bogor (Agricultural Institute in Bogor) offered crash courses on management economics, general economic theory, labour economics, and agrarian law. In September 1958 a small business

7 Bank Agro, Medan: GAPPERSU, 21-11-1958. The detailed instruction is dated 30-8-1958.
8 Bank Agro, Medan: AVROS, 28-1-1959.

school, Akademi Pemimpin Perusahaan (Academy for Business Managers), was inaugurated in Jakarta by Minister of Industry Inkiriwang (*Antara* 3 June 1958; *Suluh Indonesia* 23 September 1958). Incontrovertibly, the management vacuum was partially filled by ethnic Chinese, although this must not lead us to oversimplify and state that ethnic Chinese replaced the Dutch in the Indonesian economy in 1958 (Willmott 1960:64).

The fate of individual Dutch firms in 1958 may be illustrated by examples from sectors such as banking, shipping, and mining. The three Dutch banks were in a peculiar position. Although the SBBSI union had already assumed responsibility for day-to-day management, the government was at first hesitant to authorize a formal take-over due to the vital function these banks fulfilled in overseas financial transactions. Only in mid-April 1958 was a government ordinance issued, placing the banks under the authority of a newly created agency, Badan Pengawas Bank-Bank Pusat (Central Body for Supervision of Banks). A team of supervisors, Team Pengawas, was appointed at each of the Dutch banks to ensure that outstanding credit was not discontinued without prior consent of the authorities.

During most of 1958 the three banks continued operating as usual and, in fact, handled more than half of all foreign exchange transactions in Indonesia, despite the newest policy of LAAPLN not to accept requests in the Dutch language. Fundamental changes were announced in October 1958. Permission to process foreign exchange transactions was withdrawn at the Handelsbank, and currency operations were moved to Bank Indonesia. A full transformation into an Indonesian bank was ordered at the Escompto Bank. Equity was registered in Jakarta, not in Amsterdam, and the managing director and board members had to be Indonesian citizens as of 1 January 1959.[9]

During the early months of 1958 the Indonesian government continued to hold 34 KPM vessels in custody. However, after three months of seizure, they would become the property of Lloyd's of London, where they had been insured against expropriation. KPM would have been delighted if Lloyd's had paid out on those old, virtually written-off vessels for which it had no further use. This would have plunged the Indonesian government into an unintended conflict with the world's leading marine insurance company. Instead the KPM ships were released and sailed from Tanjung Priok (Jakarta) and Tanjung Perak (Surabaya) on 21 March 1958. Most of the recovered ships were laid up in Singapore along with the rest of the KPM fleet. The more seaworthy ones were redeployed, and those suitable only for service in Indonesian waters were sold off to an ethnic Chinese ship owner, Ek Liong

9 ANRI, Jakarta: Peraturan Pemerintah Sekretaris Kabinet 386, 16-4-1958; *Antara* 22-1-1958; Charlesworth 1959:134-6; Korthals Altes 2004:427-30.

Hin (*Antara* 30 March 1958; Palmer 1962:106; Dick 1987a:24).

Henceforth inter-island shipping was handled primarily by PELNI, along with several smaller private shipping firms. For the time being, the gap in tonnage was filled by a motley assortment of chartered ships. PELNI placed orders to purchase 42 vessels at a total cost of $ 65 million, but these ships were not delivered until late 1959, coming from shipyards in countries such as Japan and Poland. In a separate order, six ships were ordered from Dutch shipyards (Dick 1987a:141). The Indonesian government had hoped that many of KPM's Indonesian employees would be absorbed by PELNI, but even by early 1959 only slightly more than half of ex-KPM employees had found employment at PELNI, 4,800 out of 8,800. Complaints about mismanagement continued to plague PELNI even after its role in Indonesian shipping had been vastly enlarged (*Antara* 30 March and 29 August 1958; *Suluh Indonesia* 25 June 1958, 15 April 1959).

In late January 1958 temporary military management had been imposed on the Billiton tin mines, and on 1 March the transformation into a fully state-owned enterprise began. The firm's name was changed to Perusahaan Pertambangan Timah Belitung (PPTB, Belitung Tin-Mining Corporation), and an Indonesian engineer from the Department of Industry, Ukar Bratakoesoemah, replaced the last Dutch director, Herman ter Woch. A tripartite committee with representatives from Billiton and the government sat down to determine the price of the shares to be taken over, twelve out of thirteen Dutch employees at the head office departed, and Ukar assured the 8,000 Indonesian employees that only the company's status had been changed (*hanja statusnja jang berubah*). Another thing that certainly changed was the destination of deliveries. Shipments of tin ore were diverted away from the Netherlands, which allegedly caused dismissals at the Dutch smelter in Arnhem.[10]

Dutch-owned coal-mining in East Kalimantan was also affected, although KPM's Parapattan mine in Berau had already been closed down in 1956. Local authorities now tried in vain to interest Mitsubishi in helping to resume production. The Oost-Borneo Maatschappij (OBM, East Borneo Company) transferred its smaller mines to the Sebuku Company, a firm holding a property on the island of the same name on the border between Kalimantan and Sabah. Rumour had it that production had stopped, leaving hundreds of workers unemployed, but this was vehemently denied by Sebuku (*Antara* 18 January,

10 *Antara* 24-1-1958, 1-3-1958, 15-3-1958, 10-4-1958, 2-5-1958. One Dutchman, living in Monaco and a shareholder of the Billiton company, won a lawsuit against the Indonesian government. As security for payment of compensation for his losses, the court in The Hague designated the real estate owned by Bank Indonesia in central Amsterdam, which, needless, to say, evoked very angry protests from the Indonesian central bank (*Antara* 23-5-1958).

28 June 1958; *Suluh Indonesia* 6 May 1959).

Although not seized, Garuda was one of the companies most heavily affected. In December 1957, within a matter of days, nine Dutch department heads were replaced by Indonesians, while 300 Dutchmen departed in January and February 1958 alone. Garuda was compelled to suspend a large part of its operations for several months. Throughout 1958 it carried less than 60 per cent of the number of passengers recorded in 1957. Meanwhile, *Indonesianisasi* was rapidly implemented and by March 1958 the airline had only Indonesian citizens among its 3,975 employees (*Merdeka* 13 and 18 December 1957; *Antara* 31 March and 22 November 1958; Bank Indonesia 1960:233). KLM was replaced on international routes to Indonesia by European rivals such as SAS, which was quick to move in.

There was enormous uncertainty and a wealth of speculation about what the future held for the Dutch companies seized. Indonesian management under the supervision of military and civilian authorities could best be defined as running somebody else's business, a system which was obviously not suitable in the long term. Some Dutch owners wished to pull out and sell their firms. The regional authorities in East Kalimantan contemplated buying the local electricity firm, Samarinda-Tenggarongsche Electriciteits-Maatschappij (STEM, Samarinda-Tenggarong Electricity Company). In early March 1958 the North Bali estate Sumber Batok was sold to a 'Chinese from Java', and the Javanese Wirontono concern acquired a bandage factory in Surabaya. Further transactions were held up by a government ban on the use of public funds to acquire Dutch firms (*Antara* 27 January, 6, 8 and 25 March 1958).

Two more examples illustrate the atmosphere of uncertainty prevailing at the time. The Dutch-owned Tabak Export and Import Compagnie (TEIC, Tobacco Export and Import Company) was sold to a Belgian firm, but the transaction was shrouded in suspicion. In the other case, two coffee estates in Bondowoso, East Java, named Djolontoro and Kalibaru, were sold by the Dutch managing agency Kooy and Coster van Voorhout to an indigenous business in Surabaya, N.V. Wilie, but it then transpired that Wilie could not produce any proof of ownership. The estates were then secretly sold again, to another Indonesian businessman, Siswojo, who lived in Situbondo, not far from the estates. However, the military intervened, and both estates were incorporated into the PPN-Baru empire (*Antara* 18 March, 4 October 1958).

Foreign investors from countries other than the Netherlands were understandably deeply concerned about what was going on. This time the Indonesian government chose to resubmit the draft law on foreign investment already discussed by Parliament in 1956. The draft law now appeared even more liberal, in light of the draconian measures which had since been taken and retroactively legitimized by the government. In the newest version of the draft, the special government committee on foreign investment was elevated to Dewan Penanaman Modal (Council on Foreign Investment), authorized to set quotas for numbers of foreign employees and entrusted with supervision of the training of Indonesian staff. Provisions for the remittance of profits remained in force and were accompanied by long-awaited detailed instructions about the transfers of profits made in 1955 and 1956. At the introduction of the final draft in Parliament, Prime Minister Djuanda emphasized that foreign direct investment should 'serve to aid and propel' national economic development. The law was accepted by Parliament on 15 September 1958. Among the large parties only PKI voted against (*Antara* 24 April, 20 May, 20 August, 16 September 1958; Anspach 1969:195).

The year 1958 was above all one of transition. Management patterns changed profoundly and decisively in enterprises which still had Dutch owners. The next step was formal nationalization. The Indonesian government was increasingly aware that it was important that changes in ownership be legalized in a way acceptable to the international community.

Under new ownership

The popular saying in Indonesia in the late 1950s 'Hit first, regulate afterwards' (*pukul dulu, urusan belakang*) applies exceptionally well to government dealings with Dutch enterprises between late 1957 and early 1959. When these enterprises were seized, there was no blueprint for how to proceed once managerial authority had been wrested from the Dutch owners and transferred to Indonesian military and civilian authorities. The Indonesian Ambassador in London, former Minister of Foreign Affairs Sunarjo, even stated publicly that the aim of the take-overs was 'not nationalization but a measure in the interest of the people' (*bukanlah nasionalisasi melainkan tindakan untuk kepentingan rakjat*), as if there were a logical contradiction between the two (*Suluh Indonesia* 20 December 1957). In the long run the enforced separation of ownership and management was untenable, but it took the Indonesian government a strikingly long time to get around to making appropriate arrangements for the formal nationalization of the properties seized. This section surveys what happened in the wake of the take-overs.

The matter of formal nationalization did not attract much attention in the public discourse during most of 1958, a time when the regional rebellions of PRRI in West Sumatra and Permesta in Sulawesi appeared to threaten the nation's very existence. In August 1958, however, the regional parliament of West Java, Dewan Perwakilan Rakjat Daerah (DPRD, People's Regional Representative Council), during a meeting in Bandung, expressed concern about the prevailing situation and asked for the seized enterprises to be 'elevated to a more definite status' (*ditingkatkan kepada status jang lebih tegas*) (*Suluh Indonesia* 22 August 1958).

A draft law, Rancangan Undang-Undang tentang Nasionalisasi Perusahaan2 Milik Belanda di Indonesia (Draft Law concerning the Nationalization of Dutch-owned Enterprises in Indonesia), was promulgated in November 1959 and obtained immediate praise from the presidium of KENSI. It was received enthusiastically by organizations of national businessmen who 'gladly welcomed the "goal" of the law'. One member of Parliament, R.G. Doeriat, noted with satisfaction that a formal settlement would refute accusations from the outside world that Indonesia was a country 'inclined to seize or steal' (*pandai mensita2 atau mentjuri*) property belonging to another country (*Antara* 3 November 1958; *Warta Niaga dan Perusahaan* 8 and 15 November 1958; *Suluh Indonesia* 6 December 1958; Gouw Giok Siong 1960:6). The draft law stated that the take-overs in the context of the 'struggle for liberation' (*perdjuangan pembebasan*) of West Irian were in agreement with the policy which had led to the abrogation of the RTC Agreements. Nationalization applied to all Dutch-owned companies seized since 3 December 1957. These companies were all to become 'fully state-owned' (*mendjadi milik penuh negara*). This law, UU 86/1958, was promulgated on 27 December 1958 and the first unofficial guidelines were distributed a few weeks later (*Business News* 16 January 1959; Gouw Giok Siong 1960:170-7; Pelzer 1982:169).

On 6 February 1959 detailed instructions were issued on the way the law was to be implemented (PP 2/1959), stating explicitly that production should be continued at the same level and quality and on the basis of the same conditions 'as in the past' (*seperti sediakala*). Compensation for losses was to be paid to the Dutch owners, the exact amount to be determined by a committee, Panitia Penetapan Ganti Kerugian (Committee for Determination of Indemnity) set up for this purpose and composed of representatives from the Departments of Justice, Finance, and Defence. Only firms whose ownership had passed into non-Dutch hands after 15 April 1958 were exempted.[11]

Actual nationalization took place in successive waves. The first came on 23 February 1959, affecting 38 tobacco estates, of which 22 were located in North Sumatra, 14 in East Java, and 2 in Central Java. The main proprietors were the Deli Company and Senembah in North Sumatra, and the LMOD and Djelboek in East Java. A list of 98 estates pending nationalization was published (*Antara* 25 February 1959; *Suluh Indonesia* 26 February 1959; Kano 2004:table 7-5).

The second wave followed in early March 1959, affecting fifteen public utilities firms and thirteen livestock companies. The former category includ-

11 ANRI, Jakarta: Muh. Yamin 188; Gouw Giok Siong 1960:175-7.

ed those parts of the gas and electricity providers ANIEM and OGEM which had not yet been purchased by the Indonesian government and also STEM in East Kalimantan. Most of the livestock companies were in the Bandung area. A third wave followed on 14 March 1959, when no fewer than 227 agricultural estates in Java and Sumatra became the property of the Indonesian state. This time several sugar factories belonging to HVA were included and so were the estates of Michiels-Arnold, an agricultural concern of long standing in the archipelago (*Suluh Indonesia* 5, 7 and 16 March 1959; *Warta Niaga dan Perusahaan* 7 March 1959; *Antara* 16 March 1959). All nationalized estates were brought under the umbrella of PPN-Baru, which was rapidly developing into a gigantic organization.

In the midst of waves of nationalization, in late April 1959, a cable arrived from Germany which gladdened the hearts of Indonesian leaders as much as it dismayed Dutch firms. It was the final verdict of the highest regional court of justice (*Oberlandesgericht*) in Bremen in what was known as the Senembah case, which had become a test case for the legality of Indonesian take-overs of Dutch companies. In late 1958 Senembah had successfully upheld its rights of ownership to a shipment of tobacco from one of its seized estates. The tobacco was intended as collateral for a loan of Rp. 37 million to Senembah from Bank Indonesia in Medan, but had been sold on the international market by PPN-Baru, which managed the seized estate. An Amsterdam court ruled that Senembah did not have to pay back the loan, because the creditor, the Indonesian state, had already earned sufficient revenue, Rp. 51 million, from selling the tobacco. By implication, PPN-Baru had no right to sell the tobacco, as it was managing Senembah's property unlawfully.[12] Matters took a different turn in Germany.

Tobacco shipments from North Sumatra had been redirected from Amsterdam to Bremen. The Deli Company and Senembah protested jointly against the auctioning of North Sumatra tobacco in Bremen and the parties met in court. The Dutch firms called upon three experts in international law from other countries – the British Lord Arnold McNair, Professor H. Rolin from Belgium, and Professor A. Verdross from Austria. They argued that the nationalizations could not be linked to the abrogation of the RTC Agreements. The Indonesians responded with a 200-page elaboration of their motives, including a reprint of an old inflammatory booklet on colonial exploitation, entitled *De millioenen uit Deli* (*The millions from Deli*) (Van den Brand 1902), as well as a chapter written by former German central bank President Hjalmar Schacht on the difficulties surrounding the Indonesian economy. There was even a reference to German firms that had been expropriated without due

12 Bank Indonesia, Jakarta: DJB 1584; Gouw Giok Siong 1960:151-3.

compensation in the Netherlands after the Second World War. The Bremen court argued that the take-overs and nationalizations formed an integral part of the 'liberation from colonial power' (*Befreiung von kolonialer Vorherrschaft*) occurring within the context of a 'change in the social and economic structure of a new nation'. The request from the Dutch tobacco companies was interpreted as a 'demand for a compensation for the ending of colonial injustice' (*Förderung einer Entschädigung für die Beendigung von kolonialen Unrecht*) (*Antara* 21 April, 21 July, 1 August and 26 September 1959; Gouw Giok Siong 1960:124-5). This was an important decision because it acknowledged the right to take draconian measures in the name of decolonization, provided it was couched in language acceptable to international law.

Visibly strengthened by the Bremen verdict, the Indonesian government continued along its chosen path. A few sugar factories in East and Central Java, and the small tin mine on the island of Singkep, near Belitung, were nationalized on 1 June 1959. Then, on 26 June, came the long-awaited nationalization of forty Dutch firms in trading and manufacturing, including the 'Big Five'. The trading sector had in fact already reorganized in anticipation of the required legal steps. The five leading Dutch trading companies now operated as Indonesian enterprises under new names. Borsumij, with forty branch offices and 5,300 employees, became Indonesian Development Industrial and Trading Corporation (Indevitra), Internatio (61 branches, 2,000 employees) was renamed Satja Negara, Jacobson van den Berg (26 branches, 1,900 employees) was henceforth known as Judha Bhakti, Lindeteves (2,000 employees) became Indonesian Estates and Industrial Supply Corporation (Indestins), while Geo. Wehry lived on as the Triangle Corporation. Together with state-owned CTC, Usindo, and formerly Dutch-owned Mira Sari (Mirandolle Voûte), the five now became the 'Big Eight'. A military officer, usually at the rank of major or colonel, headed management in each of these trading companies, and they were in turn under the supervision of an umbrella organization called Badan Urusan Dagang (BUD, Body for Regulating Trading) (*Antara* 26 March, 29 April 1959; *Warta Niaga dan Perusahaan* 28 March 1959; *Times of Indonesia* 10 July 1959; Thomas and Panglaykim 1973:63-4; Robison 1986:73; Bondan Kanumoyoso 2001:93-4; Kano 2004:table 7-6).

Nationalized manufacturing firms were incorporated into the BAPPIT network and most company names were altered. Kolff's printing press and ink factory became Gita Karya, the metal manufacturing firm Brata in Surabaya acquired the new name Lina, the sawmills of Javahout were now called Kabana, and the chemical factory Naarden was renamed Narwasta. In Padang the cement factory revived the name Indarung, the name it had been given when it was under Indonesian management in the late 1940s. Pharmaceutical firms were likewise brought under the supervision of BAPPHAR. In Jakarta, Nurani and Nakula now replaced the once well-known brand names of Van

Gorkom and Bavosta (*Times of Indonesia* 8 December 1959, 30 January 1960; for a list of nationalized firms in Surabaya, see Dick 2003:477-8).

Eleven privately owned railways in Java were nationalized in early July 1959. Most lines had already been operated for some time by the Indonesian government, which was bound by contract to pay Rp. 6 million annually to the Dutch owners for use of the rolling stock. For some reason, nationalization of the sole remaining privately run railway, Deli Spoorweg Maatschappij (DSM, Deli Railway Company) in North Sumatra, was repeatedly postponed (*Antara* 8 July, 20 September 1959).

A tentative balance was drawn up in July 1959 by the organization of Dutch companies, the Ondernemersbond voor Indonesia (Association of Employers in Indonesia). According to the Ondernemersbond, 248 Dutch companies had so far been nationalized, 92 in mining, 77 in estate agriculture, and 32 in trading, to mention but the largest categories.[13] These 248 companies were said to represent a value of $ 1.5 billion, but the organization's chairman, J. van Oldenborgh, was pessimistic about the chances of obtaining full compensation and hoped that the Indonesian government would declare the nationalizations null and void. As Colonel Soeprajogi, Minister for Regulating Stability (*Urusan Stabilisasi*), admitted with astonishment, not even one request for compensation had thus far been submitted by a nationalized Dutch company (*Antara* 4 and 21 July 1959).

The banking sector lagged behind, as had been the case in seizing full management control in 1958. In August 1959 the directors at the Handelsbank learned that the Indonesian government had nationalized their bank; in September it was converted into Bank Umum Negara (BUNEG, State General Bank), later Bank Bumi Daya, at present Bank Mandiri (Korthals Altes 2004:431). On 1 April 1960 the Escompto Bank was liquidated, to reappear immediately as Bank Dagang Negara (BDN, State Trading Bank). The directorate at BDN was seconded by a Board of Trustees with a military man, Colonel Soehardi, as its chairman. On 21 November 1960 management of NHM was at long last transferred to Indonesian government officials, and formal nationalization followed on 30 November. Assets and activities were transferred to Bank Koperasi, Tani dan Nelayan (BKTN, Bank for Cooperatives, Farmers, and Fishermen), which had been established shortly before through a merger between BRI and a separate bank catering to the credit needs of farmers and fishermen (*Antara* 18 September 1959, 12 April 1960; Bank Indonesia 1966:59-60).

By April 1960 the waves of nationalization were nearing their conclu-

13 The total number was higher when counting the cases announced publicly since the promulgation of UU 86/1958 in December 1958. The difference lies in the estate companies, which often consisted of clusters of proprietors of individual estates.

sion, not counting joint Anglo-Dutch ventures such as BPM and Unilever. Some 700 Dutch companies had become the property of the Indonesian state, nationalization of a further 47 companies was pending (*Antara* 29 April 1960). Management at all nationalized firms was supervised by a new umbrella organization, the Badan Nasionalisasi Perusahaan2 Belanda (BANAS, Body for the Nationalization of Dutch Companies). This body began in June 1959 and was chaired by Prime Minister Djuanda himself, seconded by two deputies, Soetikno Slamet from Bank Indonesia and the aforementioned Colonel Soeprajogi. Fourteen clusters of state-owned enterprises were represented, notably PPN-Baru (estates), BAPPIT (manufacturing), BUD (trading), and BAPPHAR (pharmacies) (*Warta Niaga dan Perusahaan* 27 June 1959).

The largest branch organization, PPN-Baru, formed together with the few state-owned estates from before the take-overs, now called PPN-Lama ('Old'), a general management body for state-owned firms, Badan Pimpinan Umum Perusahaan2 Negara – Pusat Perkebunan Negara (BPU-PPN, General Management Body for State Companies – Centre for State Estates). Within PPN-Baru, estates were initially arranged by region, for instance six clusters in West Java, four in Central Java, and ten in East Java. The nine clusters in North Sumatra were very unequal in size. The largest one, SUMUT I (Sumatera Utara, North Sumatra), contained 22 estates covering almost 42,000 hectares, all originating from the Deli Company or Senembah, while the smallest cluster was SUMUT VIII, with the four estates that had once belonged to the Rotterdam-Tapanoeli Cultuur-Maatschappij (Cultivation Company), together scarcely more than 3,000 hectares. Although by no means a one-to-one correspondence, by and large the clustering did follow the lines of previous ownership, which often in turn coincided with geographic proximity.[14] This suggests a certain measure of continuity in the way the business was run.

The nationalization of Dutch enterprises had far-reaching consequences, not only for the ousted Dutch but also for Indonesia (Mackie 1971:50-1). There was a profound change in the structure of the economy, with the share of government in GDP climbing from 8 to 14 per cent, while the share of estate agriculture and private commercial services fell concomitantly (Robison 1986:64). Although it cannot be demonstrated statistically, the role of the military in the economy was greatly increased as the state now assumed responsibility for a larger part of GDP. One contemporary foreign observer, Douglas Paauw, noted that Sukarno's regulation of authority in nationalized enterprises offered the opportunity for 'real take-overs of important economic and political functions by the military elite' (Paauw 1960:46). Military

14 Bank Agro, Medan: GAPPERSU, Rapat umum anggota 2, 10-5-1962.

officers controlled state-owned enterprises and became known as 'bureaucratic socialists' (Robison 1986:95). On 1 January 1960 450 members of the armed forces took early retirement in order to work at state-owned firms, a fact noted with satisfaction by Minister Soeprajogi, who had now been promoted to the rank of general. A class of 'new rich men' (*orang kaja baru*) with firm roots in the military establishment was in the making (*Antara* 4 March 1960; Bambang Purwanto 2005).

There is a stubborn belief that things went completely wrong in the Indonesian economy as soon as the Dutch managers had left. The evidence is less conclusive. Scattered evidence testifies to the momentum in economic life being at least partially retained. Profits in the amount of Rp. 52 million were transferred to non-Dutch company owners abroad between March 1958 and September 1959.[15] Officials from PPN-Baru repeatedly claimed, although without giving figures, that production levels were not much lower in 1958 than they had been before the take-overs. Statistics show the output of, for instance, Java sugar or Sumatran palm oil to be almost identical in 1958 to what it had been in 1957 (*Antara* 29 June and 25 September 1958, 9 January 1959).

North Sumatra, with its high concentration of seized agricultural estates, may serve as an illustration of the situation at large. The production on rubber estates amounted to about 130,000 tons in both 1957 and 1958, but fell to 120,000 tons in 1959. On palm oil estates there was a decline from 160,000 tons in 1957 to 148,000 tons in 1958, and a drop to 135,000 tons in 1959. Tobacco fared worst, with a decrease in production by almost one-quarter (23 per cent) in 1958 alone.[16]

One plausible explanation for the divergence in performance from one crop to another is that many estates producing rubber or palm oil had non-Dutch foreign owners and were thus not affected by the take-overs, whereas all tobacco estates had been Dutch. In 1958 Dutch-owned estates occupied 43 per cent of the total planted area in North Sumatra's estate sector, compared to 19 per cent for British, 17 per cent for Belgian, and 11 per cent for American estates.[17] With the exception of tobacco estates, the level of output in North Sumatra's estate agriculture does not seem to have suffered dramatically as a consequence of the take-over of Dutch enterprises.

Under the new mixture of civilian and military Indonesian management, many estates laid off workers in 1958. Women in particular left. Total estate employment in North Sumatra fell from almost 196,000 labourers in January

15 Bank Indonesia, Jakarta: LAAPLN 13, no. 41.

16 GAPPERSU 1960:tables II, III. The decline in tobacco is based on recorded exports in 1957 and 1958. Regrettably, no corresponding data are available for 1959. Bank Agro, Medan: GAPPERSU, document marked *Rahasia* ('Secret'), December 1958.

17 Bank Agro, Medan: SPA, 5-11-1958.

1958 to about 192,000 by January 1959. Assuming that the lay-offs were evenly distributed over the various types of estates, we may infer that labour productivity declined somewhat in palm oil, significantly so in tobacco, but scarcely at all in rubber. The lay-offs reflected the worsening prospects for North Sumatra's key export crops on world markets. Revenues from exports were reported to have declined substantially during most of 1958, up until November, compared to the same period in 1957. The decline was 13 per cent for palm oil, 25 per cent for rubber, and 26 per cent for tobacco.[18] The far greater fall in value than in volume tells us that rubber and palm oil were fetching significantly lower prices in 1958 than in 1957, an external fluctuation that had little to do with the take-overs.

In 1959 prospects on the international market improved and estate employment rose again. By 1960 the total estate labour force in North Sumatra numbered 202,000 workers, compared to 212,000 in 1955. The total planted area in 1960 was virtually identical to what it had been in 1938 (AVROS 1956:tables I, VIII; GAPPERSU 1960:tables I, IX). In other words, the global dimensions for North Sumatra's estate agriculture remained largely unaltered despite the dramatic events of late 1957 and 1958.

These figures on estate agriculture in North Sumatra tell us that 1958 must be viewed in the context of what happened during the following years. This may be illustrated by considering several indicators of macroeconomic performance. National income, as expressed in GDP, did fall in 1958, albeit not by a staggering 13 per cent as reported at the time. But GDP recovered in 1959 and 1960, although some of the increase reflects inflation rather than an increase in real terms (Thomas and Panglaykim 1973:8; Bondan Kanumoyoso 2001:100). Nevertheless, the money supply did not expand at a higher rate in 1960 than in 1957. Moreover, Indonesia's international reserves increased by about 50 per cent between these two years (Dick et al. 2002:192). None of these indicators of macroeconomic performance suggests anything remotely resembling economic collapse as a direct consequence of the take-overs of Dutch enterprises.

An analysis of figures on foreign trade corroborates the impression of a temporary setback rather than disaster. Total export revenue declined by some 13 per cent between 1957 and 1960, but there had in fact been a recovery in 1959, which brought the value of total exports almost back to the level of 1957. The steep decline in 1960 was caused by falling oil prices and a reduced output of both smallholder and estate rubber, whereas exports of tin, tobacco, and palm oil actually rose compared to the preceding year (Appendix 2, Table 7). However, the decline in total export revenue in 1960 was accompanied

18 Bank Agro, Medan: GAPPERSU, document marked *Rahasia* ('Secret'), December 1958.

by a partial recovery of imports, which had fallen sharply in 1958 and 1959, resulting in a surplus in the balance of trade in 1960 of Rp. 3 billion, compared to more than Rp. 5 billion in 1959.

This brief analysis of foreign trade performance during the years 1957-1960 highlights two important economic trends after the take-over of Dutch firms. First, there was undeniably an immediate setback on virtually all fronts in 1958, but this setback had been largely redressed by the end of 1959. Second, the deterioration in export performance in 1958 and again in 1960 was largely caused by developments which had little or no connection with the measures taken against the Dutch – particularly the fall in oil prices and the decline in output from smallholder rubber producers, who were not at all affected by the take-over of Dutch estates.

Not surprisingly, the most adverse impact on foreign trade in 1958 and subsequent years was a sharp drop in trade with the Netherlands. After all, diverting trade away from the Netherlands was a prime target of Indonesian policy. The Dutch share in Indonesian exports plummeted from 17 per cent in 1957 to less than half of one per cent in 1960, whereas the share of the Netherlands in imports entering Indonesia fell from 10 per cent in 1957 to 3 per cent in 1959 (Bank Indonesia 1960:135-6, 1966:122-4).

When reviewing the statistical evidence on foreign trade performance in the late 1950s, it is instructive to consider Indonesia's overall competitiveness on world markets as expressed by its commodity terms of trade (export price level divided by import price level). Terms of trade declined from 85 in 1957 to 71 in 1958 but recovered rather quickly, reaching 95 in 1959 (Bank Indonesia 1960:142). This observation carries the important implication that the position of Indonesian exports on foreign markets was deteriorating in 1958 even aside from the take-overs. Indonesia had the bad fortune to be intervening profoundly in a highly export-oriented economy during a period when prospects in foreign markets were worsening anyway.

Recovery came in 1959, and the improvement in terms of trade (from 71 to 95) was aided by a steep devaluation of the Indonesian currency. On 24 August 1959 the official rate of exchange was moved from Rp. 11.40 per dollar to Rp. 45 per dollar (Bank Indonesia 1960:58-9, 119, 261-2, 266). Yet this draconian measure did not produce any enduring benefits. In 1960 terms of trade were already falling again, reaching 79 by the end of the year, which was better than in 1958 but worse than in 1957 or 1959.[19] The Indonesian economy may have succeeded reasonably well in muddling through the fundamental changes in management and ownership of large parts of its export

[19] Bank Indonesia 1966:130. Trade values for 1960 were recalculated using the exchange rate valid up until 24-8-1959 in order to facilitate a comparison between 1959 and 1960.

industry during the years 1957-1959, but it remained highly vulnerable to the vicissitudes of the world market.

Konfrontasi

Four official announcements during the second half of 1959 made abundantly clear that economic developments in Indonesia would now take a highly different course. The first was the presentation of Sukarno's *Manipol* ('Political Manifesto') on 17 August 1959, Independence Day. This document laid the foundation for the 'Guided Economy' (*Ekonomi Terpimpin*), a new economic system run in tandem with the 'Guided Democracy' introduced by Sukarno at the same time. The 'Guided Economy' stressed socialist and cooperative ideals and gave state-run operations priority over private entrepreneurship. Within half a decade, it was to alter the Indonesian economy almost beyond recognition (Mackie 1959; Tan 1967:29).

The second ominous sign was the monetary reform of 24 August 1959, which coupled the steep devaluation of the rupiah to a dramatic reduction of domestic money supply. The value of Rp. 1000 and Rp. 500 bank notes was reduced to one-tenth of their original value, Rp. 100 and Rp. 50 respectively (*Antara* 25 August 1959). This extraordinary measure demonstrated that uncontrolled inflation had become a permanent feature of Indonesian economic development, foreshadowing the extreme predicaments experienced in the monetary sphere by the mid-1960s (Arndt 1971:366-73; Mackie 1971:59-63).

The third announcement was the infamous PP 10/1959, issued on 18 November 1959, which radically altered economic conditions and social relations in rural and small-town Indonesia. PP 10/1959 was never repealed, although Sukarno did curb the anti-Chinese measures in the course of 1960. Nearly 100,000 ethnic Chinese emigrated to the People's Republic in 1960 alone (Mackie 1976:92). It was the most far-reaching expression of anti-Chinese sentiments and policies in Indonesia to date and it was a harbinger of the tragedy of the mid-1960s.

The fourth and final announcement in this series, made on 20 December 1959, is likely to have attracted a great deal less attention among Indonesians than the other three. On this day, the Dutch government made public its official protest against the nationalization of Dutch enterprises and demanded that the matter be brought before the International Court of Justice on the grounds that 'Indonesia's nationalizations were in violation of the principles of international law' (*Antara* 21 December 1959). The Dutch had given up the hope of redress or reconciliation. Only confrontations and arguments over the promised compensation lay in store in the immediate future.

The swing to the left in economic policy marked by the introduction of the 'Guided Economy' had repercussions for foreign direct investment. The quite liberal foreign investment law of September 1958 had been repealed in mid-1959, and the PKI-oriented SOBSI declared that nationalization should also be extended to include multinationals. In August 1962 Sukarno openly stated that Indonesia would no longer welcome foreign investors who wished to transfer their profits back home (Anspach 1969:196). PKI in particular wished to continue nationalization efforts and received support from organizations such as SOBSI, which had already pressed for a take-over of BPM in 1959 (*Antara* 10 August 1959). The climate for foreign investment in Indonesia was rapidly deteriorating.

Enhanced government control fitted perfectly into the framework of a 'Guided Economy'; numerous reorganizations were carried out among the major clusters of state-owned enterprises. Trading was affected in 1962. Seven of the 'Big Eight' of 1959 (all except Mira Sari) were combined with other firms to form new trading conglomerates labelled *bhakti* (literally 'loyal service'). Indevitra became Budi Bhakti (in conjunction with Moluksche Handelsvennootschap), Satja Negara turned into Aneka Bhakti, Judha Bhakti into Fadjar Bhakti (with five other firms), Indestins into Tulus Bhakti (with W.J. Stokvis and a few more companies), the Triangle Corporation became Marga Bhakti, CTC became Tri Bhakti, and Usindo, finally, lived on as Djaja Bhakti (with two other firms). Two more clusters were added, Sedjati Bhakti for trade in industrial raw materials and Sinar Bhakti for various technical deliveries, which brought the total number of *bhakti* to nine. In 1964 these nine conglomerates were rearranged into six new constellations called *niaga* ('trading') (*National business register* 1963; Panglaykim and Palmer 1969:8).

Estate agriculture was next in line, in 1963. The largely geographic arrangement of the estates in PPN-Baru was regrouped by crop, thus creating 92 clusters, including 55 rather small ones for sugar, 16 huge ones for rubber, and 7 for tobacco. In 1964 the 180-odd manufacturing firms under the umbrella of BAPPIT were split up into 121 *Perusahaan Negara* (PN, state companies), which were then rearranged into regionally defined clusters according to the very system which had just been abandoned for the agricultural estates. The largest cluster was that of East Java with 42 PNs, followed by that of Central Java with 26, while the Jakarta and West Java clusters contained 18 state companies each.[20]

In 1965 various partial rearrangements in state-run banking culminated in the creation of seven state banks. Five were relabelled units of BNI, respectively Bank Indonesia, BKTN, BNI, BUNEG, and the postal bank, Bank

20 ANRI, Jakarta: SOBSI 287, PP7/1964.

Tabungan Negara (BTN, State Savings Bank), to which were added BDN and BIN (Bank Indonesia 1966:61-2; Arndt 1971:364). BNI Unit IV later became known as Bank Bumi Daya (BBD), whereas the former NHM departments at Bank Unit II (BKTN) became Bank Exim.

Relations with the Netherlands were extremely strained, with the thorny issues of West Irian and compensation for nationalization both still unsettled. Most Dutch people had been repatriated. The houses they left behind were expropriated by the government, with 'their use allocated to the department needing them most' (*penggunanja diserahkan kepada departemen jang sangat memerlukannja*).[21] Transactions with Dutch banks were discontinued and trade unions complained when Dutchmen were found working for multinationals operating in Indonesia. In September 1961, for instance, SOBSI turned to the cabinet formally requesting the removal of Dutchmen at Unilever, as their very presence 'pained the labourers' (*menusuk hati kaum buruh*).[22] It was in this climate of undisguised hostility that in December 1961 Sukarno launched his 'Irian campaign', reiterating, as he had done consistently since 1950, the historical and legal rights of Indonesia to the western part of the island.

In the early months of 1962 landings by paratroopers on the coast of western New Guinea brought Indonesia and the Netherlands to the verge of military conflict. The international community intervened, just as it had done thirteen years earlier. Senator Robert Kennedy visited the region and persuaded the parties to attend negotiations in Washington, DC. Eventually, on 15 August 1962, formal agreement was reached in New York, stipulating a transitory administration to be installed by the United Nations Temporary Executive Authority (UNTEA), the transfer of authority to the Indonesian government on 1 May 1963, and eventually a plebiscite among the Papuans about their future. Dutch colonial officials left on 1 October 1962 and the NHM office in Merauke was abandoned in February 1963. Dutch diplomats were dismayed to see the Indonesian flag already flying in the region from 1 January 1963, four months ahead of the agreed transfer of authority.[23]

Success in the struggle against the Dutch and an increasing need to draw attention away from pressing problems at home prompted Sukarno's next diversion, the 'Crush Malaysia' (*Ganjang Malaysia*) campaign launched in

21 ANRI, Jakarta: Roeslan Abdul Gani: 113, instruction from General Gatot Subroto, 16-1-1961.

22 ANRI, Jakarta: SOBSI 278, 9-9-1961.

23 *Berita Ekonomi dan Keuangan* 13-2-1963; Mackie 1974:98-103; Huydecoper van Nigtevecht 1990:182-7. There has been deep disagreement ever since between the Indonesian government and much of the international community about the fairness of the plebiscite held in (then) Irian Jaya in 1969. For an extensive Dutch language account, see Drooglever 2005.

1963 in response to a perceived threat from the formation of the Malaysian Federation on 31 August 1963. Hostilities at home were directed at Malaysia's Western allies, Great Britain and the United States in particular. The first take-overs of partly or fully British-owned enterprises in Indonesia took place as early as mid-September 1963, accompanied by an incident in which gangs of youths attacked the British Embassy in Jakarta. The take-overs were carried out by local trade unions, with Anglo-Dutch Shell Indonesia being one of their first targets. In a move reminiscent of December 1957, the Indonesian government quickly placed all properties seized under government and military supervision. Shell's refinery at Balikpapan, East Kalimantan, for instance, came under command of Colonel Suharjo of the front forces stationed in the region, the Front Nasional Kaltim (Kalimantan Timur National Front). In contrast to 1957, however, foreign owners were assured that their property would not be nationalized.[24]

New take-overs followed in early 1964. Although they were again mainly directed at British-owned firms, Unilever, another Anglo-Dutch joint venture, was surprisingly left untouched. The long-awaited seizure of American companies took place in December 1964, but by that time Sukarno was already launching yet another campaign; this one aiming to achieve full self-reliance (*berdikari* or *berdiri di atas kaki sendiri*, 'standing on one's own feet'), which effectively implied Indonesia's withdrawal from the international economy.[25] The anti-Dutch sentiments in Indonesia, reaching a climax in the years 1957-1959, had developed into a general aversion to foreign investment in Indonesia (Lindblad 1998:105-6).

The seizure of British and American firms during the 'Crush Malaysia' campaign differed in several respects from the take-overs of Dutch enterprises, although the actual launching and subsequent regulation of management appears to have followed similar lines. The earlier operation was far more extensive, affecting more firms, larger volumes of invested capital, and a greater range of economic activity. The latter operation was more precarious, since it directly affected the three large foreign oil companies, responsible for 25 per cent of total export revenues as of 1960.[26] Facilitated by intervention from Washington, production-sharing and subcontracting agreements had been concluded with Shell, Caltex, and Stanvac in late September 1963. These arrangements allowed American capital investment to survive the hostilities during the 'Crush Malaysia' campaign. Shell was accused of sabotage and

24 ANRI, Jakarta: SOBSI 26; *Berita Ekonomi dan Keuangan* 20-9-1963; Mackie 1974:187-229.

25 ANRI, Jakarta: SOBSI 289, 15-2-1965; Sadli 1972:202.

26 Appendix 2, table 7. The distribution of oil production in 1964 was as follows: Caltex 61 per cent, Shell 18 per cent, Stanvac 12.5 per cent, three Indonesian state-owned companies (Pertamin, Permina, Permigan) together 8.5 per cent. ANRI, Jakarta: SOBSI 268, 6-6-1965.

chose, in 1965, to withdraw from Indonesia, never to return.[27]

The crucial difference lay in the link with decolonization. Nationalization of Dutch businesses could be justified on such grounds, even, as we have seen, in the eyes of the international legal community. However, this did not apply to a nationalization of British or American companies seized temporarily under the pretext of warfare. These properties were returned to their rightful owners at the conclusion of the 'war' with Malaysia in 1966, by which time the reins of power had already passed from Sukarno to Soeharto.

Considering the extraordinary circumstances surrounding the final years of Sukarno's rule, it need not be surprising that economic growth came to a virtual standstill. National income, expressed in constant 1960 prices, rose from Rp. 390 billion in 1959 to Rp. 420 billion in 1964, an increase of merely 7 per cent in half a decade (Thomas and Panglaykim 1973:8). Nevertheless, only in 1964 did inflation get completely out of hand, throwing Indonesia into a deep economic crisis, which formed the backdrop to unprecedented political and social upheaval, including the mass killings in 1965-1966 and Soeharto's rise to power. However, the time lag of several years between the take-over of Dutch firms and the economic crisis strongly indicates that the crisis of the mid-1960s cannot be directly attributed to economic decolonization.

Final settlement

The last episode in the aftermath of economic decolonization was the settlement of compensation payments for the nationalized Dutch private companies. Diplomatic relations between Indonesia and the Netherlands were restored surprisingly early, in February 1963. The newly appointed representative of the Netherlands government, C.D. Barkman, remarked afterwards that pressure was exerted to settle the compensation issue, although the highest priority was a return to more friendly relations (Barkman 1993:31-2). Yet another sign of a restoration of relations was the return of Dutch-flag shipping in Indonesian waters by 1965, albeit not in inter-island shipping

A first round of negotiations on compensation payments began in August 1964 in Bali, following a visit to Indonesia by the Dutch Minister of Foreign Affairs Luns. However, progress was slow and the talks were discontinued. A second round was initiated in late August 1965 in Bogor. On this occasion, the Indonesian spokesman, Achmat Ponsen, special assistant to the Minister of Foreign Affairs Subandrio, urged the delegates 'to forget the past in favour

27 ANRI, Jakarta: SOBSI 269, secret letter from the Attorney-General to the Deputy Prime Minister, 7-1-1964; Dick et al. 2002:189; Hunter 1971:269-70.

of a promise for the future' (De Jong and Lessing-Sutherland 2004:16-7).

However, the attempted coup on 30 September 1965 brought the negotiations to a halt for several months. On 7 September 1966 agreement was reached. The Republic of Indonesia agreed to pay 600 million guilders in compensation for the nationalized firms, plus interest accruing at a rate of one per cent annually. The total amount, 689 million guilders, was to be paid in yearly instalments over thirty years, starting in 1973. It was conceded that 600 million guilders was a far cry from the estimated real value of the property seized, 2.7 billion guilders, which in turn was far below the book value, 4.5 billion guilders, stated by the former owners (De Jong and Lessing-Sutherland 2004:9, 23-4). It was a complicated legal and commercial settlement whereby ownership of productive assets changed hands at a discount. It is also worth noting that the settlement did not come at a net cost to Indonesia, since payment was a precondition for receiving international aid through the Inter-Governmental Group on Indonesia (IGGI) beginning in 1967.

The final instalment was paid by the Indonesian government in January 2003. Dutch-Indonesian relations had come full circle since that eventful first week of December 1957.

CHAPTER IX

Conclusion

'The Dutch lion is dead but its claws are still fixed in the body of Indonesia.' If we are to believe Sjafruddin Prawiranegara, the first Indonesian President of the nation's central bank, such thinking was widespread in the early 1950s, even in the highest echelons of Indonesian society. A prominent representative of Masjumi and former Minister of Finance, Sjafruddin ascribed the disappointing economic performance to bottlenecks in production caused mainly by 'feelings of hate and repulsion' (*gevoelens van haat en afkeer*) towards foreign investors. When such sentiments prevail, Sjafruddin argued, labourers are easily persuaded to go on strike and local people are easily incited to commit theft and destroy property of foreign firms. While regretting this state of affairs, Sjafruddin admitted that such resentment was understandable, for under colonial rule foreign firms had pursued their own interests to the detriment of the Indonesian people, an attitude which 'today has still not completely vanished in certain circles of foreign businessmen' (*thans is die instelling in bepaalde buitenlandse ondernemerskringen nog niet geheel verdwenen*) (DJB 1952:26-7). Sjafruddin's analysis combines an appreciation of the historical discontinuity of the times with a perception of some measure of continuity in attitudes on both sides of the confrontation.

This book started out with a literary quotation. Although it is not mentioned in Suparto Brata's novel *Saksi mata*, we can easily imagine its protagonist, young Kuntara, crossing the Red Bridge (*Jembatan Merah*) in Surabaya, chosen as the cover illustration, and while wandering through Surabaya, sensing the momentous changes taking place in Indonesia. The image of a bridge is singularly appropriate to a discussion on decolonization and its economic aspects. Economic decolonization involved the transition from a colonial economy to a national economy. It involved reshaping economic activities into new kinds of businesses, as well as establishing business enterprises for which there had been no room in the colonial setting. Economic decolonization was about building bridges to new business.

Indonesia's economic decolonization differed from political decolonization in many ways, the most obvious differences being in chronology and in the way power was transferred. Unlike political decolonization, economic decolonization cannot be traced back to a specific moment of decisive change, such as the proclamation of Indonesian independence on 17 August 1945. Whereas the claim of sovereignty, the bloody revolution, and full international recognition of independence took almost four and a half years, the control of business enterprises was contested for much longer. Albeit unobtrusively, economic decolonization had already got underway during the Japanese occupation. It reached its climax with the take-over and nationalization of Dutch private companies in the late 1950s. Consequently, the process lasted for seventeen full years, from the end of effective Dutch colonial rule over the entire archipelago in March 1942 until July 1959, by which time almost all Dutch companies had been nationalized.

The chronology of economic decolonization consists of three phases, each with its own characteristics:

1. the initial embryonic phase during the Japanese occupation and the Indonesian Revolution, a period of about seven and a half years (March 1942-December 1949);
2. the middle phase, in which economic decolonization gained momentum, from the transfer of sovereignty up until the Indonesian government's abrogation of the Round Table Agreement, including the Finec Agreement, a period of six years (January 1950-February 1956);
3. the final phase, from the abrogation of the Round Table Agreement until most nationalizations had been effected, a period of almost three and a half years (February 1956-July 1959).

These three phases do not extend to the roots of economic decolonization during the late-colonial period nor to its aftermath in the late 1960s, when a settlement on Indonesian compensation for nationalized Dutch companies was negotiated.

The Round Table Agreement of November 1949 set the stage for economic decolonization after the transfer of sovereignty in late December 1949. It made an official separation between the political and economic aspects of decolonization. Private Dutch firms were permitted to continue operations in Indonesia provided they accepted the minimum terms of the new political sovereignty, including a commitment to promote Indonesian nationals to management and supervisory positions, that is, *Indonesianisasi* in its narrow sense.

The Round Table Agreement acknowledged a mutual interdependence between Indonesia and the Netherlands that had no parallel in political relations. It was a pragmatic compromise that allowed Dutch companies to continue making profits and Indonesia to gain access to Dutch capital, technology, and management. Indonesia's abrogation of the Round Table Agreement in 1956 changed the rules of the game and paved the way for the take-over and subsequent nationalization of Dutch firms. The implementation of the Round Table Agreement and its unilateral abrogation offer convenient lines of demarcation between the different phases of economic decolonization.

Like political decolonization, economic decolonization had its roots in the late-colonial period, but the roots were different. Apart from. Hatta, with his insistence on the virtues of cooperatives, Indonesian nationalists paid very little attention to economic issues. Something resembling a vision of the economic transformation at hand appeared only after the proclamation of independence. Yet some enterprising Indonesians were pioneers in the sense that they entered the modern world of corporate business even before independence. In the colonial economy this would generally not have been an option for indigenous Indonesians. These pioneers began to emerge in the 1910s in both the service sector (insurance, banking, trading) and manufacturing (*kretek* cigarettes, textiles).

Dutch firms, by contrast, entrusted scarcely any indigenous Indonesians with management or supervisory tasks. During the 1930s some promotion of Indonesians did occur in the colonial civil service, but only on a very limited scale. Efforts by the colonial government to modify the economy's heavy bias towards the exports of primary products by stimulating industrialization similarly began only in the 1930s, too late and with too little impact. The heritage of Dutch colonialism therefore consisted of a traditional economic structure with little potential for sustained growth and, more importantly in the short run, an acute shortage of the skills required to manage the nation's economic resources. As recognized by informed foreigners as well as the overwhelming majority of Indonesians, economic decolonization was therefore considerably more difficult to achieve than political decolonization.

Once it had been launched, economic decolonization developed a momentum of its own, characterized by a juxtaposition of external constraints, pragmatism in the management of economic assets, and political urgency. External constraints attained special importance when a higher priority was given to other targets. Pragmatism arose from the necessity to maintain continuity in production and keep the economy running. This usually meant compromising between short-term operational requirements and long-term aspirations. On various occasions, economic measures were motivated mainly or even exclusively by their political significance, often in response to economic nationalism. These three – external constraints, economic pragmatism, political urgency – were always present, but their relative importance varied in the three phases of economic decolonization.

The initial phase (1942-1949) was dominated by the extraordinary conditions prevailing during the Japanese occupation and the Indonesian Revolution. On occasion the displacement of Dutch management personnel in 1942 and 1943 offered senior Indonesian staff opportunities to assume responsibility for run-

The Surabaya office of Borsumij which after the takeover in 1957 was converted into the state-owned trading company Indevitra (KITLV 4243)

ning business units, but only to the extent permitted by the Japanese military command. Enterprising Indonesian traders, often from Sumatra, were likewise able to expand their activities under Japanese rule but, again, their scope of action was highly restricted as Indonesia was integrated into the Japanese war economy and tendencies to autarky were reinforced. Only towards the very end of the occupation did the Japanese authorities take some propaganda initiatives aimed at greater Indonesian participation in managing their own economy.

External constraints also played a decisive role during the Indonesian Revolution. The Republican government gave highest priority to the political and military struggle against the returning Dutch, and it was becoming increasingly evident that the Dutch were intent on retaining control of their economic assets in Indonesia, whether still a colony or a sovereign nation. Despite strong socialist leanings, the Republican government gave repeated assurances that Dutch firms would be able to continue operations after the recognition of independence. The overriding aim was to obtain Dutch acknowledgement of Indonesian independence, but there was also awareness that independence would be very difficult in the short run without Dutch know-how.

Indonesians did manage economic assets in Republican territory until they were returned to their Dutch owners, while enterprising traders from Sumatra kept expanding their businesses, often in conjunction with smuggling and business dealings by military units. However, when it came to choosing the nation's central bank, preference was given to the Dutch-controlled Java Bank over the Republic's own BNI. *Indonesianisasi* of the bureaucracies in Dutch-controlled territory was accelerated, although little *Indonesianisasi* took place in the Dutch firms. At the same time, the climate was gradually improving for Indonesians wishing to set up a new business either in the Republic or in Dutch-controlled territory. On balance, however, the initial phase of economic decolonization delivered very disappointing results, attributable to the predominance of external constraints.

The middle phase (1950-1956) saw pragmatism prevailing in most areas. Successive Indonesian cabinets faced the dilemma of how to respond to demands for radical measures voiced by political parties and pressure groups, while fulfilling the government's obligations to honour the guarantees given to foreign, especially Dutch, firms and taking care not to jeopardize the smooth functioning of the economy. This called for compromises that often failed to satisfy either the Dutch firms or the Indonesian economic nationalists. A pragmatic approach was also required by the other actors in the economy. Economic prospects in the early to mid-1950s were generally favourable for Indonesia as a major supplier of raw materials such as rubber, oil, and tin on the world market. There was potential for rapid expansion of operations in business ventures set up by Indonesian businessmen, who nevertheless had to find ways to deal with the shortage of investment funds and working capital, as well as the lack of accumulated business experience and long-standing market connections. Dutch companies wished to profit from the opportunities opening up, but faced unprecedented bottlenecks in daily operations and had to reformulate business strategies to adjust to the new situation. These three actors – the Indonesian government, Indonesian businessmen, Dutch firms – all figure prominently in this book.

After the transfer of sovereignty the Indonesian government was especially keen to secure control of symbolic economic institutions. Its approach of cooperation and take-over by purchase of equity succeeded in the case of the central bank, national aviation, and a range of public utilities (electricity, urban transport), but not in inter-island shipping, where fierce competition on unequal terms ensued between the Dutch shipping concern KPM and its state-owned rival, PELNI. Voluntary nationalization emerged as a possible model for a harmonious transition of economic assets, but it presupposed the cooperation of Dutch firms and sufficient financial resources in Indonesia to purchase equity at a price acceptable to owners. Neither of these two preconditions were met. In an international comparative perspective, it is worth noting that such an approach was used successfully in Malaysia in the 1970s, with Malaysia using oil revenues to buy out the British. Harmonious economic decolonization is expensive, but so is the alternative. The price paid reflected expectations of future profits. Public utilities, for instance railroads and tramways, were subject to government price controls and were not very profitable, whereas plantations and trading companies were likely to generate handsome profits.

The Indonesian government acknowledged the importance of reducing the excessive dependence of the economy and the government budget on primary exports, especially as the Korean War boom in world trade proved short-lived. Ambitious plans for industrialization were drawn up shortly after the transfer of sovereignty, but implementation was erratic. One critical bottleneck was access to credit, in part due to the banking sector being in the midst of transformation and adjustment, resulting in the remaining foreign banks, three of them Dutch, coexisting with newly established Indonesian institutions. The latter were more inclined to actively support business ventures by indigenous Indonesians, but they had fewer resources and grew increasingly dependent on political connections. The statistical record on structural economic change during the 1950s is not conclusive, but it is clear that the sectoral composition of the economy did not change significantly. Indonesia's thrust towards industrialization only occurred under Soeharto.

In the early and mid-1950s economic nationalism found its most overt manifestation in the Benteng policy of positive discrimination of indigenous Indonesians. Pragmatism also played a role here, notably in attempts to mitigate the worst consequences when the policy was already backfiring. Yet the political urgency that predominated from the beginning precluded a positive outcome. The Benteng policy became a national scandal, notorious for little achievement and much corruption. It provided an environment which on occasion fostered anti-Chinese sentiments, while in the long run it seriously discredited indigenous Indonesian entrepreneurship. In this way, the Benteng policy paved the way for the rigorous measures taken against ethnic Chinese in 1959 and the strengthening of state involvement in the economy in the early 1960s. Again, a comparison with Malaysia is instructive. The New Economic Policy, launched in 1970 in response to racial unrest, significantly enhanced the position of indigenous Malays, *bumiputera,* in the economy, often through para-state institutions, but not primarily at the expense of the economic interests of Malaysian Chinese.

The ill-fated Benteng policy was not an isolated measure. It was part of a wider package of far-reaching state regulations and a general tendency in favour of a socialist economy. In such an economy, private enterprise was increasingly seen as an anomaly. Trade regulations served to boost indigenous Indonesian participation and to allow indigenous Indonesians, *pribumi,* to share in the profits reaped from trading. However, trade policies had already been distorted by an excessive dependence on trade taxes for financing the government budget, not to mention the absurdly complex system of multiple exchange rates enforced in Indonesia during the 1950s. The pragmatism shown in tapping the most easily accessible sources of government revenue while setting targets which were fundamentally political was not a happy combination. There were too many priorities to be pursued simultaneously and they were usually incompatible.

Yet, despite the failure of the Benteng policy, there was a new dynamism in indigenous entrepreneurship in Indonesia during the 1950s. Large numbers of new enterprises were established, covering a broad spectrum of economic activity. The indigenous share in the total number of both incorporated business ventures and newly established firms was high, even in sectors where positive discrimination did not apply. Examples from Central Java at a local level testify to the great diversity of new business ventures and show a shift in ownership patterns from ethnic Chinese to Javanese in the 1950s. Indigenous entrepreneurship frequently benefited from support by the local authorities. Auspiciously, the cooperative movement continued to expand. The rapid increase in participation by Indonesians, particularly indigenous Indonesians, in corporate business was an important part of the *Indonesianisasi* effort. As such, it represented a major step forward in achieving economic decolonization.

This new dynamism applied to both small-scale entrepreneurship at the local level and large concerns operating on a national scale. This was the time of famous empire builders, among them Agoes Moesin Dasaad, Achmad Bakrie, Hasjim Ning, and Soedarpo Sastrosatomo at the national level, and Haji Kalla and T.D. Pardede in Sulawesi and North Sumatra, respectively. The top 200 conglomerates identified in the Indonesian economy several decades later included about twenty indigenous businesses that had been active as early as the 1950s, most having been founded shortly after the transfer of sovereignty. Nonetheless, political connections were becoming increasingly important to continued expansion. Several of the businessmen with prominent positions in the Indonesian corporate world during the 1950s disappeared from the public eye during the Soeharto regime. The role of the military in business was also increasing at this time, mostly through joint ventures with private ethnic Chinese entrepreneurs.

Economic decolonization was directed primarily against the Dutch, not Indonesia's ethnic Chinese. However, the ethnic Chinese did become easy additional targets of economic nationalism due to their strong economic position, their record of collaboration with Dutch colonialism, and their lack of involvement in the Indonesian nationalist movement. Difficulties were aggravated due to the issue of dual Chinese citizenship not yet having been resolved when policies were implemented which drew a sharp distinction between Indonesian and foreign nationals. *Indonesianisasi* was not by definition the same as *pribumisasi*, although that is what it effectively became in the most vigorous applications of the Benteng policy. There was an anti-Chinese side to economic decolonization and it was a strong latent force at all times, but it only tended to surface sporadically.

Ethnic Chinese business was in a particularly vulnerable position whenever economic nationalism took precedence over pragmatism or, for that matter, over adherence to the Republic's constitutional commitment not to discriminate on the basis of race. Nevertheless, the evidence does not suggest that ethnic Chinese business firms were held back by discrimination. The world of small-scale entrepreneurship saw numerous new firms established by ethnic Chinese, especially in trading and manufacturing, occasionally set up in cooperation with local indigenous businessmen, as shown by examples from Central Java. Among the top 200 conglomerates identified later, twenty had ethnic Chinese owners, and almost all their firms were founded in the 1950s. Here we encounter the origins of well-known business concerns such as the Salim group, Astra, Sinar Mas, Rodamas, and Mantrust, to name but a few. In the 1950s the foundations were laid for the development of conglomerates which were to become characteristic of the Indonesian economy in the late twentieth and early twenty-first century.

Dutch companies had reason to be content with the safeguards offered by the Finec Agreement. However, the reality of daily operations in Indonesia after the transfer of sovereignty entailed innumerable difficulties, especially in labour relations, land use, and currency regulations. The firms faced 'exorbitant' wage demands, strikes, occupations of estate land by locals, and restrictions on remitting profits. Despite these hindrances, most stayed on and adjusted to the new situation. Very few quietly sold off their assets and closed the door behind them. Several leading firms, including the famous 'Big Five' in trading, tried out alternative locations outside Indonesia, which almost invariably met with little success. The rationale behind the pragmatic policy of accommodation was a firm conviction that Dutch management was indispensable to the Indonesian economy and likely to remain so. At the same time, Dutch businessmen in Indonesia often showed a greater understanding of Indonesian independence and nationalist aspirations than policy makers in the Netherlands. The scant statistical evidence available suggests that handsome profits were remitted to the Netherlands, despite the restrictions. There was a tendency to give priority to short-term gains over undertaking long-term investment. Strategies formulated by Dutch businesses in Indonesia became increasingly focused on short-term profits.

Indonesianisasi in the narrow sense of promoting Indonesian staff to management and supervisory positions played a peculiar role in business policies pursued by Dutch firms. The lack of such a policy in the past provided a rationale for continuing operations in Indonesia, whereas accommodation to changing conditions appeared to imply efforts to train higher-level Indonesian staff. The record of achievements during the years 1950-1956 is mixed. Among firms with a leading position in their sector and a high profile, the oil giant BPM set an example by investing heavily in training and indeed succeeding in adjusting the ethnic composition of its staff. Others, notably in banking and tin-mining, gained a certain notoriety for a less cooperative attitude. Firms attracting less public attention often felt less urge to incorporate *Indonesianisasi* effectively in management strategies, but again the record shows great variation. The trading concern Internatio is an example of firms that declined to differentiate between indigenous Indonesians and ethnic Chinese, and it was criticized for initiating only superficial changes. Others, for instance the LMOD estate in East Java, implemented a form of *Indonesianisasi* fitting with other priorities of the firm.

Indonesianisasi in Dutch companies offers perhaps the best illustration of how a pragmatic approach was adopted by all involved. The Indonesian government exerted pressure through stiffer immigration policies, and Dutch companies did what they considered inevitable without losing full control of operations. On occasion, the process was speeded up by external factors such as difficulties in recruiting staff from the Netherlands. In the end, however, no one was satisfied. Progress was too slow for the economic nationalists and too fast for Dutch business. A comparative perspective, using examples from non-Dutch foreign corporations, is illuminating as it suggests that much more could have been done to promote indigenous Indonesian personnel than what was actually achieved in most Dutch companies. A combination of stubbornness, ethnocentricity, and the usual reluctance of business to admit outsiders in management explains why Dutch business was not more accommodating.

By the time Indonesia abrogated the Round Table Agreement in 1956 the obvious failure of the Benteng policy and the overall unimpressive record of *Indonesianisasi* underscored that economic decolonization was lagging seriously behind both official and popular expectations. Dutch control over vital parts of the economy was still largely intact, and it was too early to appreciate the gains promised by the new dynamism in Indonesian entrepreneurship. Pragmatism had exacted its toll, but more had probably been achieved during the middle phase of economic decolonization than what surfaced at the time.

The final phase (1956-1959) witnessed the primacy of politics over all other factors in determining the momentum of economic decolonization. The showdown for Dutch business erupted in a highly explosive atmosphere in which politics had become all-pervasive. Constitutional democracy was replaced by Sukarno's Guided Democracy, regional rebellions appeared to threaten the very existence of the nation, martial law ruled. Most importantly for our purposes, Sukarno chose the path of direct, and if need be military, confrontation in the controversy with the Dutch over western New Guinea, a matter which, regrettably, had been left unresolved by the Round Table Conference.

The switch to Sukarno's Guided Economy was a further step in achieving an economy inspired by socialism, which had formed the ideal for leading policy makers ever since the proclamation of independence. The most surprising facet of the massive take-over of Dutch corporate assets which began in the first week of December 1957 is that it had not been foreseen by most Dutchmen living in Indonesia at the time. This testifies to the Dutch conviction of being indispensable in independent Indonesia, and perhaps also to a perception of reality which differed fundamentally from that of the Indonesians, who in a highly charged political atmosphere perceived only Dutch intransigence. The road to take-over was marked by public statements containing undisguised threats. With the benefit of hindsight, it appears clear where the road would lead.

The historical evidence is not conclusive with respect to a number of issues surrounding the take-overs. Although it is not certain, the Sukarno government probably knew something was about to happen without actually orchestrating the seizures. It is also likely that the government was encouraged by the successful completion of negotiations with Japan on war reparations and generous development aid. However, it is not clear why a full year passed before the legal basis was created, in December 1958, for the nationalization of expropriated Dutch assets. It is important to differentiate between the initial event, the seizure of Dutch companies, and the follow-up, the nationalizations.

There were several actors on the political stage at the time: President Sukarno, who had survived an assassination attempt; the PKI, trade unions, and the left wing of PNI, all urging for immediate and decisive action; and finally, the military, which under martial law was in control of the country. The divergent interests of those involved coincided in increasing pressure on the government to seize the opportunity to achieve full economic decolonization through nationalization as it presented itself.

Throughout 1958 and the first half of 1959 the situation within the expropriated Dutch companies was highly unusual. Although the companies were still Dutch property, they were fully managed by Indonesian personnel under military supervision. Operating performance deteriorated, which was inevitable given the utter lack of experience and skill of most of the Indonesian military men suddenly entrusted with the management of these companies. The downturn in performance may also be partially explained by detrimental external developments at that time. Although a recovery did come about fairly quickly, in 1959, it is hazardous to attribute the take-overs directly to the extreme deterioration of the Indonesian economy in the early and mid-1960s. Both military business and management by ethnic Chinese flourished in the wake of the take-overs. The final phase of economic decolonization would provoke an exodus of the Dutch, taking with them Dutch capital, technology, know-how, and management experience. The process of economic decolonization reached completion, but only through draconian measures and at a high price.

During the immediate aftermath of economic decolonization, a small number of Dutch firms continued operations, either because the change of ownership was postponed or because they had escaped nationalization by virtue of being partially British, as was the case with BPM and Unilever. During Indonesia's ill-fated *konfrontasi* with Malaysia in 1963 and 1964 British and American firms were seized in a fashion reminiscent of the take-overs of Dutch businesses in 1957. Yet these take-overs were not linked to decolonization or followed up by a formal change of ownership. The companies were handed back to their owners as soon as the military campaign ended.

The aftermath to economic decolonization also embraced the settlement of Indonesia's payment of compensation for the nationalized Dutch firms. Negotiations began shortly after the Dutch surrender of western New Guinea, and an agreement was reached in 1966. The key issue here is whether the Indonesian payments formed anything approaching an adequate compensation for the nationalized assets. Total payments fell far short of the demands made by the Dutch owners, although it should be borne in mind that the Indonesian argument that Dutch economic assets had been substantially written off during the 1950s still needs to be substantiated. The dispute concerned whether compensation should be paid according to the book value of assets or expected future earnings. The arguments brought forward by the Indonesians are not at variance with the strategy geared towards short-term gain pursued by many Dutch firms prior to the take-overs.

Economic decolonization was a three-pronged process encompassing *Indonesianisasi* in its various forms, nationalization, and a change of orientation in the economy. These three bridged the gap between the colonial economy inherited from Dutch rule and the national economy which has since prevailed in Indonesia. There was considerable variation in the degree to which targets were met. Some forms of *Indonesianisasi*, notably the establishment of new enterprises in sectors previously closed to Indonesians and the transfer of formerly colonial public enterprises to the state, met with considerable success. Other forms of *Indonesianisasi*, in particular attempts to wrest control from foreign-owned business in trading and the promotion of Indonesians to higher positions in Dutch firms, either backfired or produced meagre results on balance. Nationalization of Dutch enterprises, which may be viewed as the most extreme form of *Indonesianisasi*, was implemented in a dramatic and costly fashion, but with the important corollary that it was acknowledged as not being in violation of international law. The large-scale conversion of private Dutch firms to state-owned enterprises accounts for the exceptionally strong involvement by the state in the Indonesian economy from the late 1950s onwards. Structural economic change, finally, scarcely occurred at all during this phase of transition in Indonesia's economic development.

Causal links between the three prongs of the decolonization process draw our special attention. It would be stretching the argument too far to assert that the Dutch companies were nationalized because they had not done enough to promote Indonesians to higher positions. Such a facile analysis fails to take into account the pragmatism often demonstrated by the Indonesian authorities and the highly explosive political situation in which the take-overs and nationalizations happened. Neither can it be said that the path to forced nationalization was eased by *Indonesianisasi* in those firms in which it met with some success. Voluntary nationalization was not a viable model for application on a large scale, and the newly emerging Indonesian businesses had not yet had time to acquire sufficient capabilities to replace the Dutch. Take-over and nationalization were the inevitable corollary of political urgency in a very tense situation, in which Dutch companies quickly became scapegoats, held responsible for everything that had gone wrong.

In hindsight, it is easy to argue that it might have been better for Indonesia to turn to nationalization only after more had been accomplished in terms of *Indonesianisasi*, that is, to wait for a time when it was better positioned to replace Dutch with Indonesians, whether of indigenous origin or not. But such a scenario presupposes a continued pragmatism which was incompatible with the volatile political situation prevailing in the late 1950s, caused by steady deterioration in the relationship with the Netherlands and an increasingly sharp cleavage in domestic politics between the radical PKI and the radical wing of PNI, supported by the President, on the one hand and the religious parties and the armed forces on the other. Furthermore, the expulsion of the Dutch did not plunge Indonesia into deep economic crisis immediately. Managing the nation's resources and keeping the economy afloat became more difficult, but not impossible.

Our final impression draws on intuition. Looking at the evidence on Indonesian economic life during the 1940s and 1950s, it seems that we are faced with two realities coexisting side by side. There was the reality of the Dutch, rooted in the past and coloured by the conviction of being indispensable, while focused on the pursuit of short-term gain. And there was the reality of the Indonesians, oriented towards the future and filled with increasing self-confidence and a growing awareness of the necessity of a complete emancipation from the heritage of colonial rule. In the end, the Dutch had to cede considerable material assets and many Dutch people were expelled from a place they considered home. The Indonesians gained what they wanted but lost a wealth of expertise and easy access to investment capital and modern technology. Both groups paid a high price.

Appendices

Appendix 1. Cabinets and political parties, 1945-1959

Period	Prime minister	Political parties
11 Nov. 1945 – 27 June 1947	Sjahrir	PSI, Masjumi, PNI
27 June 1947 – 23 Jan. 1948	Amir Sjarifuddin	Masjumi, PNI, PSII
29 Jan. 1948 – 19 Dec. 1949	Hatta (RI)	PNI, Masjumi
19 Dec. 1949 – 6 Sept. 1950	Hatta (RSI)	PNI, Masjumi
6 Sept. 1950 – 21 March 1951	Natsir	Masjumi, PSI
18 April 1951 – 23 Febr. 1952	Sukiman	Masjumi, PNI
30 March 1952 – 2 June 1953	Wilopo	PNI, Masjumi
31 July 1953 – 24 July 1955	Ali Sastroamidjojo	PNI, NU
Aug. 1955 – 3 March 1956	Harahap	Masjumi, NU, PSI
March 1956 – 14 March 1957	Ali Sastroamidjojo	PNI, Masjumi, NU
9 April 1957 – 9 July 1959	Djuanda	*kabinet kerdja*
9 July 1959 –	Sukarno	*kabinet kerdja*

Notes: RI = Republik Indonesia (Republic of Indonesia), RIS = Republik Indonesia Serikat (United States of Indonesia, 27 Dec. 1949 – 17 Aug. 1950), *kabinet kerdja* (working cabinet) = extra-parliamentary cabinet. 'Guided Democracy' (*Demokrasi Terpimpin*) was proclaimed on 17 August 1959.

Main political parties with share of votes in the general election of September 1955 and number of seats in parliament

	Party	% of votes	Seats
PNI	Partai Nasional Indonesia	22.3	57
	Masjumi	20.9	57
NU	Nahdlatul Ulama	18.4	45
PKI	Partai Komunis Indonesia	16.4	39
PSII	Partai Sarikat Islam Indonesia	2.9	8
Parkindo	Partai Kristen Indonesia	2.6	8
	Partai Katholik	2.0	6
PSI	Partai Sosialis Indonesia	2.0	6
	Total of eight largest parties	87.5	226

Sources: Ricklefs 1981:238; Cribb 2000:164.
Note: Total number of seats in parliament was 257.

Appendix 2. Foreign trade, 1940-1960

Table 1. Foreign trade of the Netherlands Indies in 1940 and of Dutch-controlled Indonesia, 1946-1949 (in millions of guilders)

	Exports			Imports	Balance
	Rubber	Oil	Total	Total	
1940	392	170	883	437	+ 446
1946	70	6	155	282	- 127
1947	68	62	343	810	- 467
1948	256	260	1044	1134	- 90
1949	248	412	1478	1574	- 96

Sources: 1940: Korthals Altes 1991:56, 75, 163; 1946-1948: ANRI, Jakarta: NEFIS, 18-5-1949; 1949: DJB 1951:63, 1953:123.

Table 2. Foreign trade, 1950-1957 (Rp. million)

	Exports			Imports	Balance
	Rubber	Oil	Total	Total	
1950	1,284	560	3,038	1,673	1,365
1951[1]	2,483	703	4,908	3,318	1,590
1951[2]	7,449	2,109	14,724	9,954	4,770
1952	4,778	2,181	10,652	10,806	- 154
1953	3,080	2,291	9,343	8,584	759
1954	3,013	2,579	9,759	7,172	2,587
1955	4,888	2,421	10,620	6,888	3,732
1956	4,028	2,560	10,055	9,755	300
1957	3,983	3,677	11,052	9,086	1,966

Source: Bank Indonesia 1955:93, 96, 1958:128-9.
Exchange rate: [1] Rp. 3.80/$, [2] Rp. 11.40/$.

Table 3. Exports by sector, 1950-1956 (Rp. million)

	Total	Non-oil	Agricultural	Smallholder	Estate
1950	3,038	2,478	2,175	1,425	750
1951	4,908	4,205	3,719	2,422	1,297
1952	10,652	8,471	7,124	3,792	3,332
1953	9,343	7,052	5,886	3,007	2,879
1954	9,759	7,180	6,110	3,342	2,768
1955	10,620	8,199	7,198	4,006	3,192
1956	10,055	7,495	6,476	3,488	2,988

Sources: Bank Indonesia 1955:93, 1957:127; Bank Agro, Medan: AVROS, 9-7-1957.
Exchange rate: 1950-1951: Rp. 3.80/$, 1952-1956: Rp. 11.40/$.

Table 4. Imports by type of commodity, 1951-1956 (Rp. million)

	Total	Raw materials	Textiles	Capital goods
1951	3,318	1,148	1,701	469
1952	10,806	3,440	5,377	1,989
1953	8,584	3,232	3,740	1,612
1954	7,172	3,048	2,686	1,425
1955	6,888	3,451	2,133	1,279
1956	9,755	3,775	4,050	1,893

Sources: Bank Indonesia 1955:93, 1957:33.
Exchange rate: 1950-1951: Rp. 3.80/$, 1952-1956: Rp. 11.40/$.

Table 5. Geographic composition of foreign trade, 1951-1957 (given as percentage)

	Destination of exports			Origin of imports		
	Asia	Europe	Americas	Asia	Europe	Americas
1951	41	35	17	42	33	21
1952	33	33	27	40	36	21
1953	35	35	22	43	35	19
1954	40	34	18	46	35	15
1955	34	36	24	36	44	16
1956	39	38	17	42	37	18
1957	44	33	16	42	38	17

Source: Bank Indonesia 1955:98-9, 1959:174-5.

Table 6. Trade with the Netherlands, 1951-1957

	Exports to Netherlands			Imports from Netherlands		
	Value (Rp. million)	Share (%) Europe	Share (%) Total	Value (Rp. million)	Share (%) Europe	Share (%) Total
1951	1012	59	21	395	36	12
1952	2278	65	21	1417	37	13
1953	2104	64	23	1007	34	12
1954	1882	56	19	750	30	10
1955	1675	43	16	808	26	12
1956	1956	51	19	1038	29	11
1957	1854	51	17	892	26	10

Source: Bank Indonesia 1955:98-9, 1958:133-4.

Table 7. Foreign trade performance, 1957-1960

	1957	1958	1959	1960
Total exports (Rp. million)	11,052	8,612	10,613	9,578
- Rubber	3,983	2,978	4,780	4,296
- Oil	3,677	3,219	3,257	2,515
- Tin	631	431	412	829
- Tobacco	383	345	278	329
- Palm oil	347	314	273	276
Imports (Rp. million)	9,086	5,851	5,494	6,583
- Capital goods	1,895	1,259	1,122	1,447
Balance of trade (Rp. million)	1,966	2,761	5,119	2,995
Export production (thous. tons)				
- Smallholder rubber	418	377	485	444
- Estate rubber	261	223	233	190
- Tin	39	28	26	33
- Tobacco	15	22	16	23
- Palm oil	170	168	136	143

Sources: Bank Indonesia 1958:128-9, 1960:132-6, 139, 1966:109-11, 120-4.

Appendix 3. Exchange rates, 1950-1960 (Rp./$)

	Official	Exports	Imports	Black market
1950	3.80	6.70	9.50	14.50
1951		7.60	11.40	16.50
1952	11.40	11.10	11.70	21.70
1953		11.40	14.50	25.30
1954		11.40	13.90	34.30
1955		11.40	15.30	33.30
1956		12.00	21.40	31.00
1957		19.60	27.60	45.80
1958		30.40	47.00	95.00
1959	45.00	32.90	60.60	225.00
1960		41.60	80.00	150.00

Source: Rosendale 1978:164.

Appendix 4. Labour conflicts, 1950-1957

	All of Indonesia			North Sumatra	
	Strikes	Strikers (thousands)	Lost days (thousands)	Strikes	Lost days (thousands)
1950	144	491	1112		
1951	541	319	531		
1952	349	133	(125)	65	194
1953	280	420	687	115	341
1954	319	158	(340)	287	366
1955	(469)	239	585	500	446
1956	(505)	340	996	729	560
1957	(128)	1080	1132	231	90

Sources: Indonesia: Bank Indonesia 1955:166, 1958:218; North Sumatra: AVROS 1956:table xii; GAPPERSU 1960:table xii.

Bibliography

Sources

Arsip Nasional Republik Indonesia (ANRI), Jakarta
- Algemeene Secretarie: 147, 148, 258, 373, 474, 482, 538, 763, 776, 789, 799, 806, 808, 912, 1283.
- Delegasi Indonesia: 1217, 1251.
- Kabinet Presiden: 18, 63, 1479, 1505, 1526, 1550, 1658, 1695.
- Kementerian Keuangan 1950-1959: 313, 351, 418.
- Kementerian Penerangan: 207.
- Kementerian Perburuhan dan Sosial 1945-1949: 69.
- Muh. Yamin: 72, 89, 188, 346.
- NEFIS: 29, 75, 121.
- Peraturan Pemerintah Pengganti Undang-Undang: 32.
- Peraturan Pemerintah Sekretaris Kabinet: 386.
- Risalah Rapat Dewan Perwakilan Rakjat (DPR): 127, 132, 222.
- Sekretariat Negara RI: 375, 378, 781.
- Roeslan Abdul Gani: 113.
- Sentral Organisasi Buruh Seluruh Indonesia (SOBSI): 268, 269, 278, 287.

Bank Indonesia, Jakarta:
- De Javasche Bank (DJB): 125, 126, 128, 129, 130, 131, 132, 133, 181, 183, 184, 197, 198, 1581, 1583, 1584, 3233, 3234, 3235, 3236, 3322, 3352, 3353.
- Lembaga Alat-Alat Pembajaran Luar Negri (LAAPLN) 13.

Bank Mandiri, Jakarta: Nederlandsche Handel-Maatschappij (NHM, Factorij).

Bank Agro, Medan: Algemeene Vereeniging van Rubberplanters ter Oostkust van Sumatra (AVROS), Gabungan Pengusaha Perkebunan Sumatera Utara (GAPPERSU)/Sumatra Planters' Association (SPA).

PT Semen Padang, Indarung, West Sumatra.

Bibliography

Abdullah, Taufik
2005 'Indonesianisasi; Sebuah wacana dan serentetan peristiwa', *Lembaran Sejarah* 8-2:1-14.

Abeyasekere, Susan
1989 *Jakarta; A history*. Singapore: Oxford University Press.

Abriyanto, M.
1995 *Garuda Indonesia; Pengisi kemerdekaan bangsa*. Jakarta: Garuda Indonesia.

Agung, Ide Anak Agung Gde
1973 *Twenty years Indonesian foreign policy, 1945-1965*. The Hague: Mouton.

Alers, H.J.H.
1958 *Rubberplantage; Indische roman uit de dagen van de grote uittocht*. 's-Gravenhage: Van Stockum.

Amstutz, N.G.
1958 *Development of indigenous importers in Indonesia, 1950-1955*. PhD thesis, Tufts University, Boston, MA.

Anspach, Ralph
1969 'Indonesia', in: Frank Golay et al. (eds), *Underdevelopment and economic nationalism in Southeast Asia*, pp. 111-201. Ithaca, NY: Cornell University Press.

Antlöv, Hans and Thommy Svensson
1991 'From rural home weavers to factory labour; The industrialization of textile manufacturing in Majalaya', in: Paul Alexander, Peter Boomgaard and Ben White (eds), *In the shadow of agriculture; Non-farm activities in the Javanese economy. Past and present*, pp. 113-26. Amsterdam: Royal Tropical Institute.

Apriyanto, Tri Chandra
2004 'Warisan kolonial yang belum (di)selesaikan; Nasionalisasi perusahaan perkebunan di Jember', Paper presented at an international workshop on 'The economic side of decolonization', Yogyakarta, 18-19 August.
2005 'The decolonization process in Jember', Paper presented at an international conference on 'The economic decolonization of Indonesia in regional perspective', Leiden, 18-19 November.

Arndt, H.W.
1971 'Banking in hyperinflation and stabilisation', in: Bruce Glassburner (ed.), *The economy of Indonesia*, pp. 359-95. Ithaca, NY: Cornell University Press.

Asmulyadi
1994 'Nasionalisasi pabrik semen Padang dan dampaknya terhadap peningkatan kapasitas produksi 1958-1977', BA thesis, Faculty of Arts, Andalas University, Padang.

AVROS
1956 *Statistische gegevens*. Medan: Algemeene Vereeniging van Rubberplanters ter Oostkust van Sumatra.

Aziz, M.
1955 *Japan's colonialism and Indonesia*. The Hague: Nijhoff.

Backman, Michael
1999 *Asian eclipse; Exposing the dark side of business in Asia*. Singapore: Wiley.

Bangun, Tridah
1983 *T.D. Pardede; Wajah seorang pejuang wiraswasta*. Jakarta: Gunung Agung.
1987 *Dr. T.D. Pardede 70 tahun; Pejuang-patriot*. Jakarta: Haji Masagung.

Bank Indonesia
1954 *Laporan tahun pembukuan 1953/54*. Djakarta: Kolff.
1955-1966 *Report for the year 1954/55, 1955/56, 1956/57, 1957/58, 1958/59, 1959/60, 1960/65*. Djakarta: Kolff.

Barkman, C.D.
1993 *Bestemming Jakarta; Het herstel der Nederlands-Indonesische betrekkingen*. Amsterdam: Van Soeren.

Bartlett III, A.G.
1972 *Pertamina: Indonesia National Oil*. Jakarta: Amerasian.

Basundoro, Purnawan
2004 'Menjadi tu(h)an di rumah sendiri; Pancaroba usaha pertambangan minyak di Indonesia 1945-1960', *Lembaran Sejarah* 7-1:173-95.

Baudet, H. and C. Fasseur
1977 'Koloniale bedrijvigheid', in: J.H. van Stuijvenberg (ed.), *De economische geschiedenis van Nederland*, pp. 309-50. Groningen: Wolters-Noordhoff.

Baudet, H. and M. Fennema et al.
1983 *Het Nederlands belang bij Indië*. Utrecht: Aula.

Baudet, M.J. and G.J. Wijers
1976 'De economische betekenis van Nederlands-Indië voor Nederland', *Economisch-Statistische Berichten* 61:885-8.

B.B.L.
1931 *De B.B.L. en Indianisatie*. Batavia: Plantijn.

Bertocchi, G. and F. Canova
2002 'Did colonization matter for growth?; An empirical exploration into the historical causes of Africa's underdevelopment', *European Economic Review* 46:1815-71.

Boeke, J.H.
1953 *Economics and economic policy of dual societies as exemplified by Indonesia*. New York: Institute of Pacific Relations.

Boomgaard, Peter
2000 'Surviving the slump; Developments in real incomes during the depression of the 1930s in Indonesia, particularly Java', in: Peter Boomgaard and Ian Brown (eds), *Weathering the storm; The economies of Southeast Asia in the 1930s depression*, pp. 23-52. Singapore: Institute of Southeast Asian Studies.

Boomgaard, Peter and A.J. Gooszen
1991 *Changing economy in Indonesia; XI. Population trends, 1795-1942*. Amsterdam: Royal Tropical Institute.

Booth, Anne

1988 *Agricultural development in Indonesia*. Sydney: Allen and Unwin.

1990 'Foreign trade and domestic development in the colonial economy', in: Anne Booth, W.J. O'Malley and Anne Weidemann (eds), *Indonesian economic history in the Dutch colonial era*, pp. 267-95. New Haven, CT: Yale University Press.

1998 *The Indonesian economy in the nineteenth and twentieth centuries; A history of missed opportunities*. London: Macmillan.

2002 'Growth collapses in Indonesia; A comparison of the 1930s and the 1990s', *Itinerario. European Journal of Overseas History* 26-3/4:73-99.

BPS

1959 *Perusahaan-perusahaan industri (Manufacturing industries) 1957*. Jakarta: Biro Pusat Statistik.

Brand, J. van den

1902 *De millioenen uit Deli*. Amsterdam: Höveker and Wormser.

Brata, Suparto

2002 *Saksi mata*. Jakarta: Kompas.

Burger, D.H.

1939 *De ontsluiting van Java's binnenlanden voor het wereldverkeer*. Wageningen: Veenman.

1975 *Sociologisch-economische geschiedenis van Indonesia*. Amsterdam: Royal Tropical Institute; Leiden: KITLV Press. [Vol. 1 translated as *Sejarah ekonomis sosiologis Indonesia*. Djakarta 1957.]

Business directory

1956 *Business directory of Indonesia*. Jakarta.

Campo, J.N.F.M. á

1998 'Business not as usual; Dutch shipping in independent Indonesia', *International Journal of Maritime History* 10-2:1-39.

Charlesworth, Harold Karr

1959 *A banking system in transition; The origin, concept and growth of the Indonesian banking system*. Jakarta: New Nusantara Publishing.

Cholil, M.

1971 *Sejarah operasi-operasi pembebasan Irian Barat*. Jakarta: Pusat Sejarah ABRI.

CISI

1990 *A study of top 200 national private business groups in Indonesia, 1989*. Jakarta: CISI Raya Utama.

Claver, Alex

2006 *Commerce and capital in colonial Java; Trade, finance and commercial relations between Europeans and Chinese, 1820s-1942*. PhD thesis, Free University of Amsterdam.

Clerx, J.M.M.J.

1992 'De financiële verhouding tussen Nederland en Indonesië opnieuw bezien (1945-1967)', *Politieke Opstellen* 11/12:59-71.

Coppel, Charles A.

1997 'Revisiting Furnivall's "Plural society"; Colonial Java as a Mestizo society?', *Ethnic and Racial Studies* 20:562-79. [Reprinted in: Charles

A. Coppel, *Studying ethnic Chinese in Indonesia*, pp. 136-56. Singapore: Singapore Society of Asian Studies, 2002.]

Corden, W.M. and J.A.C. Mackie
1962 'The development of the Indonesian exchange rate system', *Malayan Economic Review* 7-1:37-60.

Creutzberg, P.
1975 *Changing economy in Indonesia; I. Indonesia's export crops, 1816-1940*. The Hague: Nijhoff.
1977 *Changing economy in Indonesia; III. Expenditure on fixed assets*. The Hague: Nijhoff.
1979 *Changing economy in Indonesia; V. National income*. The Hague: Nijhoff.

Cribb, Robert
1981 'Political dimensions of the currency question, 1945-1947', *Indonesia* 31:131-6.
1988 'Opium and the Indonesian revolution', *Modern Asian Studies* 22:701-22.
2000 *Historical atlas of Indonesia*. Richmond: Curzon.

Data Consult
1991 *Anatomy of Indonesian conglomerates*. Jakarta: Data Consult.

Daulay, Amir Husin et al.
1993 *William Soerjadjaja; Kejayaan dan kejatuhannya; Studi kasus eksistensi konglomerasi bisnis di Indonesia*. Jakarta: Bina Rena Pariwara.

Derksen, J.B.D. and J. Tinbergen
1945 'Berekeningen over de economische betekenis van Nederlandsch-Indië voor Nederland', *Maandschrift van het Centraal Bureau voor de Statistiek* 40:210-6.

Dick, Howard W.
1987a *The Indonesian interisland shipping industry; An analysis of competition and regulation*. Singapore: Institute of Southeast Asian Studies.
1987b 'Prahu shipping in Eastern Indonesia in the interwar period', *Bulletin of Indonesian Economic Studies* 23-1:104-21.
1989 'Japan's economic expansion in the Netherlands Indies between the First and Second World Wars', *Journal of Southeast Asian Studies* 20-2:244-72.
1993a 'Nineteenth-century industrialization; A missed opportunity?', in: J. Thomas Lindblad (ed.), *New challenges in the modern economic history of Indonesia*, pp. 123-48. Leiden: Programme of Indonesian Studies.
1993b 'Oei Tiong Ham', in: John Butcher and Howard Dick (eds), *The rise and fall of revenue farming; Business elites and the emergence of the modern state in Southeast Asia*, pp. 272-80. New York: St. Martin's Press.
2003 *Surabaya, city of work; A socioeconomic history, 1900-2000*. Singapore: Singapore University Press.
2004 'The Indonesian economy in the 1950s; Multiple exchange rates, business networks and centre-region relations', in: Hanneman Samuel and Henk Schulte Nordholt (eds), *Indonesia in transition; Rethinking civil society, region and crisis*, pp. 175-94. Yogyakarta: Pustaka Pelajar.

Dick, Howard W., Vincent J.H. Houben, J. Thomas Lindblad and Thee Kian Wie
2002 *The emergence of a national economy; An economic history of Indonesia 1800-2000*. Crows Nest, NSW: Allen and Unwin.

Dieleman, Marleen
2007 *The rhythm of strategy: A corporate biography of the Salim group in Indonesia*. Amsterdam: Amsterdam University Press.

DJB
1940-1953 *Verslag van de President van De Javasche Bank en van de Raad van Commissarissen over het boekjaar 1939/40, 1940/41, 1941/46+1946/47, 1947/48+1948/49, 1949/50, 1950/51, 1951/52, 1952/53*. Batavia: Kolff.

Doel, Wim van den
2000 *Afscheid van Indië; De val van het Nederlandse imperium in Azië*. Amsterdam: Prometheus.

Donnithorne, Audrey
1954 'Western enterprise in Indonesia today', *Pacific Affairs* 27:27-40.

Doorn, J.A.A. van
1994 *De laatste eeuw van Indië; Ontwikkeling en ondergang van een koloniaal project*. Amsterdam: Bert Bakker.

Drooglever, P.J.
2005 *Een daad van vrije keuze: De Papoea's van westelijk Nieuw-Guinea en de grenzen van het zelfbeschikkingsrecht*. Amsterdam: Boom.

Elson, R.E.
2001 *Suharto; A political biography*. Cambridge: Cambridge University Press.

Eng, Pierre van der
1987 *De Marshall-hulp*. Houten: De Haan.
1992 'The real domestic product of Indonesia, 1880-1989', *Explorations in Economic History* 29:343-73.
1994 *Food supply in Java during war and decolonisation, 1940-1949*. Hull: Centre for Southeast Asian Studies.
1998 'Exploring exploitation; The Netherlands and colonial Indonesia 1870-1940', *Revista de Historia Económica* 16:291-321.
2001 'Indonesia's economy and standard of living in the 20th century', in: Grayson Lloyd and Shannon Smith (eds), *Indonesia today; Challenges of history*, pp. 181-99. Singapore: Institute of Southeast Asian Studies.
2002 'Indonesia's growth performance in the twentieth century', in: Angus Maddison, D.S. Prasada Rao and William F. Shepherd (eds), *The Asian economies in the twentieth century*, pp. 143-79. Cheltenham/Northampton, MA: Elgar.

Erniwati
2004 'Posisi ekonomi orang Cina di Padang pada masa dekolonisasi', Paper presented at an international workshop on 'The economic side of decolonization', Yogyakarta, 18-19 August.

Fasseur, C.
1994 'Cornerstone and stumbling block; Racial classification and the late colonial state in Indonesia', in: Robert Cribb (ed.), *The late colonial state in Indonesia; Political and economic foundations of the Netherlands Indies 1880-1942*, pp. 31-56. Leiden: KITLV Press. [Verhandelingen 163.]

Feith, Herbert
1962 *The decline of constitutional democracy in Indonesia*. Ithaca, NY: Cornell University Press.

Fennema, M. and J. Rhijnsburger
1981 'Nederland, Indië en de wereldmarkt', in: Ferd Crone and Henk Overbeek (eds), *Nederlands kapitaal over de grenzen; Verplaatsing van produktie en gevolgen voor de nationale ekonomie*, pp. 72-93, Amsterdam: SUA.

Fieldhouse, D.K.
1978 *Unilever overseas; The anatomy of a multinational, 1895-1965*. London: Croom Helm.

Fischer, Louis
1959 *The story of Indonesia*. New York: Harper.

Furnivall, J.S.
1939 *Netherlands India; A study of plural economy*. Cambridge: Cambridge University Press.
1943 *Educational progress in Southeast Asia*. New York: Institute of Pacific Relations.

GAPPERSU
1960 *Angka-angka statistik*. Medan: Gabungan Pengusaha Perkebunan Sumatera Utara/Sumatra Planters' Association.

Gardner, Paul F.
1997 *Shared hopes, separate fears; Fifty years of U.S.-Indonesian relations*. Boulder, CO: Westview.

Gase, Ronald
1984 *Misleiding of zelfbedrog; Het Nederlandse beleid ten aanzien van Nieuw Guinea*. Baarn: In den Toren.

Gelderen, J. van
1961 'The economics of the tropical colony', in: J.H. Boeke et al., *Indonesian economics; The concept of dualism in theory and policy*, pp. 111-64. The Hague: Van Hoeve.

Gerungan, J.B.
1952 'The cigarette industry in Indonesia', *Economic Review of Indonesia* 6:64-6.

Geus, P.B.R. de
1984 *De Nieuw-Guinea kwestie; Aspecten van buitenlands beleid en militaire macht*. Leiden: Nijhoff.

Glassburner, Bruce
1971 'Economic policy-making in Indonesia, 1950-1957', in: Bruce Glassburner (ed.), *The economy of Indonesia*, pp. 70-98. Ithaca, NY: Cornell University Press.

Goedkoop, J.A.M.
1990 'Handelsvereeniging "Amsterdam" 1945-1958; Herstel en heroriëntatie', *Jaarboek voor de Geschiedenis van Bedrijf en Techniek* 7:219-40.

Gooszen, Hans
1999 *A demographic history of the Indonesian archipelago, 1880-1942*. Leiden: KITLV Press. [Verhandelingen 183.]

Gould, J.W.
1961 *Americans in Sumatra*. The Hague: Nijhoff.
Gouw Giok Siong
1960 *Segi-segi hukum internasional pada nasionalisasi di Indonesia*. PhD thesis, University of Indonesia, Jakarta.
Graaf, H.J. de, A.H. Joustra and A.G. Vromans
1960 *Nederlandsch-Indië onder Japanse bezetting*. Franeker: Wever.
Graaff, Bob de
1997 *'Kalm temidden van woedende golven'; Het Ministerie van Koloniën en zijn taakomgeving, 1912-1940*. Den Haag: SDU.
Griffiths, Richard T.
1996 'The Dutch economic miracle', in: Jan Luiten van Zanden (ed.), *The economic development of the Netherlands since 1870*, pp. 173-86. Cheltenham/Brookfield, MA: Elgar.
Groeneboer, Kees
1998 *The Dutch language in colonial Indonesia, 1600-1950; A history of language*. Amsterdam: Amsterdam University Press.
Hack, Karl
2003 'Theories and approaches to British decolonization in Southeast Asia', in: Marc Frey, Ronald W. Pruessen and Tan Tai Yong (eds), *The transformation of Southeast Asia; International perspectives on decolonization*, pp. 105-62. Armonk/London: Sharpe.
Hadinoto, Soejono
1949 *Ekonomi Indonesia; Dari ekonomi kolonial ke ekonomi nasional*. Djakarta: Jajasan Pembangunan.
Harper, T.N.
1999 *The end of empire and the making of Malaya*. Cambridge: Cambridge University Press.
Hatta, Moh.
1957 *The co-operative movement in Indonesia*. Ithaca, NY: Cornell University Press.
Hersumpana
2004 '*Indonesianisasi* of the rural industry in Moyudan, Yogyakarta, 1945-1957', Paper presented at an international workshop on 'The economic side of decolonization', Yogyakarta, 18-19 August.
2005 'Indigenous entrepreneurs in the wave of the free market; Transition from colonial to national economy, 1945-1967', Paper presented at an international conference on 'The economic decolonization of Indonesia in regional perspective', Leiden, 18-19 November.
Higgins, Benjamin
1957 *Indonesia's economic stabilization and development*. New York: Institute of Pacific Relations.
Hikita, Yasuyuki
1997 'Japanese companies' inroads into Indonesia under Japanese military domination', in: Peter Post and Elly Touwen-Bouwsma (eds), *Japan,*

Indonesia and the war; Myths and realities, pp. 134-76. Leiden: KITLV Press. [Verhandelingen 173.]

Hunter, Alex
1971 'The Indonesian oil industry', in: Bruce Glassburner (ed.), *The economy of Indonesia*, pp. 254-314. Ithaca, NY: Cornell University Press.

Huydecoper van Nigtevecht, J.L.R.
1990 *Nieuw-Guinea; Het einde van een koloniaal beleid*. 's-Gravenhage: SDU.

Indisch Verslag
1932-1941 *Indisch Verslag over 1931, 1934, 1938, 1940*. Batavia: Landsdrukkerij.

Iwatake, Teruhiko
1995 *Nanpo gunseika no keizai shisak – Malai, Sumatera, Jawa no kiroku*. Second edition. Tokyo: Ryukei Shosha. [First published 1981.]

Jacob, M. (see also Vredenbregt, Jacob)
1986 *Sesuai petang*. Jakarta: Djambatan.

Japanese military administration
1963 *Japanese military administration in Indonesia* [Indonesia ni okeru Nihon gunsei no kenkyu]. Washington, DC: Department of Commerce. [Originally published in 1959 by Okuma Memorial Social Sciences Research Institute, Tokyo: Kinokuniya Shoten.]

Johnson, Harry
1972 'The ideology of economic policy in new states', in: David Wall (ed.), *Chicago essays in economic development*, pp. 23-40. Chicago: University of Chicago Press.

Jong, J.J.P. de and D.M.E. Lessing Sutherland
2004 *To forget the past in favour of a promise for the future; Nederland, Indonesië en de financiële overeenkomst van 1966; Onderhandeling, regeling, uitvoering*. Den Haag: Buitenlandse Zaken.

Jong, L. de
2002 *The collapse of a colonial society; The Dutch in Indonesia during the Second World War*. Leiden: KITLV Press. [Verhandelingen 206.]

Jonker, Joost and Keetie Sluyterman
2000 *Thuis op de wereldmarkt; Nederlandse handelshuizen door de eeuwen heen*. Den Haag: SDU.

Kahin, Audrey R.
1997 'Trade and taxes; Aspects of the West Sumatra economy during the Revolution', in: Taufik Abdullah (ed.), *The heartbeat of Indonesian Revolution*, pp. 199-210. Jakarta: Gramedia.

Kahin, Audrey R. and George McT. Kahin
1995 *Subversion as foreign policy; The secret Eisenhower and Dulles debacle in Indonesia*. New York: Norton.

Kahin, George McT.
1952 *Nationalism and revolution in Indonesia*. Ithaca, NY: Cornell University Press.

Kano, Hiroyoshi
2004 *Gendai Indoneshia keizaishi ron; Yushutsu keizai to nogyo mondai*. Tokyo: Tokyo University Press.

Kanumoyoso, Bondan

2001 *Nasionalisasi perusahaan Belanda di Indonesia*. Jakarta: Sinar Harapan.

Keppy, Peter

2001 *Hidden business; Indigenous and ethnic Chinese entrepreneurs in the Majalaya textile industry, West Java, 1928-1974*. PhD thesis, Free University of Amsterdam.

2006 *Sporen van vernieling; Oorlogsschade, roof en rechtsherstel in Indonesië, 1940-1957*. Amsterdam: Boom.

Kerkhof, Jasper van de

2005a '"Defeatism is our worst enemy"; Rehabilitation, reorientation and *indonesianisasi* at Internatio and HVA, 1945-1958', *Lembaran Sejarah* 8-2:109-28.

2005b '*Indonesianisasi* of Dutch economic interests, 1930-1960; The case of Internatio', *Bijdragen tot de Taal-, Land- en Volkenkunde* 161:181-209.

2005c 'Onmisbaar maar onbemind; De Koninklijke Paketvaart Maatschappij en de Billiton Maatschappij in het onafhankelijke Indonesië (1945-1958)', *Tijdschrift voor Sociale en Economische Geschiedenis* 2-4:122-46.

Kindleberger, C.P.

1962 *Foreign trade and the national economy*. New Haven, CT: Yale University Press.

Klinken, Gerry van

2001 'The battle for history after Suharto; Beyond sacred dates, great men and legal milestones', *Critical Asian Studies* 33:323-50.

Kolff, G.H. van der

1961 'Brown and white economy; Unity in diversity', in: *Indonesian economics; The concept of dualism in theory and policy*, pp. 215-50. 's-Gravenhage: Van Hoeve.

Korthals Altes, W.L.

1987 *Changing economy in Indonesia; VII. Balance of payments, 1822-1939*. Amsterdam: Royal Tropical Institute.

1991 *Changing economy in Indonesia; XIIA. General trade statistics 1822-1940*. Amsterdam: Royal Tropical Institute.

2004 *Tussen cultures en kredieten; Een institutionele geschiedenis van de Nederlandsch-Indische Handelsbank en Nationale Handelsbank, 1863-1964*. Amsterdam: NIBE.

Kurasawa, Aiko

1990 *Gunseika Jawa sangyo sokan*. Tokyo: Ryukei Shosha. [Reprint of a publication by Djawa Gunsei Kanbu, 1944.]

1997 'Rice shortage and transportation', in: Peter Post and Elly Touwen-Bouwsma (eds), *Japan, Indonesia and the war; Myths and realities*, pp. 111-33. Leiden: KITLV Press. [Verhandelingen 173.]

Liem Tjwan Ling

1979 *Raja gula Oei Tiong Ham*. Surabaya: Liem.

Lindblad, J. Thomas

1988a *Between Dayak and Dutch; The economic history of Southeast Kalimantan, 1880-1942*. Dordrecht/Providence, RI: Foris. [KITLV, Verhandelingen 134].

1988b 'De handel tussen Nederland en Nederlands-Indië, 1874-1939', *Economisch- en Sociaal-Historisch Jaarboek* 51:240-98.

1989a 'Economic aspects of the Dutch expansion in Indonesia, 1870-1914', *Modern Asian Studies* 23-1:1-24.

1989b 'The petroleum industry in Indonesia before the Second World War', *Bulletin of Indonesian Economic Studies* 25-2:53-77.

1990 'The process of economic development in the Outer Provinces of the Dutch East Indies', *Journal of the Japan-Netherlands Institute* 2:208-34.

1993 'Economic growth in the Outer Islands, 1910-1940', in: J. Thomas Lindblad (ed.), *New challenges in the modern economic history of Indonesia*, pp. 233-63. Leiden: Programme of Indonesian Studies.

1996a 'Business strategies in late colonial Indonesia', in: J. Thomas Lindblad (ed.), *Historical foundations of a national economy in Indonesia, 1890s-1990s*, pp. 207-28. Amsterdam: North-Holland.

1996b 'The economic relationship between the Netherlands and colonial Indonesia, 1870-1940', in: Jan Luiten van Zanden (ed.), *The economic development of the Netherlands since 1870*, pp. 109-19. Cheltenham/ Brookfield, MA: Elgar.

1998 *Foreign investment in Southeast Asia in the twentieth century.* London: Macmillan.

2001 'Politieke economie en de dekolonisatie in Indonesië', in: J. Thomas Lindblad and Willem van der Molen (eds), *Macht en majesteit; Opstellen voor Cees Fasseur*, pp. 132-46. Leiden: Talen en Culturen van Zuidoost-Azië en Oceanië.

2002 'The importance of *indonesianisasi* during the transition from the 1930s to the 1960s', *Itinerario. European Journal of Overseas History* 26-3/4:51-72.

2003 'The economic impact of decolonization in Southeast Asia; Economic nationalism and foreign direct investment, 1945-1965', in: Marc Frey, Ronald W. Pruessen and Tan Tai Yong (eds), *The transformation of Southeast Asia; International perspectives on decolonization*, pp. 35-51. Armonk/ London: Sharpe.

2004a 'Beyond Benteng; Indonesian entrepreneurship in Central Java in the 1950s', *Lembaran Sejarah* 7-1:85-100.

2004b 'Van Javasche Bank naar Bank Indonesia; Voorbeeld uit de praktijk van *indonesianisasi*', *Tijdschrift voor Sociale en Economische Geschiedenis* 1:28-46.

2005a 'From Java Bank to Bank Indonesia; A case study of *indonesianisasi* in practice', *Lembaran Sejarah* 8-2:15-32.

2005b 'Structural characteristics of Japanese investment in Indonesia', *Economics and Finance in Indonesia/Ekonomi dan Keuangan Indonesia* 53:195-214.

2007 'Conglomerates in Indonesia; The road to power and beyond', in: Alex E. Fernandez Jilberto and Barbara Hogenboom (eds), *Big business and economic development; Conglomerates and economic groups in developing countries and transition economies under globalization*, pp. 65-85. London/ New York: Routledge.

Locher-Scholten, Elsbeth

1994 'Dutch expansion in the Indonesian archipelago around 1900 and the imperialism debate', *Journal of Southeast Asian Studies* 25-1:91-111.

Lockhart, Bruce M.

2003 'Monarchy and decolonization in Indochina', in: Marc Frey, Ronald W. Pruessen and Tan Tai Yong (eds), *The transformation of Southeast Asia; International perspectives on decolonization*, pp. 52-71. Armonk/London: Sharpe.

Lubis, Mochtar

1963 *Twilight in Djakarta*. London: Hutchinson. [Translation of Lubis 1964.]

1964 *Senja di Djakarta*. Kuala Lumpur: Pustaka Antara. [Appeared in 1963 in Dutch translation as *Schemer over Djakarta*. Baarn: Hollandia.]

MacIntyre, Andrew

1990 *Business and politics in Indonesia*. North Sydney: Allen and Unwin.

Mackie, J.A.C.

1959 'The political economy of guided democracy', *Australian Outlook* 13:285-92.

1961 'Indonesia's government estates and their masters', *Pacific Affairs* 34:337-60.

1971 'The Indonesian economy, 1950-1963', in: Bruce Glassburner (ed.), *The economy of Indonesia*, pp. 16-69. Ithaca, NY: Cornell University Press.

1974 *Konfrontasi; The Indonesian-Malaysian dispute, 1963-1966*. Kuala Lumpur: Oxford University Press.

1976 'Anti-Chinese outbreaks in Indonesia, 1959-1968', in: J.A.C. Mackie (ed.), *The Chinese in Indonesia; Five essays*, pp. 77-138. Melbourne: Nelson.

Mackie, J.A.C. and Charles A. Coppel

1976 'A preliminary survey', in: J.A.C. Mackie (ed.), *The Chinese in Indonesia; Five essays*, pp. 1-18. Melbourne: Nelson.

Maddison, Angus

1989 'Dutch income in and from Indonesia, 1700-1938', in: Angus Maddison and Gé Prince (eds), *Economic growth in Indonesia, 1820-1940*, pp. 15-42. Dordrecht/Providence, RI: Foris. [KITLV, Verhandelingen 137].

1990 'Dutch colonialism in Indonesia; A comparative perspective', in: Anne Booth, W.J. O'Malley and Anne Weidemann (eds), *Indonesian economic history in the Dutch colonial era*, pp. 322-35. New Haven, CT: Yale University Press.

Mangkusuwondo, Suhadi

1975 'Indonesia', in: Shinichi Ichimura (ed.), *The economic development of East and Southeast Asia*, pp. 1-57. Honolulu: University of Hawaii Press.

1976 *Industrialization efforts in Indonesia; The role of agriculture and foreign trade in the development of the industrial sector*. PhD thesis, University of California, Berkeley.

McMahon, Robert J.

2003 'The United States and Southeast Asia', in: Marc Frey, Ronald W. Pruessen and Tan Tai Yong (eds), *The transformation of Southeast Asia;*

International perspectives on decolonization, pp. 213-25. Armonk/London: Sharpe.

Meek, John P.
1956 *The government and economic development in Indonesia, 1950-1954* PhD thesis, University of Virginia, Charlottesville, VA.

Meijer, Hans
1994 *Den Haag – Jakarta; De Nederlands – Indonesische betrekkingen 1950-1962*. Utrecht: Aula.

Meyer Ranneft, J.W.
1937 'Hollands fout in Indië', *De Gids* 101-1:289-326.

Moedjanto, G.
1988 *Indonesia abad ke-20* [2 vols.]. Yogyakarta: Kanisius.

Mozingo, David
1961 'The Sino-Indonesian dual nationality treaty', *Asian Survey* 1:25-7.

Muhaimin, Y.A.
1990 *Bisnis dan politik; Kebijaksanaan ekonomi Indonesia 1950-1980*. Jakarta: LP3ES.

Nakamura, Mitsuo
1976 *The crescent arises over the banyan tree; A study of the Muhammadiyah movement in a Central Javanese town*. Ithaca, NY: Cornell University Press.

Narny, Yenny
1996 'Bank Nasional Bukittinggi sebelum dan sesudah kemerdekaan (1930-1965)', BA thesis, Faculty of Arts, Andalas University, Padang.

National business register
1963 *National business register of Indonesia 1962/63*. Jakarta: Indonesian Trade Directory.

Navis, A.A.
1986 *Pasang surut pengusaha pejuang; Otobiografi Hasjim Ning*. Jakarta: Grafitipers.

Nederlandsch-Indische Padang Portland Cement Maatschappij
1949 *Verslag over het jaar 1948*. Amsterdam: Gebr. Veth.

Neuman, A.M. de
1956 'On the promotion of indigenous Indonesian industries with special reference to credit facilities for private business and for local government enterprises', *Ekonomi dan Keuangan Indonesia* 9:683-728.

Neumark, S.D.
1954 'The national income of Indonesia, 1951-1952', *Ekonomi dan Keuangan Indonesia* 7:348-91.

Nishihara, Masashi
1976 *The Japanese and Sukarno's Indonesia; Tokyo-Jakarta relations, 1951-1966*. Kyoto: Centre of Southeast Asian Studies.

Nota
1935 *Nota betreffende de Indianisatie van 's lands dienst*. Batavia: Centraal Kantoor voor de Statistiek.

Oey Beng To
1991 *Sejarah kebijaksanaan moneter Indonesia; I. 1945-1958*. Jakarta: Lembaga Pengembangan Perbankan Indonesia.

Oorschot, H.J. van
1956 *De ontwikkeling van de nijverheid in Indonesië*. 's-Gravenhage/Bandung: Van Hoeve.

Paauw, Douglas S.
1960 *Financing economic development; The Indonesian case*. Glencoe, IL: Free Press.

Palmer, Ingrid
1972 *Textiles in Indonesia; Problems of import substitution*. New York: Praeger.

Palmer, Leslie H.
1962 *Indonesia and the Dutch*. London: Oxford University Press.

Panggabean, Maraden
1993 *Berjuang dan mengabdi*. Jakarta: Sinar Harapan.

Panglaykim, J. and I. Palmer
1969 *State trading corporations in developing countries*. Rotterdam: Rotterdam University Press.

Pelzer, Karl J.
1982 *Planters against peasants; The agrarian struggle in East Sumatra, 1947-1958*. 's-Gravenhage: Nijhoff. [KITLV, Verhandelingen 97].

Penders, C.L.M.
2002 *The West New Guinea debacle; Dutch decolonisation and Indonesia 1945-1962*. Hindmarsh, SA: Crawford, Leiden: KITLV Press.

Perbanas
1974 *Perkembangan situasi dan masalah-masalah perbankan nasional swasta di Indonesia 1973/74*. Jakarta: Perbanas.

Perron, E. du
1996 *Het land van herkomst*. Amsterdam: Van Oorschot. [First published 1935.]

Pidato
1949 *Pidato ketua delegasi Republik Indonesia pada pembukaan Konperensi Medja Bundar (23-08-1949)*. Jakarta.

Poelgeest, L. van
1999 *Japanse besognes; Nederland en Japan, 1945-1975*. Den Haag: SDU.

Pohan, Syafruddin
1992 *Achmad Bakrie; Sebuah potret kerja keras, kejujuran dan keberhasilan*. Jakarta: Kelompok Usaha Bakrie.

Post, Peter
1991 *Japanse bedrijvigheid in Indonesië, 1868-1942; Structurele elementen van Japan's economische expansie in Zuidoost-Azië*. PhD thesis, Free University of Amsterdam.
1997 'The formation of the pribumi business elite in Indonesia, 1930s-1940s', in: Peter Post and Elly Touwen-Bouwsma (eds), *Japan, Indonesia and the war; Myths and realities*, pp. 87-110. Leiden: KITLV Press. [Verhandelingen 173].

Postma, T.F.H. et al.
1946 'De Javasuikerindustrie gedurende de Japanse bezetting', *Mededeelingen van het Departement van Economische Zaken in Nederlandsch-Indië* 12:1-163.

Prillwitz, P.M.
1946 'De ondernemingslandbouw tijdens de Japansche bezetting', *Economisch Weekblad voor Nederlandsch-Indië*, 2 March.

Pruessen, Ronald W.
2003 'John Foster Dulles and decolonization in Southeast Asia', in: Marc Frey, Ronald W. Pruessen and Tan Tai Yong (eds), *The transformation of Southeast Asia; International perspectives on decolonization*, pp. 226-40. Armonk/London: Sharpe.

Purwanto, Bambang
2003 'In search of new opportunity; The *indonesianisasi* of economic life in Yogyakarta in the 1950s', Paper presented at an international conference on 'Decolonizing societies; The reorientation of Asian and African livelihoods under changing regimes', Amsterdam, 10-13 December.
2004 'Sejarawan akademik dan disorientasi historiografi; Sebuah otokritik', Inaugural professorial address, Faculty of Arts, Gadjah Mada University, Yogyakarta, 28 September.
2005 'Economic decolonization and the rise of Indonesian military business', Paper presented at an international conference on 'The economic decolonization of Indonesia in regional perspective', Leiden, 18-19 November.
2006 *Gagalnya historiografi Indonesiasentris?!* Yogyakarta: Ombak.

Rahardjo, M. Dawam et al.
1995 *Bank Indonesia dalam kilasan sejarah bangsa*. Jakarta: LP3ES.

Ranken, E.A.
1989 'De niet-Europese bijdrage tot de economische ontwikkeling van West-Borneo, 1900-1940', in: Adriaan Clemens and J. Thomas Lindblad (eds), *Het belang van de Buitengewesten; Economische expansie en koloniale staatsvorming in de Buitengewesten van Nederlands-Indië, 1870-1942*, pp. 177-209. Amsterdam: NEHA.

Rasiah, Rajah
1997 'Class, ethnicity and economic development in Malaysia', in: Garry Rodan, Kewin Hewison and Richard Robison (eds), *The political economy of Southeast Asia; An introduction*, pp. 121-47. Melbourne: Oxford University Press.

Reijden, B. van der
1936 'Rapport betreffende eene gehouden enquête naar de arbeidstoestanden in de industrie van strootjes en inheemsche sigaretten op Java; Deel III, Oost-Java'. Bandoeng: Kantoor van Arbeid. [Publicatie 12].

Ricklefs, M.C.
1981 *A history of modern Indonesia*. Houndmills: Macmillan.

Robison, R.
1986 *Indonesia; The rise of capital*. Sydney: Allen and Unwin.

Rochijat, Pipit
1985 'Am I PKI or non-PKI?', *Indonesia* 40:37-56.
Rodenburg, G.
1946 'De suikerindustrie op Java tijdens de Japansche bezetting', *Economisch Weekblad voor Nederlandsch-Indië*,13 and 20 April.
Ronde Tafel Conferentie
1949 *Ronde Tafel Conferentie te 's-Gravenhage; Feiten en documenten*. 's-Gravenhage: Secretariat of the Round Table Conference.
Rosendale, Phyllis
1978 *The Indonesian balance of payments, 1950-1966; Some new estimates*. PhD thesis, Australian National University, Canberra.
Round Table Conference
1950 *Results as accepted in the second plenary meeting held on 2 November 1949 in the Ridderzaal at The Hague*. Djakarta: Kolff.
Runturambi, F.
1959 'Politik keuangan serta pengaruhnja', *Ekonomi dan Masjarakat* 2/3:6-32.
Sadli, Moh.
1972 'Foreign investment in developing countries; Indonesia', in: Peter Drysdale (ed.), *Direct foreign investment in Asia and the Pacific*, pp. 201-25. Canberra: Australian National University Press.
Said, Salim
1991 *Genesis of power; General Sudirman and Indonesian military in politics, 1945-1949*. Singapore: Institute of Southeast Asian Studies.
Sartono Kartodirdjo
1984 *Modern Indonesia; Tradition and transformation*. Yogyakarta: Gadjah Mada University Press.
1986 'The modern Indonesian intelligentsia as protagonist of political modernization', *Itinerario* 10-1:197-212.
2001 *Indonesian historiography*. Yogyakarta: Kanisius.
Sato, Shigeru
1994 *War, nationalism and peasants; Java under the Japanese occupation, 1942-1945*. Sydney: Allen and Unwin.
2003 'Japanization in Indonesia re-examined; The problem of self-sufficiency in clothing', in: Li Narangoa and Robert Cribb (eds), *Imperial Japan and national identities in Asia, 1895-1945*, pp. 270-95. London: RoutledgeCurzon.
Schwarz, Adam
1999 *A nation in waiting; Indonesia's search for stability*. St. Leonards, NSW: Allen and Unwin.
Segers, W.A.I.M.
1987 *Changing economy in Indonesia; VIII. Manufacturing industry 1870-1942*. Amsterdam: Royal Tropical Institute.
Selosoemardjan
1962 *Social changes in Jogjakarta*. Ithaca, NY: Cornell University Press.
Shibata, Yoshimasa
1997 'The monetary policy in the Netherlands East Indies under the Japa-

nese administration', in: Peter Post and Elly Touwen-Bouwsma (eds), *Japan, Indonesia and the war; Myths and realities*, pp. 177-202. Leiden: KITLV Press. [Verhandelingen 173].

Siahaan, Bisuk
1996 *Industrialisasi di Indonesia; Sejak hutang kehormatan sampai banting stir.* Jakarta: Pustaka Data.

Sitsen, P.H.W.
1943 *Industrial development of the Netherlands Indies.* New York: Institute of Pacific Relations.

Sjahrir, Sutan
1956 *Perdjuangan kita.* Bandung: Pendidikan Rakjat.

Skinner, G. William
1963 'The Chinese minority', in: Ruth T. McVey (ed.), *Indonesia*, pp. 97-108. New Haven: Yale University Press.

Sluyterman, Keetie E.
2003 *Kerende kansen; Het Nederlandse bedrijfsleven in de twintigste eeuw.* Amsterdam: Boom.

Soemitro Djojohadikoesoemo (see also Sumitro Djojohadikusumo)
1943 *Het volkscredietwezen in de depressie.* Haarlem: Bohn.

Somers Heidhues, Mary F.
1988 'Citizenship and identity; Ethnic Chinese and the Indonesian Revolution', in: Jenifer W. Cushman and Wang Gungwu (eds), *Changing identities of the Southeast Asian Chinese since World War II*, pp. 115-39. Hong Kong: Hong Kong University Press.

Steijlen, Fridus
2002 *Memories of 'the East'; Abstracts of the Dutch interviews about the Netherlands East Indies, Indonesia and New Guinea (1930-1962) in the oral history project collection.* Leiden: KITLV Press.

Stoler, Laura Ann
1985 *Capitalism and confrontation in Sumatra's plantation belt, 1870-1979.* New Haven, CT: Yale University Press.

Sukarman, Widigdo
2005 'Upaya membentuk perbankan nasional; Peran bank BNI pada tahun 1950an', *Lembaran Sejarah* 8-2:47-68.

Sulistiyono, Singgih Tri
2005 'In the shadow of nationalism; PELNI during the period of *Indonesianisasi*', *Lembaran Sejarah* 8-2:85-108

Sumitro Djojohadikusumo
1946 'Apa arti Indonesia bagi Nederland, diukur dengan uang?', *Patriot* 28 September.
1986 'Recollections of my career', *Bulletin of Indonesian Economic Studies* 22-3:27-39.

Suryadinata, Leo
1992 *Pribumi Indonesians, the Chinese minority and China.* Third edition. Singapore: Heinemann Asia.

1997 *The culture of the Chinese minority in Indonesia*. Singapore: Times Books International.

Sutter, John O.

1959 *Indonesianisasi; A historical survey of the role of politics in the institutions of a changing economy from the Second World War to the eve of the general election, 1940-1955*. PhD thesis, Cornell University, Ithaca, NY.

Suwardi

2005 'Nasionalisasi perusahaan minyak di Riau, 1930-1970', Paper presented at an international seminar on 'Dekolonisasi di Pulau Sumatera', Padang, 1-2 August.

Suytino, Heru

1996 'Pabrik gula Gonandwinangun sebelum dan sesudah nasionalisasi tahun 1950-1963', MA thesis, Department of History, Gadjah Mada University, Yogyakarta.

Sjafruddin Prawiranegara

1987 'Recollections of my career', *Bulletin of Indonesian Economic Studies* 23-3:100-8.

Tamara, Nasir (ed.)

1998 *Aburizal Bakrie; Bisnis dan pemikirannya*. Jakarta: Pustaka Sinar Harapan.

Tan Tjin Kie

1967 'Sukarnian economics', in: Tan Tjin Kie (ed.), *Sukarno's guided Indonesia*, pp. 29-45. Brisbane: Jacaranda.

Taselaar, Arjen

1998 *De Nederlandse koloniale lobby; Ondernemers en de Indische politiek: 1914-1940*. Leiden: CNWS.

Thee Kian Wie

1996 `Economic policies in Indonesia during the period 1950-1965, in particular with respect to foreign investment', in: J. Thomas Lindblad (ed.), *Historical foundations of a national economy in Indonesia, 1890s-1990s*, pp. 315-29. Amsterdam: North-Holland.

2003 *Recollections; The Indonesian economy, 1950s-1990s*. Singapore: Institute of Southeast Asian Studies.

2005 'Indonesia's first affirmative policy; The "Benteng" program in the 1950s', *Lembaran Sejarah* 8-2:33-46.

Thomas, Kenneth D. and J. Panglaykim

1973 *Indonesia; The effects of past policies and President Suharto's plans for the future*. Melbourne: CEDA.

Thompson, Virginia

1945-1946 'Japan's blueprint for Indonesia', *Far Eastern Quarterly* 5:200-7.

Thompson, Virginia and Richard Adloff

1955 *Minority problems in Southeast Asia*. Stanford, CA: Stanford University Press.

Toer, Pramoedya Ananta

1960 *Hoa kiau di Indonesia*. Jakarta: Bintang Press.

Touwen, Jeroen
2001 *Extremes in the archipelago; Trade and economic development in the Outer Islands of Indonesia, 1900-1942*. Leiden: KITLV Press. [Verhandelingen 190].

Twang Peck Yang
1998 *The Chinese business elite in Indonesia and the transition to independence, 1940-1950*. Kuala Lumpur: Oxford University Press.

Van der Werff and Hubrecht
1951 'De nationalisatie van De Javasche Bank', *Extra Bericht* [August].

Verslag Commissie staatsrechterlijke hervormingen
1941 *Verslag van de Commissie tot bestudering van staatsrechterlijke hervormingen ingesteld bij Gouvernementsbesluit van 14 September 1940*. Batavia: Landsdrukkerij.

Voigt, J.H.
1946 'Aanteekeningen betreffende de thee-ondernemingen op Java gedurende de Japansche bezetting' , *Economisch Weekblad voor Nederlandsch-Indië*, 24 August.

Vredenbregt, Jacob
1989 *Aan het einde van de middag*. Second impression. Amsterdam: Nijgh and Van Ditmar. [First published 1984.].

Wahid, Abdul
2004 'Pribumisasi dan ironi ekonomi non-pertanian di pedesaan; Industri batik Cirebon tahun 1940an-1950an', Paper presented at an international workshop on 'The economic side of decolonization', Yogyakarta, 18-19 August.

Wardhana, Ali
1964 *Monetary problems of an underdeveloped economy, with special reference to Indonesia*. PhD thesis, University of California, Berkeley.

Warmelo, W. van
1946 'De Indische industrie gedurende de Japansche bezetting', *Economisch-Statistische Berichten*, 27 March.

Wasino
2005 'Nasionalisasi pabrik gula Mangkunegaran', *Lembaran Sejarah* 8-2:69-84.

White, N.J.
1996 *Business, government and the end of empire; Malaya, 1942-1957*. Oxford: Oxford University Press.

Willmott, Donald W.
1960 *The Chinese of Semarang; A changing minority community in Indonesia*. Ithaca, NY: Cornell University Press.

World Bank
1976 *World tables*. Washington, DC: World Bank.

Yong Mun Cheong
1997 'Indonesia's Singapore connection, 1945-1948', in: Taufik Abdullah (ed.), *The heartbeat of Indonesian Revolution*, pp. 232-50. Jakarta: Gramedia.

Yoshihara, Kunio (ed.)
1989 *Oei Tiong Ham concern; The first business empire of Southeast Asia*. Kyoto: Centre for Southeast Asian Studies.

Yulianto, Ibrahim
2005 'Politik ekonomi pendudukan Jepang di Surakarta, 1942-1945', Paper presented at an international workshop on 'Indonesia during the Japanese occupation', Yogyakarta, 28-29 July.

Zed, Mestika
2003 *Kepialangan politik dan Revolusi; Palembang 1900-1950*. Jakarta: LP3ES.

Zed, Mestika, Hasril Chaniago and Khairul Jasmi
2001 *Indarung; Tonggak sejarah industri semen Indonesia*. Jakarta: Pustaka Sinar Harapan.

Zubir, Zaiyardam
2004 'Nasionalisasi atau bukan, apa bedanya; Studi tentang buruh tambang batubara Ombilin Sawahlunto Sumatera Barat pasca-kolonialisasi', Paper presented at an international workshop on 'The economic side of decolonization', Yogyakarta, 18-19 August.

Zwaag, J. van der
1991 *Verloren tropische zaken; De opkomst en ondergang van de Nederlandse handel- en cultuurmaatschappijen in het voormalige Nederlands-Indië*. Meppel: Feniks Pers.

Index